# Writing About Screen Media

*Writing About Screen Media* presents strategies for writing about a broad range of media objects – including film, television, social media, advertising, video games, mobile media, music videos, and digital media – in an equally broad range of formats.

The book's case studies showcase media studies' geographical and industrial breadth, with essays covering topics as varied as: Brazilian telenovelas, K-pop music videos, Bombay cinema credit sequences, global streaming services, film festivals, archives, and more. With the expertise of over forty esteemed media scholars, the collection combines personal reflections about writing with practical advice. *Writing About Screen Media* reflects the diversity of screen media criticism and encourages both beginning and established writers to experiment with content and form.

Through its unprecedented scope, this volume will engage not only those who may be writing about film and other screen media for the first time but also accomplished writers who are interested in exploring new screen media objects, new approaches to writing about media, and new formats for critical expression.

**Lisa Patti** is Associate Professor in the Media and Society Program at Hobart and William Smith Colleges. She is co-author (with Glyn Davis, Kay Dickinson, and Amy Villarejo) of *Film Studies: A Global Introduction* (2015) and co-editor (with Tijana Mamula) of *The Multilingual Screen: New Reflections on Cinema and Linguistic Difference* (2016).

# Writing About Screen Media

Edited by Lisa Patti

LONDON AND NEW YORK

First published 2020
by Routledge
2 Park Square, Milton Park, Abingdon, Oxon OX14 4RN

and by Routledge
52 Vanderbilt Avenue, New York, NY 10017

*Routledge is an imprint of the Taylor & Francis Group, an informa business*

© 2020 selection and editorial matter, Lisa Patti; individual chapters, the contributors

The right of Lisa Patti to be identified as the author of the editorial material, and of the authors for their individual chapters, has been asserted in accordance with sections 77 and 78 of the Copyright, Designs and Patents Act 1988.

All rights reserved. No part of this book may be reprinted or reproduced or utilised in any form or by any electronic, mechanical, or other means, now known or hereafter invented, including photocopying and recording, or in any information storage or retrieval system, without permission in writing from the publishers.

*Trademark notice*: Product or corporate names may be trademarks or registered trademarks, and are used only for identification and explanation without intent to infringe.

*British Library Cataloguing in Publication Data*
A catalogue record for this book is available from the British Library

*Library of Congress Cataloging-in-Publication Data*
Names: Patti, Lisa, editor.
Title: Writing about screen media / edited by Lisa Patti.
Description: London ; New York : Routledge, 2019. |
Includes bibliographical references and index. |
Identifiers: LCCN 2019012236 (print) | LCCN 2019018917 (ebook) | ISBN 9780815393924 (ebook) | ISBN 9780815393511 | ISBN 9780815393511(hardback :alk. paper) | ISBN 9780815393528(paperback : alk. paper) | ISBN 9780815393924(ebk)
Subjects: LCSH: Mass media criticism.
Classification: LCC P96.C76 (ebook) | LCC P96.C76 W75 2019 (print) | DDC 302.23--dc23
LC record available at https://lccn.loc.gov/2019012236

ISBN: 978-0-8153-9351-1 (hbk)
ISBN: 978-0-8153-9352-8 (pbk)
ISBN: 978-0-8153-9392-4 (ebk)

Typeset in Goudy
by Taylor & Francis Books

Visit the companion website: writingaboutscreenmedia.net

Printed and bound by CPI Group (UK) Ltd, Croydon, CR0 4YY

# Contents

*List of figures* x
*List of contributors* xii
*Acknowledgements* xxii

**PART I**
**New frameworks for writing about screen media** 1

1 Introduction 3
   LISA PATTI

   *(Still) learning to write about screen media* 3
   *How to read this book* 6
   *In practice* 13

2 The big picture: Strategies for writing about screen media 15
   LISA PATTI

   *Collaborate* 15
   *Frame* 18
   *Curate* 19
   *Follow (up)* 20
   *In practice* 21

3 From screen aesthetics to site design: Analyzing form across screen media 25
   LISA PATTI

   *Taking notes* 25
   *Close readings: case studies* 27
   *In practice* 39

4  Entering the conversation: How and where to develop a critical argument  43
   LISA PATTI

   *What is an argument?* 43
   *Thinking on the page: free writing* 45
   *Structuring your argument: outlines* 46
   *Setting the scene: introductions* 48
   *Telling a story: evidence* 53
   *Making a last(ing) impression: conclusions* 55
   *In practice* 57

5  From notebook to network: When and how to use digital tools  59
   LISA PATTI

   *Digital resources: reading, watching, writing* 59
   *In praise of paper* 64
   *Citation* 65
   *Fair use* 67
   *In practice* 68

# PART II
# Writers on writing about screen media  71

## Objects and events  73

6  Writing about transnational cinema: *Crazy Rich Asians*  75
   OLIVIA KHOO

7  Capturing moments: Writing about film festivals as events  79
   KIRSTEN STEVENS

8  Writing about experimental cinema: Andy Warhol's *Empire* (1964)  84
   GLYN DAVIS

9  From meaning to effect: Writing about archival footage  88
   JAIMIE BARON

10  Making the absent present: Writing about nonextant media  92
    ALLYSON NADIA FIELD

11  Expressing race in Brazilian telenovelas  96
    JASMINE MITCHELL

12  Writing about music video: Tracing the ephemeral            100
    CAROL VERNALLIS

13  Writing across divides: Locating power in K-pop music videos   104
    S. HEIJIN LEE

14  Playing to write: Analyzing video games                       109
    TREAANDREA M. RUSSWORM AND JENNIFER MALKOWSKI

15  When it all clicks: Writing about participatory media         113
    LAUREN S. BERLINER

16  Feeling out social media                                      117
    JULIE WILSON AND EMILY CHIVERS YOCHIM

17  "A Very Black Project": A method for digital visual culture   122
    LAUREN MCLEOD CRAMER

18  Writing about transnational media: From representation to
    materiality                                                   126
    FAN YANG

19  Writing about digital and interactive media                   131
    DALE HUDSON AND PATRICIA R. ZIMMERMANN

20  (Un)limited mobilities                                        137
    RAHUL MUKHERJEE

21  Context is key: How (and why) you should write about outdoor
    advertising                                                   142
    BETH CORZO-DUCHARDT

## Methods and locations                                          147

22  How sound helps tell a story: Sound, music, and narrative in
    Vishal Bhardwaj's *Omkara*                                    149
    NILANJANA BHATTACHARJYA

23  Writing outside the text: A cultural approach to exhibition and
    moviegoing                                                    154
    JASMINE NADUA TRICE

24  Writing about streaming portals: The drama of distribution    159
    RAMON LOBATO

25  Analyzing and writing about credit sequences                  163
    MONIKA MEHTA

viii  Contents

26 "We are not thinking frogs": The archive, the artifact, and the task of the film historian  169
KATHERINE GROO

27 Show me the data!: Uncovering the evidence in screen media industry research  173
BRONWYN COATE AND DEB VERHOEVEN

28 Researching and writing across media industries  177
DEREK JOHNSON

29 The value of surprise: Ethnography of media industries  182
TEJASWINI GANTI

30 Listen up!: Interviewing as method  186
ALICIA KOZMA

31 The need for translation: Difference, footnotes, hyperlinks  190
TIJANA MAMULA

**Forms and formats**  197

32 Words and more: Strategies for writing about and with media  199
VIRGINIA KUHN

33 Best practices for screen media podcasting  206
CHRISTINE BECKER AND KYLE WRATHER

34 Confessions of an academic blogger  211
HENRY JENKINS

35 The research and the remix: Video essays as creative criticism  216
JEFFREY MIDDENTS

36 Foregrounding the invisible: Notes on the video essay review  221
CHIARA GRIZZAFFI

37 Review, edit, repeat: Writing and editing book reviews  226
ALICE LEPPERT

38 Extracurricular scholarship: "Writing" my audio commentary of *Losing Ground*  230
TERRI FRANCIS

39 The short, sweet art of blurb writing  234
LEAH SHAFER

40 Bridging the gaps between scholarly essays and mass-market film
   writing 238
   NICK DAVIS

41 Writing across the page without a line 243
   HOLLY WILLIS

# Figures

| | | |
|---|---|---|
| 3.1 | The opening title for the television show *Lost* (2016) | 28 |
| 3.2a–b | The extreme close-ups at the beginning of the *Lost* pilot episode | 28 |
| 3.3 | An extreme low angle, point of view shot from Jack's perspective in *Lost's* pilot episode | 28 |
| 3.4a–b | High angle shots from *Lost* | 29 |
| 3.5 | Shot that begins a shot/reverse shot sequence in *Lost* | 29 |
| 3.6 | Reverse shot in *Lost* | 30 |
| 3.7 | The camera stops following Jack to examine the *mise-en-scène* in *Lost*. | 30 |
| 3.8 | The first shot of the beach in *Lost* | 30 |
| 3.9 | A horizontal pan scans the beach in *Lost* | 31 |
| 3.10 | A long tracking shot in *Lost* | 31 |
| 3.11a–b | Shots of Ralph Angel and Blue looking directly at each other and at the camera in the pilot episode of *Queen Sugar* (2016) | 34 |
| 3.12a–c | Centered compositions in Kogonada's video essay *Wes Anderson: Centered* (2014) | 35 |
| 3.13a–c | Low angle shots in Kogonada's video essay *Quentin Tarantino: From Below* (2012) | 35 |
| 3.14a–c | Shots from Kogonada's video essay *What is neorealism?* (2013) | 36 |
| 3.15a–b | Menus for the Criterion Collection DVD edition of the film *In the Mood for Love* (2000) | 37 |
| 3.16a–b | *Criterion Collection DVD bonus features for* In the Mood for Love *(2000)* | 38 |
| 7.1 | Photograph by Jaklene Vukasinovic, courtesy of Melbourne Women in Film Festival. Festival panel "Making a film on a micro-budget," Australian Centre for the Moving Image, February 2018 | 82 |
| 9.1 | A found image from *A Movie* (1958) | 89 |
| 9.2 | Bruce at seven years old in *Seven Up!* (1964) | 91 |

List of figures xi

| | | |
|---|---|---|
| 13.1 | PSY's performance with MC Hammer at the 2013 Billboard Music Awards | 105 |
| 13.2 | PSY on a tour bus in the "Gangnam Style" music video | 106 |
| 18.1 | The sleek packaging of information in *Under the Dome*; Source: Jonathan Papish, Part 3 of 8 "Under The Dome" Documentary on China's Pollution by Chai Jing (Best English Subtitles), available at https://www.youtube.com/watch?v=BXMZpF0K1ME | 127 |
| 19.1 | Design of home page to navigate media and other information. Engage Media, Indonesia/Australia | 132 |
| 20.1 | Airtel ad promising unlimited calls and data at New Delhi airport. Source: Photo by Author | 139 |
| 21.1 | A newspaper illustration from "Couldn't Stand the Posters: Webster City People Drape Pictures of Scantily-Dressed Women," clipping from unknown newspaper, ca. 1898, scrapbook, p. 41, box HI5, courtesy of the Outdoor Advertising Association of America Archives, David M. Rubenstein Rare Book & Manuscript Library, Duke University | 145 |
| 22.1a–b | Extreme close-ups of Dolly's face in *Omkara* (Vishal Bhardwaj, 2006) | 151 |
| 25.1a–b | Images from the credit sequence for *Kaagaz Ke Phool/Paper Flowers* (Guru Dutt, 1959) | 165 |
| 25.2 | Image from the credit sequence for *Luck by Chance* (Zoya Akhtar, 2009) | 166 |
| 31.1a–b | Images from *Annihilation* (Alex Garland, 2018) with Italian subtitles presented by Netflix | 193 |
| 32.1a–b | Screen shots from *Filmic Texts and the Rise of the Fifth Estate* showing Scalar's pop-up display | 202 |
| 32.2a–b | Screen shots of the interface of MoMLA | 203 |
| 35.1 | Still from the author's video essay "Memories of C/Leo: On Auteurism and *Roma*" | 219 |
| 36.1a–b | Images from *Success*, a video essay by Jaap Kooijman published on *[in]Transition - Journal of Videographic Film & Moving Image Studies*, 2.4, 2016 | 223 |

# Contributors

**Jaimie Baron** is an Associate Professor of Film Studies at the University of Alberta. Her first book, *The Archive Effect: Found Footage and the Audiovisual Experience of History*, was published in 2014. She is currently working on a new book entitled *Misuse: The Ethics of Audiovisual Appropriation in the Digital Era*. She is the founder, director, and co-curator of the Festival of (In)appropriation, a yearly international festival of short experimental found footage films and videos. She is also a co-founder of *Docalogue*, an online space for scholars and filmmakers to engage in conversations about contemporary documentary, soon to also be a book series published by Routledge Press.

**Christine Becker** is an Associate Professor in the Department of Film, Television, and Theatre at the University of Notre Dame specializing in film and television history and critical analysis. Her book *It's the Pictures That Got Small: Hollywood Film Stars on 1950s Television* (Wesleyan University Press, 2009) won the 2011 IAMHIST Michael Nelson Prize for a Work in Media and History. She is currently working on a research project exploring issues of cultural taste in contemporary American and British television. She is also a co-host and co-producer of *Aca-Media*, the official podcast for the Society for Cinema and Media Studies.

**Lauren S. Berliner** is an Associate Professor at University of Washington Bothell where she teaches in the Media & Communication and Cultural Studies programs. She is the author of *Producing Queer Youth: The Paradox of Digital Media Empowerment* (Routledge, 2018) and co-editor (with Ron Krabill) of *Feminist Interventions in Participatory Media: Pedagogy, Publics, Practice* (Routledge, 2018). She is also a co-curator of The Festival of (In)Appropriation, an annual showcase of experimental films.

**Nilanjana Bhattacharjya** is an Honors Faculty Fellow and Senior Lecturer at Barrett, the Honors College at Arizona State University in Tempe. Her research focuses on the relationship between music and narrative in popular Hindi films, as well as on how music helps define identity in South Asian diasporic locations. Her writing has appeared in the journals *Framework: The Journal of Cinema and Media*, *South Asian Popular Culture*, *Asian Music*, and

*South Asian History and Culture*, as well as in the edited volumes *From Bombay to Bollywood: Tracking Cinematic and Musical Tours* (Minnesota, 2008) and *South Asian Transnationalisms: Cultural Exchange in the Twentieth Century* (Routledge, 2012).

**Bronwyn Coate** is a cultural economist and Senior Lecturer in the School of Economics, Finance and Marketing at RMIT University with expertise in the economic analysis of the arts and creative industries. She applies a range of economic and econometric techniques to cultural data and works with multidisciplinary teams to develop innovative approaches and techniques that are data driven and empirically based. Bronwyn is a member of the Kinomatics Project.

**Beth Corzo-Duchardt** holds a PhD in Screen Cultures from Northwestern University and has taught media studies and gender studies courses at Northwestern University, DePaul University, Muhlenberg College, and Lafayette College. She is currently working on two book projects related to screen media. The first, *Primal Screen: Primitivism and American Silent Film Spectatorship*, investigates how popular ideas about the early cinema's universal appeal were shaped by colonialist and primitivist discourses. The second is a media history of outdoor advertising in North America that aims to provide crucial historical context for understanding contemporary multi-media outdoor landscapes.

**Lauren McLeod Cramer** is an Assistant Professor in the Cinema Studies Institute at the University of Toronto. Her current research project, "A Hip-Hop Joint: The Architecture of Blackness," uses architectural design to theorize about hip-hop's "joints," the points of articulation between the aesthetics of Blackness and visual culture. Lauren is a founding member of *liquid blackness*, a research collective and peer-reviewed journal focused on Blackness and aesthetics, and currently serves on its Editorial Board. Her writing has appeared in *The Black Scholar, Black Camera, Film Criticism, liquid blackness,* and *In Media Res*.

**Glyn Davis** is Reader in Screen Studies at the University of Edinburgh. He is the co-editor, with Gary Needham, of *Warhol in Ten Takes* (BFI, 2013) and the co-author, with Kay Dickinson, Lisa Patti, and Amy Villarejo, of *Film Studies: A Global Introduction* (Routledge, 2015). His writing has been published in journals including *Aniki, Cinema Journal, MIRAJ,* and *Screen*. From 2016 to 2019, Glyn was the Project Leader of "Cruising the 1970s: Unearthing Pre-HIV/AIDS Sexual Cultures," a pan-European queer history project funded by HERA (www.crusev.ed.ac.uk).

**Nick Davis** is Associate Professor of English and Gender & Sexuality Studies at Northwestern University, with a courtesy appointment in Radio/TV/Film. His book *The Desiring-Image* (Oxford University Press, 2013) developed new aesthetic and theoretical paradigms for contemporary queer cinema, drawing heavily on Deleuzian philosophies of cinema, desire, and collective formations. He has published additional essays on work by James Baldwin, Leos Carax, David Cronenberg, Alfonso Cuarón, Julie Dash, John Cameron Mitchell, and the actresses Julie Christie and Vanessa Redgrave, and is developing a new book project based on movies produced and released in the year 1999. He is currently a Contributing Editor at *Film Comment* Magazine and writes the film reviews at www.Nick-Davis.com.

**Allyson Nadia Field** is Associate Professor of Cinema and Media Studies at The University of Chicago. A scholar of African American cinema, her work combines archival research with concerns of film form, media theory, and broader cultural questions of representation across periods and practices. She is the author of *Uplift Cinema: The Emergence of African American Film and the Possibility of Black Modernity* (Duke University Press, 2015) and co-editor with Jan-Christopher Horak and Jacqueline Stewart of *L.A. Rebellion: Creating a New Black Cinema* (University of California Press, 2015). With Marsha Gordon, she is the co-editor of *Screening Race in American Nontheatrical Film* (Duke University Press, 2019).

**Terri Francis** directs the Black Film Center/Archive at Indiana University, Bloomington. Her interview with transformative lesbian filmmaker Cheryl Dunye appears in the 2018 winter issue of *Film Quarterly*. She guest edited a close-up on Afrosurrealism in film and video for the 2013 fall issue of *Black Camera*. In 2011, Francis published her study of Jamaican nontheatrical films in "Sounding the Nation: Martin Rennalls and the Jamaica Film Unit, 1951–1961" in *Film History*. Her book *The Cinematic Prism of Josephine Baker*, a study of how the entertainer used humor to master her precarity, is forthcoming from Indiana University Press. Francis's film commentary can be found on NPR, in the *Chicago Tribune*, and in *The Guardian*.

**Tejaswini Ganti** is Associate Professor in the Department of Anthropology and core faculty in the Program in Culture & Media at New York University. A cultural and visual anthropologist specializing in South Asia, her research and teaching interests include anthropology of media, Indian cinema, media industries, production cultures, visual culture, neoliberalism and globalization. She has been conducting ethnographic research about the social world and filmmaking practices of the Hindi film industry since 1996 and is the author of *Producing Bollywood: Inside the Contemporary Hindi Film Industry* (Duke University Press 2012) and *Bollywood: A Guidebook to Popular Hindi Cinema* (Routledge 2004; 2$^{nd}$ edition 2013). Her current research examines the politics of language and translation within the Bombay film industry; the formalization and professionalization of film training through film schools in India; and a social history of Indian cinema in the U.S.

**Chiara Grizzaffi** is adjunct faculty at Università IULM, in Milan, where she obtained her PhD in 2015. Her book on video essays, *I film attraverso I film. Dal "testo introvabile" ai video essay* was published in 2017 by

Mimesis; her essays have appeared in journals such as *Bianco e Nero* and *Cinergie*, and in books such as *Critofilm. Cinema che pensa il cinema*, edited by Adriano Aprà (2016), and *Harun Farocki. Pensare con gli occhi*, edited by Luisella Farinotti and Barbara Grespi (2017). She is co-editor of *[in]Transition*, and member of the editorial staffs of *Cinergie* and *L'avventura*. As a film critic, she has collaborated with the magazines *8 ½*, *Duellanti*, and *Rolling Stone*.

**Katherine Groo** is an Assistant Professor of Film and Media Studies at Lafayette College. Her essays have appeared in *Discourse*, *Cinema Journal*, *Framework*, and *Frames* as well as several edited collections. She is co-editor of *New Silent Cinema* (Routledge/AFI, 2015) and author of *Bad Film Histories: Ethnography and the Early Archive* (University of Minnesota Press, 2019).

**Dale Hudson** is an associate professor of Film and New Media at New York University Abu Dhabi and digital curator for the Finger Lakes Environmental Film Festival (FLEFF). His research examines film and digital media, globalization, migration, and environmentalism, particularly in relation to the Middle East, South Asia, and North America. He is author of *Vampires, Race, and Transnational Hollywoods* (Edinburgh, 2017) and co-author with Patricia R. Zimmermann of *Thinking through Digital Media: Transnational Environments and Locative Places* (Palgrave Macmillan, 2015). His essays and other writings appear in *Afterimage*, *American Quarterly*, *Cinema Journal*, *Film Quarterly*, *French Cultural Studies*, *Immerse*, *Jadaliyya*, *Screen*, *Studies in Documentary Film*, and other journals and anthologies.

**Henry Jenkins** is the Provost's Professor of Communication, Journalism, Cinematic Art, and Education at the University of Southern California and the founder and former co-director of the MIT Comparative Media Studies Program. He blogs at henryjenkins.org, and he is the co-host of the podcast, *How Do You Like It So Far?* He has written or edited more than 20 books on various aspects of media and cultural studies, including *Textual Poachers: Television Fans and Participatory Culture* (Routledge, 1992), *Convergence Culture: Where Old and New Media Collide* (New York University Press, 2006), *Spreadable Media: Creating Meaning and Value in a Networked Society* (New York University Press, 2013), *By Any Media Necessary: The New Youth Activists* (New York University Press, 2016), and the forthcoming *Popular Culture and the Civic Imagination: Case Studies of Creative Social Change*.

**Derek Johnson** is Professor of Media and Cultural Studies in the Department of Communication Arts at the University of Wisconsin-Madison. He is the author of *Transgenerational Media Industries: Adults, Children, and the Reproduction of Culture* (University of Michigan Press, 2019) as well as *Media Franchising: Creative License and Collaboration in the Culture Industries* (New York University Press, 2013).

xvi  *List of contributors*

**Olivia Khoo** is Associate Professor in Film and Screen Studies at Monash University, Australia. She is the author of *The Chinese Exotic: Modern Diasporic Femininity* (Hong Kong University Press, 2007), and co-author (with Belinda Smaill and Audrey Yue) of *Transnational Australian Cinema: Ethics in the Asian Diasporas* (Lexington, 2013).

**Alicia Kozma** is Assistant Professor of Communication and Media Studies at Washington College. Her research focuses on women's labor in the entertainment industries. Her recent project documents women's labor across the neo-art house movement, alongside a book manuscript that examines the links between Hollywood's historical and contemporary hiring and employment practices and their impact on institutionalized gendered labor disparities. Dr. Kozma's recent work has been published in *Television & New Media*, *Camera Obscura*, and *Film Comment*. She is the series editor of *New Histories of Women in Entertainment* (Peter Lang) and the editor of *ReFocus: The Films of Doris Wishman* (U of Edinburgh).

**Virginia Kuhn** is a Professor in the USC School of Cinematic Arts. Her work centers on visual and digital rhetoric, feminist theory, and algorithmic research methods. She leads the Video Analysis Tableau project, a tool that uses machine-reading algorithms to facilitate research with video archives. Kuhn defended a media-rich digital dissertation in 2005, and has since published several collections of peer reviewed digital scholarship. Kuhn serves on the editorial boards of several journals and directs a graduate certificate in Digital Media + Culture and an undergraduate multimedia Honors program.

**S. Heijin Lee** is Assistant Professor of Social and Cultural Analysis at New York University. Lee is co-editor of *Fashion and Beauty in the Time of Asia* (NYU Press, 2019) and *Pop Empires: Transnational and Diasporic Flows of India and Korea* (University of Hawai'i Press, 2019) as well as author of *The Geopolitics of Beauty: Transnational Circulations of Plastic Surgery, Pop, and Pleasure* (forthcoming). Lee has been featured on National Public Radio's *Code Switch* as well as The Korea Society's "K-Pop 101" Series.

**Alice Leppert** is Assistant Professor of Media and Communication Studies at Ursinus College. Her work has appeared in *Television and New Media*, *Cinema Journal*, *Celebrity Studies*, and *Genders* and in several edited collections. She serves as the book review editor for *Film Criticism*, and her first book, *TV Family Values: Gender, Domestic Labor, and 1980s Sitcoms* is forthcoming from Rutgers University Press.

**Ramon Lobato** is Senior Research Fellow in the School of Media and Communication at RMIT University, Melbourne. His books include *Shadow Economies of Cinema* (BFI, 2012), *The Informal Media Economy* (Polity, 2015), *Geoblocking and Global Video Culture* (INC, 2016) and *Netflix Nations* (NYU Press, 2019).

*List of contributors* xvii

**Jennifer Malkowski** is an Assistant Professor of Film and Media Studies at Smith College. They are the author of *Dying in Full Detail: Mortality and Digital Documentary* (Duke University Press, 2017) and the co-editor of *Gaming Representation: Race, Gender, and Sexuality in Video Games* (Indiana University Press, 2017). Their work has also been published in *Cinema Journal*, *Jump Cut*, *Film Quarterly*, and the edited collections *Queers in American Popular Culture*, *Unwatchable*, and *A Tumblr Book: Platform and Cultures*.

**Tijana Mamula** is a film scholar, filmmaker, and translator. She is currently engaged in a second, practice-based doctorate at Newcastle University, exploring the ways in which literary adaptation might be conceived and produced as a mode of film theory. She is the author of *Cinema and Language Loss: Displacement, Visuality and the Filmic Image* (Routledge, 2013) and co-editor, with Lisa Patti, of *The Multilingual Screen: New Reflections on Cinema and Linguistic Difference* (Bloomsbury, 2016).

**Monika Mehta** is Associate Professor of English at State University of New York, Binghamton. Her research and teaching interests include new media and film studies; cinema in South Asia; theories of nation-state; feminist studies; postcolonial critique; and globalization and cultural production. She is the author of *Censorship and Sexuality in Bombay Cinema* (University of Texas Press, 2011; Permanent Black, 2012). Her articles and chapters examining trans/national film regulation; globalization and cultural production in India; DVD compilations; music awards; cinephilia; and authorship have appeared in journals such as *The Velvet Light Trap*, *Studies in South Asian Film and Media*, *South Asian Popular Culture* as well as edited collections such as *Global Bollywood: Travels of Hindi Song and Dance*, *Music in Contemporary Indian Film*, and *Postcolonial Studies Meets Media Studies*. Her co-edited collection, *Pop Empires: Transnational and Diasporic Flows of Korea and India* (University of Hawai'i Press) is forthcoming.

**Jeffrey Middents** is Associate Professor of Literature at American University in Washington, DC, where he studies and teaches film and world literature. His book, *Writing National Cinema: Film Journals and Film Culture in Peru* (UPNE, 2009) investigates the historical place of cultural writing within a national discourse by tracing how Peruvian cinema was shaped by local film criticism. He has also published essays – in print and video versions – on a variety of other topics, including documentary aesthetics in the work of Chilean filmmaker Patricio Guzmán, Peruvian director Luis Llosa's films made under producer Roger Corman, the sense of place in contemporary Latin American cinema, movie stardom and "the indigenous" in the works of Dolores del Rio and Magaly Solier, and the pedagogy of teaching "world cinema." He is currently working on a monograph on transnational auteurism and the work of Alfonso Cuarón.

xviii  *List of contributors*

**Jasmine Mitchell** is an Assistant Professor of American Studies at the State University of New York-Old Westbury. She holds a PhD in American Studies from the University of Minnesota. Professor Mitchell's research focuses on transnational constructions of race, gender, sexuality, and national identity in U.S. and Brazilian media. Her book, Imagining the Mulatta: Blackness in U.S. and Brazilian Media is forthcoming from University of Illinois Press.

**Rahul Mukherjee** has been researching and teaching about environmental media and global media at University of Pennsylvania. He has been part of two collaborative projects, one concerned with circulation of local music videos through memory cards in India and the other dealing with ICT (platform jumping) practices in Zambia. He is presently working on two book projects: one concerned with mediations of radiation emitting technologies and their environmental impact titled *Radiant Infrastructures: Media, Environment, and Cultures of Uncertainty* (forthcoming, Duke University Press) and the other about aspirational mobilities unleashed by mobile media technologies called *(Un)Limited India: Memory Card, WhatsApp, and Jio*. During 2017–2018, Rahul was at Cornell University's Society for the Humanities as the Atkinson Center for a Sustainable Future Fellow. He is part of the editorial board of the *Journal of Visual Culture*.

**TreaAndrea M. Russworm**, an Associate Professor of English at the University of Massachusetts, Amherst, teaches classes on video games, digital cultural studies, and African American popular culture. She is the author of *Blackness is Burning: Civil Rights, Popular Culture, and the Problem of Recognition* (Wayne State University Press, 2016) and a co-editor of *From Madea to Media Mogul: Theorizing Tyler Perry* (University of Mississippi Press, 2016) and *Gaming Representation: Race, Gender, and Sexuality in Video Games* (Indiana University Press, 2017). She is currently writing a fourth book on race, technology, and the politics of play.

**Leah Shafer** is Associate Professor in the Media and Society Program at Hobart and William Smith Colleges. Her criticism appears in: *FLOW: A Critical Forum on Television and Media Culture, Film Criticism, The Journal of Interactive Technology and Pedagogy,* and *Cinema Journal Teaching Dossier*. She has published in anthologies including *The 25 Sitcoms that Changed Television: From I Love Lucy to Modern Family* and *Feminist Interventions in Digital Pedagogy*. A scholar/artist, she was awarded a residency with media art collaborative Signal Culture and her experimental documentary *Declaration of Sentiments Wesleyan Chapel* was screened in the Finger Lakes Environmental Film Festival.

**Kirsten Stevens** is Lecturer in Arts and Cultural Management at the University of Melbourne. Her research explores film festivals and film culture events with particular interests in the impacts of digital technology and the influence of festivals within national screen industries. She is the author of *Australian Film Festivals: Audience, Place and Exhibition Culture* (Palgrave Macmillan, 2016) and has taught extensively in screen and media studies. She is deputy director of the Melbourne Women in Film Festival and Vice President of *Senses of Cinema* journal.

**Jasmine Nadua Trice** is an Assistant Professor of Cinema and Media Studies at the University of California, Los Angeles, where she researches and teaches on Asian cinemas, transnational media, urban film cultures, and exhibition and moviegoing. Her book, *Speculative Publics: Cinema Circulation and Alternative Film Culture in Manila, Philippines*, is under contract with Duke University Press. From 2016–2018, she was Co-Investigator of the "Southeast Asian Cinemas Research Network (SEACRN): Promoting Dialogue Across Critical and Creative Practice," funded through the Arts and Humanities Research Council. Her academic work has been published in *Asian Cinema*, the *International Journal of Cultural Studies*, the *Quarterly Review of Film and Video*, *Feminist Media Studies*, *Projector: Journal of Media and Culture*, and *Feminist Media Histories*. Her research has been funded through the American Association for University Women, the Asian Cultural Council, and the Hellman Fellows.

**Deb Verhoeven** is Canada 150 Research Chair in Gender and Cultural Informatics at the University of Alberta. She is Director of the Kinomatics Project.

**Carol Vernallis** teaches at Stanford University. Her books include *Experiencing Music Video: Aesthetics and Cultural Context* (Columbia University Press, 2004) and *Unruly Media: YouTube, Music Video, and the New Digital Cinema* (Oxford University Press, 2013), as well as two co-edited handbooks on contemporary audiovisual aesthetics, *The Oxford Handbook of New Audiovisual Aesthetics* and *The Oxford Handbook of Sound and Image in Digital Media* (Oxford University Press, 2013). Her articles have appeared in *American Music*, *Cinema Journal*, *The Journal of Popular Music Studies*, *Journal of the Society for American Music*, *Music Sound and the Moving Image*, *Popular Music*, the *Quarterly Review of Film and Video*, and *Screen*.

**Holly Willis** is a Research Professor in the School of Cinematic Arts at the University of Southern California where she served as the founding chair of the Media Arts + Practice division. She teaches courses on new and emerging media forms, especially as they relate to moving-image storytelling. She is the author of *Fast Forward: The Future(s) of the Cinematic Arts* and *New Digital Cinema: Reinventing the Moving Image*, as well the editor of *The New Ecology of Things*, a collection of essays about ubiquitous computing. The co-founder of *Filmmaker Magazine*, dedicated to independent film, she served as the editor of *RES Magazine* and co-curator of RESFEST, a festival of experimental media, for several years, and she writes frequently for diverse publications about experimental film, video, new media and creative nonfiction. Her work has appeared in publications as diverse as *Film Comment, Afterimage, ArtWeek, Variety* and *The Normal School*.

**Julie Wilson** is Associate Professor of Communication Arts and Community and Justice Studies at Allegheny College where she teaches courses in media and cultural studies. She is co-author, with Emily Chivers Yochim, of *Mothering through Precarity: Women's Work and Digital Media* (Duke University Press, 2017). Julie is also author of *Neoliberalism* (Routledge, 2017) and has published articles in numerous journals including *Cinema Journal, Cultural Studies, Television and New Media*, and *Celebrity Studies*.

**Kyle Wrather** is a PhD Candidate at the University of Texas at Austin in the Department of Radio-Television-Film. He holds a BA in English and BA in Communication with a focus on journalism and a minor in broadcasting from Mississippi State University. His MA thesis at Georgia State University examined regulation modalities of network neutrality. His research interests include podcasting and the intersection of media industries and new technologies.

**Fan Yang** is an Associate Professor in the Department of Media and Communication Studies at the University of Maryland, Baltimore County (UMBC). She is the author of *Faked in China: Nation Branding, Counterfeit Culture, and Globalization* (Indiana University Press, 2016). Yang works at the intersection of transnational media studies, globalization and communication, postcolonial studies, and contemporary China. Her scholarship on cultural studies and global China, transnational media culture, and urban visual culture has appeared in *Critical Studies in Media Communication, Theory, Culture & Society, positions: asia critique, Journal of Asian American Studies, Quarterly Review of Film and Video*, and *Verge: Studies in Global Asias*, among others. She is working on a new book that examines the growing number of transnational media artifacts that bring the imaginary amalgamation of China and America – or "Chimerica" – into being.

**Emily Chivers Yochim** is Associate Professor of Communication Arts and Women's, Gender, and Sexuality Studies at Allegheny College where she teaches courses in media and cultural studies. She is co-author, with Julie Wilson, of *Mothering through Precarity: Women's Work and Digital Media* (Duke University Press, 2017). Emily is also author of *Skate Life: Re-Imagining White Masculinity* (University of Michigan Digital Culture Books) and has published articles in numerous journals including *Cultural Studies, Communication and Critical/Cultural Studies*, and *The Sociology of Sport Journal*.

**Patricia R. Zimmermann** is Professor of Screen Studies in the Roy H. Park School of Communications at Ithaca College and Codirector of the Finger Lakes Environmental Film Festival (FLEFF). Her most recent books exploring new media, independent film and video history, and experimental and documentary theory include *Thinking Through Digital Media: Transnational Environments and Locative Places* with Dale Hudson (Palgrave Macmillan, 2015); *Open Spaces: Openings, Closings, and Thresholds of Independent Public Media* (University of St. Andrews, 2016); *The Flaherty: Decades in the Cause of Independent Film* with Scott MacDonald (Indiana University Press, 2017); and *Open Space New Media Documentary: A Toolkit for Theory and Practice* with Helen De Michiel (Routledge, 2018).

# Acknowledgements

This book emerged from my collaborations with the many writers – teachers, students, and colleagues – who showed me how to write about screen media and how to share those lessons with others.

Amy Villarejo helped me transition from writing about literature to writing about film, and she invited me to collaborate with her, Glyn Davis, and Kay Dickinson on the book *Film Studies: A Global Introduction*. Amy, Glyn, and Kay generously taught me how to write (and publish) a book. I first developed the ideas that I share in this volume when working on the "Writing about cinema" chapter in *Film Studies: A Global Introduction*. I am grateful for their mentorship and friendship.

I have had the pleasure of writing with three scholars who loom large in my life as collaborators and friends (and contributors to this book): Tijana Mamula, Monika Mehta, and Leah Shafer. They bring rigor and style to their work as writers and teachers, and this book has benefited immensely from their insights and support.

My students and colleagues in the Media and Society Program at Hobart and William Smith Colleges have contributed in many different ways to this project. Every idea that I present in the opening section was shaped by feedback from students; our classes have been laboratories for experiments with writing about screen media. The ability to watch my students transform as writers – both within the arc of a single class and over the course of their careers as Media and Society students – has been one of the greatest pleasures of teaching at HWS. I am fortunate to work in a program where all of my colleagues are dedicated pedagogues. In formal reviews and informal chats, they have each guided my development as a teacher; and they have helped me navigate the ever-changing landscape of media studies pedagogy with unwavering support and reliably sharp humor. Rebecca Burditt, Lester Friedman, Grant Holly, Marilyn Jimenez, Liz Lyon, Ashwin Manthripragada, Linda Robertson, Leah Shafer, and Iskandar Zulkarnain are a teaching dream team. As much as I enjoy their company and camaraderie, I am also grateful for the generous support of the Office of Academic and Faculty Affairs for the sabbatical leave that enabled me to spend a semester away from campus completing this book. At HWS, I wrote sections of this

Acknowledgements xxiii

manuscript during "Pop-up Writing Days" organized by Susan Pliner. I am grateful to Susan for creating time and space for faculty to focus on writing and to the colleagues that joined me for our writing sessions. I also received crucial support from the staff of the Warren Hunting Smith Library at HWS – especially Sara Greenleaf who worked closely with me to develop many of the writing assignments included in this book – and the staff of the Digital Learning Center at HWS – especially Jen Webb who fielded my questions about images, file storage, and other always-pressing concerns with great skill, speed, and patience. Finally, I thank my HWS colleague Nick Ruth for his permission to include his striking print "Better than Ever" (2017) on the book's cover.

As I explain in the introduction, my early teaching collaborations provided the foundation for the ideas in this book. Sidney Orlov taught me how to teach students to write, and Patty Zimmermann (in collaboration – of course – with Dale Hudson and Anna Siomopoulos) taught me how to teach outside of my comfort zone.

I gained valuable experience as an editor working on collections large and small with wonderful co-editors: Ted Hovet, Tijana Mamula, Monika Mehta, Jasmine Mitchell, Stanka Radović, and Erin Copple Smith. The success of those collaborations helped me to launch this project.

Editing *Writing About Screen Media* was much less challenging than I expected it to be thanks to the diligence of all of the book's contributors. This volume is a massive collaboration, and each of the forty-one authors who wrote and co-wrote chapters confirmed the value of collaborative scholarship.

I am grateful to the excellent team at Routledge. I knew from my experience working with Natalie Foster on *Film Studies: A Global Introduction* that she and Routledge would be the perfect fit for this project. Her enthusiasm for the book and her feedback at crucial points in the book's development were essential. Jennifer Vennall was an ideal editorial assistant, keeping the book on track and addressing every question and concern as if this were the only book she had to shepherd to publication.

Finally, I thank my family and friends for their patience and support throughout the writing process. I extend special thanks to Byron Suber who invited me to lead a faculty writing workshop funded by the Central New York Humanities Corridor (helping others to write is surely one of the best ways to improve your own writing), to Joyce Jesionowski who helped me to brainstorm book titles, and to Marcela Romero Rivera who offered encouragement throughout the writing process.

This book is dedicated to Jim, Steven, and Nica – my most important collaborators.

Part I
# New frameworks for writing about screen media

# 1 Introduction

*Lisa Patti*

**(Still) learning to write about screen media**

Like many of my colleagues in the sprawling field of media studies, I followed a long and winding path learning to write about cinema and other media. When I began a Ph.D. program at Cornell University in comparative literature, I planned to study contemporary novels and critical theory. But I was stopped in my tracks almost immediately by one of the first graduate seminars I took – "Sex and the Politics of Representation" – taught by Professor Amy Villarejo who would eventually become my dissertation advisor. In addition to an ambitious reading list, we also watched a feature film every week. Rather than analyzing each film through the critical framework provided by the paired reading assignments, we analyzed all of these texts together, in a critical matrix that opened up many interpretive possibilities.

I was hooked. But I was also stumped. When I began to write my first essay for that seminar, I realized that while I had something to say about the film I was analyzing (Liliana Cavani's 1974 film *The Night Porter*), I had no idea *how* to say it. After spending years learning the specialized language used to describe literary forms (from *alliteration* to *synecdoche*), I discovered that I did not know how to describe cinematic form. My professor referred me to one of the most vital reference books in the field – David Bordwell and Kristin Thompson's *Film Art*. I immediately bought a well-used copy at the campus bookstore and began to read their detailed explanations of cinematography, sound design, editing, and other elements of film style. My crash course in film aesthetics did not immediately position me to write a sophisticated analysis, but it was a start.

Over the next few years, I took as many film courses and read as much film criticism as possible. Just as I was starting to feel confident as a film critic, I began teaching as an adjunct instructor for Ithaca College's Department of Cinema and Photography. I co-taught two courses there – "Introduction to Film Aesthetics and Analysis" and "Hollywood and American Film." Each class meeting included: a lecture, the screening of a feature film and multiple shorts, and a post-screening discussion. During these classes, I learned the value of collaboration. Each instructor analyzed the films we watched from unique vantage points since they too had discovered film through idiosyncratic itineraries that included French literature, theatre, communications, English, and art history. At first, I found the course format to be very intimidating because it was difficult to prepare fully for each class meeting. When we were scheduled to discuss films that were widely available on DVD and VHS (long before the days of widespread online streaming), I would borrow the films from the library and watch them multiple times in order to prepare for lectures and discussions. I would then bring to class typed outlines and detailed screening notes to use as resources. However, the department rented some films from important archives and distributors such as the Museum of Modern Art. These films would typically arrive just before class began so that we barely had enough time to thread the 16mm prints through the projector. We certainly did not have the luxury of advanced screenings to prepare for class. I found myself in the unfamiliar position of participating in post-screening discussions with no preparation, responding to the film we had just watched without an opportunity to plan or refine my observations and arguments. Over time I grew to appreciate this forced spontaneity, and I developed confidence in my observations and interpretations. The relevance and persuasiveness of my interpretations varied, but those post-screening discussions freed me from my anxiety about being wrong and sharpened my analytical instincts.

When I began teaching for the Media and Society Program at Hobart and William Smith Colleges, I encountered new challenges as a writer and teacher. The first course that I taught at HWS was Introduction to Media and Society. After several years of teaching film, I felt comfortable guiding students through discussions of film aesthetics, history, and theory. At HWS, I was asked to teach an interdisciplinary course with the following description:

> This course provides an introduction to various media and their modes, methods, and themes. We will explore the role of media in shaping social consciousness, global economies, and material culture. Examples drawn from film, television, print media, and digital environments will be contextualized, analyzed, and theorized as crucial elements of our media culture. Students will gain an appreciation for the social, cultural, economic, and political influences of global communications while performing close readings of conventional media objects. Writing assignments, exams, presentations, and projects will help to cement insights gained through close investigation of films, TV shows, advertisements, video games, music videos, and more.

Film led a long list of media objects. Hired in May to begin teaching that August, I spent the summer learning as much as I could about "TV shows, advertisements, video games, music videos, and more." That experience changed not only my teaching but also my writing as I shifted from researching film to a broader focus on screen media. Even the one film course that I teach now – Global Cinema – includes television shows, trailers, and other media objects as supplementary texts; and I have published essays on commercials, video games, and music videos.

As I moved from teaching and writing about film to teaching and writing about screen media, I often found myself without the reference tools that had guided my earlier disciplinary turns. Film studies scholars may consult several excellent reference volumes for writers. Film scholar Timothy Corrigan's book *A Short Guide to Writing about Film* (now in its ninth edition) provides a comprehensive overview of relevant methods and resources. For example, the book includes in its discussion of note-taking a useful guide for developing a shorthand system for taking notes (for example, "cu"= "close-up"). The more recent book *Writing about Movies* (already in its fifth edition) similarly combines suggestions for writing about film with more general advice about academic writing. For example, the book contains both a comprehensive "thesis statement checklist" and an illustrated glossary of film terms. Combined with Bordwell and Thompson's *Film Art* (now in its eleventh edition), these books provide aspiring film critics with the critical tools necessary for writing both reviews and scholarly essays about cinema. I had a difficult time, however, finding similar books to guide me through the transition to teaching and writing about other screen media. Media scholars have published important books that provide critical foundations for analyzing specific media objects – including, for example, Carol Vernallis' *Experiencing Music Video: Aesthetics and Cultural Context* and Jeremy Butler's *Television: Critical Methods and Applications*. However, no single volume covers writing about the many different media objects students analyze in Media and Society classes.

I simultaneously realized that writing itself was morphing into different formats. My first forays into writing about film were unsteady as I experimented with using terms like *mise-en-scène* and *high key lighting* for the first time, but I was writing in a familiar format – the scholarly essay – where my experience as a literature student – generating close readings, structuring an argument, and citing sources – remained relevant. As I continued to write and assign scholarly essays, the field of media studies started to change. I assigned more and more blog posts, podcast episodes, video essays, and practitioner interviews as required "readings." I also expanded the "writing" assignments in my classes to include different formats for critical inquiry – for example, screencasts, trailer remixes, and blogs. I found wonderful sources that addressed specific writing formats, such as Christian Keathley and Jason Mittell's book *The Videographic Essay: Criticism in Sound & Image*, a co-authored guide to creating video essays, and the dossier "In Focus: The Practitioner Interviewer" in *Cinema Journal*, a collection of articles edited by media scholar Christine Cornea that introduces scholars to methods for interviewing directors and other media artists and practitioners. The idea for this book emerged from my desire to have a reference volume that would gather this expertise – providing insight and guidance about the growing array of media objects that we encounter in our field and the range of formats in which we might analyze those objects.

## How to read this book

Digital distribution challenges the divisions between film, television, and new media as objects of critical inquiry. As new media platforms have expanded the range of exhibition environments in which audiences encounter media content, new publication formats and platforms for scholars and critics have emerged in turn. This book reflects media studies' heterogeneity and encourages writers to experiment across formats and platforms.

In the first part of the book – "New frameworks for writing about screen media" – I offer general strategies for writing about screen media. In this chapter, I introduce my experience as a writer and provide an overview of the book. In Chapter 2 – "The big picture: Strategies for writing about screen media" – I encourage readers to adopt four writing practices – collaborating, framing, curating, and following up – that can be used to analyze any screen media object. In Chapter 3 – "From screen aesthetics to site design: Analyzing form across screen media" – I discuss the value of taking screening notes and present case studies for the analysis of form across screen media, expanding formal analysis to include the design of digital spaces. In Chapter 4 – "Entering the conversation: How and where to develop a critical argument" – I explain how to develop a critical argument in the context of various writing projects – from a traditional written essay to a video essay to a podcast. The chapter discusses free writing, outlines, introductions, evidence, and conclusions. Finally, in Chapter 5 – "From notebook to network: When and how to use digital tools" – I discuss digital resources for watching, reading about, and writing about screen media and compare them to their print counterparts. The chapter also explores best practices for citation and considers the fair use of copyrighted material in media criticism.

The second part of the book – "Writers on writing about screen media" – includes short chapters from several dozen media scholars. Featuring emerging and established scholars from a wide range of disciplinary and geographic locations, this part of the book explores different media objects from the perspective of writers who have produced some of the most exciting recent work in their respective fields. Each contributor discusses one media object (for example, music videos or film credit sequences) or writing format (for example, film reviews or video essays), combining personal reflections about writing with practical advice. This part of the book includes three sections: "Objects and events" features chapters that focus on specific media texts (such as found footage films or television shows) or media events (such as film festivals or video gameplay); "Methods and locations" includes chapters that present specific media studies methodologies (such as ethnographic interviews or data analysis) and spaces (such as media archives or streaming platforms); and "Forms and formats" presents chapters that consider different modes of critical expression (such as podcasts and blurbs).

You may opt to read this book in a linear fashion, from cover to cover, to gain an overview of different approaches to writing about screen media. However, the book also enables modular reading. Below you will find a series of proposed units – collections of several chapters that allow you to explore a particular topic from multiple vantage points. These units make visible the points of intersection and tension between and among the chapters. Each writer pays careful attention to the contexts in which they write – the personal, historical, cultural, and institutional factors that have led them to write about screen media in particular ways. Combining these chapters affords you an opportunity to consider key topics within different writing contexts.

While *Writing About Screen Media* provides an extensive survey of writing about screen media, this book is not exhaustive or comprehensive. As a reader, you can expand the scope of the book by following each chapter's lead to other examples and resources. In a recent article in *Cinema Journal* (since renamed the *Journal of Cinema and Media Studies*), media scholar Jennifer Malkowski (one of the contributors to this volume), argues in favor of exploring the breadth of media studies. They write,

> Cinema and media studies has grown so vast that none of us sees its whole panorama anymore, if we ever could. That doesn't excuse us from making the effort of climbing at least a few stories skyward to get a better vantage point.
>
> (130)

Whether you are a student who is about to write about screen media for the first time or an accomplished writer who would like to experiment with a new format or subject, the chapters in this book invite you to try something new. The implicit – and at times explicit – argument throughout the book is "Try this!" Readers will find additional resources and links on the book's companion website: writingaboutscreenmedia.net.

## *Formal analysis and design*

Formal analysis entails the close reading of aesthetic details – from visual style to sound-image relationships. Chapter 3 presents strategies for analyzing screen aesthetics across a range of media objects. This chapter stresses the importance of note-taking and demonstrates comparative approaches to formal analysis through a series of case studies that examine the formal qualities of media texts (cinematography, editing, *mise-en-scène*, and sound) and the design of the digital spaces where we often encounter screen media (such as websites for individual texts and streaming platforms).

Many of the chapters in the second part of the book also analyze form: Nilanjana Bhattacharjya presents a close reading of the sound-image relationships in a song sequence from the film *Omkara* (Vishal Bhardwaj, 2006); Jeffrey Middents discusses the editing decisions he made when producing a video essay on Alfonso Cuarón's film *Roma* (2018); Chiara Grizzaffi complements his essay by discussing the formal attributes of successful video essays from her perspective as a reviewer; TreaAndrea M. Russworm and Jennifer Malkowski consider strategies for analyzing the aesthetics and mechanics of games; Carol Vernallis offers a toolkit for the formal analysis of music videos, including an excerpt from her close reading of Lady Gaga's "Bad Romance" video; and Christine Becker and Kyle Wrather discuss sound, editing, and other formal features of podcasts.

Turning to questions of design, Dale Hudson and Patricia R. Zimmermann analyze the design features (and interactive possibilities) of new media art; Lauren McLeod Cramer analyzes "The Very Black Project" on Instagram; Virginia Kuhn explores the design features of online essays; and Ramon Lobato considers the structure of global streaming portals.

A series of chapters focuses specifically on analyzing text/image relationships: Grizzaffi discusses the use of text in video essays; Hudson and Zimmermann discuss the textual elements of digital media projects in relation to other design features; Kuhn discusses different approaches to designing text for the screen; Tijana Mamula discusses screen media subtitles; and Monika Mehta analyzes the textual elements in film credit sequences.

## *Ethnography*

Ethnographic methods – including participant observation and interviews – move beyond textual analysis to research specific cultures (for example, regional, institutional, or industrial cultures) and the people who live and work within them. Several essays in Part II explore ethnographic approaches to screen media criticism. Tejaswini Ganti explains what she has learned through her ethnographic research on Bombay cinema; Lauren S. Berliner recounts her research on participatory media projects; Alicia Kozma shares best practices for interviewing based on her experiences interviewing the women staff members of independent arthouse theatres; Rahul Mukherjee includes anecdotes from his ethnographic research on mobile phone use in India; Kirsten Stevens discusses the ethnographic research methods necessary to analyze film festivals as events; Jasmine Nadua Trice discusses her ethnographic research on film exhibition in Manila, Philippines; Julie Wilson and Emily Chivers Yochim discuss their interviews with mothers about social media; and Fan Yang considers social media research as ethnography. The emphasis on best practices for conducting interviews in the chapters by Ganti, Wilson and Yochim, and Kozma also surfaces in Christine Becker and Kyle Wrather's overview of podcast interviews and Henry Jenkins' guidelines for publishing interviews on a blog. In addition, the chapters by Berliner and Kozma offer specific guidelines for applying for approval from your institution's IRB (Institutional Review Board) for ethnographic research projects.

## History

Part I focuses on contemporary (primarily twenty-first century) examples of screen media as do many of the chapters in Part II. However, several chapters offer guidance for conducting historical research. Kirsten Stevens discusses strategies for historical research about international film festivals; Beth Corzo-Duchardt shares resources for finding information about outdoor advertisements, including open access digital archives; Allyson Nadia Field explores early film from an archaeological perspective, explaining how writers can find information about *nonextant media*; Katherine Groo shares her experiences visiting film archives in different countries and provides starting points and critical questions for archival research; and Glyn Davis considers the differences between watching historical experimental films online and in museums.

## Access

Studying media history reveals the varying degrees of access we have to the media objects we want to study. Glyn Davis, Allyson Nadia Field, and Katherine Groo all consider access to historical media objects in relation to archives (both online archives and physical archives housed in museums and other spaces.) Terri Francis considers her role working on the DVD release of the film *Losing Ground* (Kathleen Collins, 1982), previously unavailable to her and other teachers. Jaimie Baron discusses found footage films and the "archive effect" they produce. TreaAndrea M. Russworm and Jennifer Malkowski acknowledge the difficulty of accessing many games, pointing to alternative ways to access gaming experiences (for example, gameplay walkthrough videos). Fan Yang explores issues of access in relation to censorship, discussing the history of the Chinese online documentary *Under the Dome* (Chai Jing, 2015). Field, Francis, and Russworm and Malkowski also consider the role of *format obsolescence*, the ways new technologies make old ones obsolete or even extinct, in preventing our access to media objects produced in formats no longer supported by the technologies we regularly use.

## Authorship

Many studies of screen media either explicitly or implicitly engage theories of media authorship. Several chapters in the second part of the book consider the role of media authors: Jeffrey Middents analyzes the authorship of film director Alfonso Cuarón, discussing his recent film *Roma* (2018) in relation to his earlier films and noticing the narrative and stylistic connections among his films; Derek Johnson considers corporate authorship and transmedia franchises; Lauren McLeod Cramer discusses the authorship of "The Very Black Project" on Instagram; and Monika Mehta considers *above-the-line* (directors, writers, etc.) and *below-the-line* (artisans, technicians, etc.) authorship as revealed in film credit sequences. Mehta's chapter is one of several that consider media *paratexts*, texts such as trailers, posters, and commentaries that circulate in relation to other media texts. Other analyses of media paratexts include: Nilanjana Bhattacharjya's analysis of film song sequences (which often circulate separately from the films in which they appear); Tijana Mamula's analysis of subtitles and dubbing; Terri Francis's account of recording the audio commentary for the DVD release of the film *Losing Ground* (Kathleen Collins, 1982); Leah Shafer's guidelines for writing film blurbs; and Beth Corzo-Duchardt's historical analysis of billboards and other outdoor advertisements. Paratexts extend the storytelling worlds of films, television shows, games, and other screen media objects, complicating our understanding of authorship and providing multiple points of entry for our analysis.

**Media industries**

Several chapters employ ideas and methods from the field of *media industries studies*: Bronwyn Coate and Deb Verhoeven model the use of data to understand film industry trends and recommend policy changes; Derek Johnson outlines a framework for analyzing media franchises; Olivia Khoo considers the reception of the global blockbuster film *Crazy Rich Asians* (John M. Chu, 2018) in relation to its production and distribution history; Ramon Lobato offers guidelines for studying global streaming platforms such as Netflix; Monika Mehta shows that film credit sequences contain important information about the industrial history of films; Jasmine Mitchell reveals that the official corporate policies of major television networks regarding cultural representation may contradict their programming; and Rahul Mukherjee uses ethnographic fieldwork and a close reading of mobile phone advertisements to consider the discourses of "unlimited data" circulated by mobile phone network providers. Mukherjee and Coate and Verhoeven explore data's role in media analysis from different vantage points, with Mukherjee considering the discourses surrounding "unlimited" data and Coate and Verhoeven demonstrating the value of data for industry analysis. Complementing their chapters, Alicia Kozma discusses the collection of data through interviews, and Dale Hudson and Patricia R. Zimmermann analyze data in relation to digital and interactive media projects.

**Exhibition**

Chapter 3 explores formal analysis, paying attention to the exhibition (and distribution) conditions in which we encounter media objects. Several chapters in the second part of the book similarly explore media exhibition. Allyson Nadia Field reminds readers that *nonextant media* that are no longer accessible to us as primary sources were in fact viewed by specific audiences, encouraging us to locate as much information as possible about the exhibition histories of those lost media objects. Alicia Kozma discusses her interviews with the female employees of contemporary independent arthouse cinemas, inviting us to think about the ways that ethnographic research yields insights about theatrical exhibition's labor conditions. Jasmine Nadua Trice shares her experiences researching contemporary film exhibition and distribution practices in Manila,

Philippines. Kirsten Stevens shifts our analytical focus from films to film festivals, pointing to the different elements of a festival as an event that invite our analysis. Glyn Davis discusses the different exhibition contexts for experimental films – from gallery installations to laptop screenings; and Jaimie Baron explains the value of including in our writing an account of our experience watching a film. Ramon Lobato considers the role of global streaming services in the exhibition landscape. Finally, Fan Yang discusses the online release of the documentary project *Under the Dome* (Chai Jing, 2015) as an event, best tracked in real time as viewers respond to the event on social media platforms.

## *Digital media*

In the first part of the book, multiple chapters directly address digital media. Chapter 2 presents strategies for analyzing screen media in digital environments; Chapter 3 considers formal analysis in relation to the design of digital presentation spaces; Chapter 4 compares the formulation of critical arguments in print and digital forms; and Chapter 5 provides an overview of digital resources for reading, watching, and writing.

Many of the chapters in Part II consider digital screen media (such as Dale Hudson and Patricia R. Zimmermann's exploration of digital and interactive media projects), while others consider media with longer histories through the lens of digital distribution (such as Ramon Lobato's chapter on Netflix and other global streaming services.) The list of chapters that address digital media includes: Lauren S. Berliner's discussion of participatory media; Lauren McLeod Cramer's analysis of "The Very Black Project" on Instagram; Christine Becker and Kyle Wrather's discussion of podcasts; Henry Jenkins' chapter on blogs; Terri Francis' account of recording the audio commentary for the DVD release of the film *Losing Ground* (Kathleen Collins, 1982); Virginia Kuhn's assessment of writing for online publication; Tijana Mamula's review of digital translation practices and opportunities; Jeffrey Middents' account of producing a video essay; Rahul Mukherjee's exploration of mobile phones; Carol Vernallis' discussion of music videos; Julie Wilson and Emily Chivers Yochim's research on mothering and social media; and Fan Yang's discussion of the online circulation of *Under the Dome* (Chai Jing, 2015).

## *Representation*

Several chapters focus directly on issues of *representation*. Lauren S. Berliner, Olivia Khoo, Lauren McLeod Cramer, S. Heijin Lee, and Jasmine Mitchell consider the ways in which *stereotypes* shape media criticism, discussing participatory media, film, social media, music videos, and television respectively. They explore the ways our assumptions about racial and ethnic representation inform the production and reception of screen media. Bronwyn Coate and Deb Verhoeven show that an analysis of industry data can lead to policy changes that encourage diversity within the film industry.

## 12  Lisa Patti

### Transnational media

Many chapters employ a *transnational media* framework, tracing the production or circulation of media texts across geographic borders. Chapter 2 argues for the importance of considering media objects in a comparative framework and for doing so, whenever relevant, on a global scale. Chapter 3 presents case studies of formal analysis that model comparison in global frameworks. In Part II of the book, multiple chapters adopt a transnational perspective: Olivia Khoo considers the film *Crazy Rich Asians* (John M. Chu, 2018) as a global blockbuster; S. Heijin Lee discusses PSY's "Gangnam Style" music video in relation to its American and South Korean reception; Tijana Mamula argues for the importance of translation for both screen media and media criticism; Fan Yang explores the transnational circulation of the Chinese documentary project *Under the Dome* (Chai Jing, 2015); and Jeffrey Middents approaches the films of Alfonso Cuarón through a comparative framework. A second set of chapters explores national case studies: Bronwyn Coate and Deb Verhoeven examine film exhibition in Australia; Jasmine Mitchell discusses Brazilian television; and Rahul Mukherjee examines mobile phone use in India. Readers may combine several chapters into a single national case study explored through multiple perspectives and methodologies by reading together three chapters about cinema in India: Monika Mehta's analysis of film credit sequences; Tejaswini Ganti's analysis of Bombay cinema production cultures; and Nilanjana Bhattacharjya's analysis of Bollywood song and dance sequences.

### Comparative case studies

Readers may opt to compare case studies that focus on media objects linked by their medium or format. Beth Corzo-Duchardt and Rahul Mukherjee both discuss advertisements. Carol Vernallis and S. Heijin Lee both discuss music videos, and Nilanjana Bhattacharjya's analysis of a film song sequence complements their readings of music performances. Lauren McLeod Cramer, Fan Yang, and Julie Wilson and Emily Chivers Yochim all discuss social media.

Readers may similarly combine chapters that explore specific writing modes. Multiple chapters discuss writing reviews: Nick Davis compares writing film reviews for popular publications like *Film Comment* to writing scholarly essays; Terri Francis considers the range of observations one can share when crafting an audio commentary; Chiara Grizzaffi discusses the process of writing an open access peer review of a video essay; Alice Leppert presents best practices for writing an academic book review; and Leah Shafer guides readers through blurb writing.

### Research

The chapters in this book employ different forms of media research – from visiting media archives to reading media criticism. Chapter 4 discusses the development of a research question and a thesis statement in the early phases of your writing process and the importance of locating and presenting evidence to support your argument. Chapter 5 discusses digital research resources and citation strategies. Several chapters in the second part of the book directly address different elements of the research process. Lauren McLeod Cramer, Olivia Khoo, Kirsten Stevens, and Jasmine Nadua Trice explain how to formulate a research question, and Holly Willis considers the different (and creative) ways writers can present their research. Beth Corzo-Duchardt, Allyson Nadia Field, and Fan Yang point out the value of specific online research resources; and Glyn Davis and Katherine Groo explain the importance of visiting media archives.

*Writing style*

In her book *Stylish Academic Writing*, Helen Sword argues that "stylish academic writers achieve abstract ends such as *engagement, pleasure,* and *elegance* not through mystical displays of brilliance and eloquence [...] but by deploying some very concrete, specific, and transferable techniques" (8). Sword urges writers to follow the lead of their stylish peers by using "first-person anecdotes," "numerous examples," and "visual illustrations," among other techniques (8). Each chapter in Part II models stylish writing, but several chapters directly discuss writing style. Henry Jenkins focuses on the best writing style to adopt for blogs, and Leah Shafer presents the 4 C's of writing an engaging blurb. Nick Davis reflects on the differences between writing for scholarly publications and popular publications. Jenkins, Shafer, and Davis all consider the issue of writing style in relation to length as does Alice Leppert in her discussion of the challenges of writing book reviews. Finally, Holly Willis explores "creative critical writing" and the importance of focusing on questions of form and style in our writing across formats and platforms rather than focusing only on the critical arguments we present.

### In practice

*Write your (writing) autobiography*

In the opening section of this introduction, I shared my writing autobiography – a narrative account of the different stages in my ongoing project of learning how to write about screen media. For me, each stage involves self-assessment: what kind of writer have I been so far? What do I need and want to learn about writing? To begin, assess the types of media objects you have written about, the critical methods that have informed your writing, and the writing formats that you have used. Turn this account – which might include a single entry such as "scholarly written essays about film" or an extensive list such as "written essays, video essays, and interviews about film, television, and new media" into a short narrative essay. In your essay, present a brief chronological account of the path that you followed to this book.

Your writing autobiography should define your strengths as a writer – for example, "discussing complex ideas in a lively and accessible prose style" – and should link those strengths to goals for expanding your writing portfolio – for example, "starting a weekly blog with a colleague" or, more modestly, "writing a television episode recap to share with a friend." Revising your autobiography at regular intervals – for example, at the end of every semester or at the end of every academic year – will help you to track your progress. Remember, however, that disciplinary and creative breadth for the sake of breadth is not the goal of this exercise (or this book.) Instead, an inventory of your writing allows you to define more clearly for yourself and for those reading your work how you position yourself as a writer in relation to the field of media studies and how the depth and/or breadth of your work contributes to the field.

**Accept invitations to experiment with your writing**

"In practice" sections at the end of every chapter in Part I invite you to participate in writing exercises that put the book's recommendations into practice. The later chapters do not include formal "In practice" sections, but each chapter directly or indirectly invites you to experiment with a new writing practice. When you encounter these invitations, accept them, adjusting their scope whenever necessary in order to make them more manageable and more relevant for you.

# References

Bordwell, David, Kristin Thompson, and Jeff Smith. *Film Art: An Introduction*. 11th edition. McGraw Hill, 2017.

Butler, Jeremy. *Television: Critical Methods and Applications*. 4th edition. Routledge, 2012.

Cornea, Christine, editor. "In Focus: The Practitioner Interview." *Cinema Journal*, vol. 47, no. 2, 2008.

Corrigan, Timothy. *A Short Guide to Writing About Film*. 9th edition. Pearson, 2015.

Gocsik, Karen, Dave Monahan, and Richard Barsam. *Writing About Movies*. 5th edition. Norton, 2019.

Keathley, Christian, and Jason Mittell. *The Videographic Essay: Criticism in Sound & Image*. caboose, 2016.

Malkowski, Jennifer. "Against Expertise: The Current Case for Breadth Over Depth." *Cinema Journal*, vol. 57, no. 2, 2018.

Sword, Helen. *Stylish Academic Writing*. Harvard UP, 2012.

Vernallis, Carol. *Experiencing Music Video: Aesthetics and Cultural Context*. Columbia UP, 2004.

# 2 The big picture
## Strategies for writing about screen media

*Lisa Patti*

This chapter presents four strategies for analyzing screen media. First, *collaborate* with other writers, approaching writing as a critical conversation between you and your writing partners. Second, *frame* your analysis, using different frames to define the scope of your work and the critical methodologies it deploys. Third, *curate* media objects into sets or series that facilitate comparisons and provoke questions. Finally, *follow* the critical conversations that your work enters, soliciting and engaging feedback and seeking out new work that other scholars and artists produce.

## Collaborate

Five of the chapters in Part II of this volume were co-authored by two writers reflecting on their previous co-writing experiences. The labor of co-writing may take different forms. My experiences as a co-author have followed this basic model: first, the co-authors generate ideas through various forms of pre-writing which may include: exchanging ideas via e-mail, having pre-writing meetings via phone or video conference, and sharing preliminary writing plans in the form of notes and outlines. Second, the co-authors devise a formal writing plan that clearly divides the writing tasks. This often involves designating each author as the primary author for some sections of the writing project and the secondary author for other sections. The authors then begin to work independently on their respective sections. Third, the authors trade their drafts back and forth, offering comments and suggestions in response to each other's drafts. Finally, the authors edit and proofread the final merged draft of the writing project, usually through several stages of revision, first addressing big picture issues of argument and organization and eventually addressing close-up issues such as spelling and grammar. This work flow may vary among different writing partnerships (and collaborative writing may involve more than two writers), but several basic principles of co-writing apply to most collaborations: a clear division of labor; openness to giving and accepting rigorous feedback; and frequent communication between the writers during all three major phases of writing – pre-writing, writing, and revision.

Collaborative writing draws our attention to the ways that all scholarly writing proceeds as a critical conversation. Often that conversation may seem remote or abstract. If you are writing a scholarly essay about a classical Hollywood film such as *Singin' in the Rain* (Gene Kelly and Stanly Donen, 1952), you are entering into a critical dialogue with the many scholars and critics who have previously written about the film. However, it might be difficult to bring the liveliness of an actual conversation into your prose or to imagine that your work is in fact contributing to a critical conversation. I have found it much easier to remain aware of the critical conversations I am entering when I write with one or more collaborators. The conversations that we have behind the scenes during the writing process acknowledge the wider critical conversations that our work engages and the new conversations we hope to generate. As we debate arguments and counter-arguments, share sources to consult, or consider the best choice of words to convey a particular idea, we enact critical conversations that shape our writing.

Collaboration can influence writing projects even when you are writing independently. While I strongly advocate for the value of collaborative writing, there are many times when a single-authored project makes more sense, either because you have been assigned to produce an independent project by an editor or teacher or because your research positions you to present a specific argument emerging from your work. In these cases, you can still adopt a collaborative approach even if your name will be the only one below the title.

Building on my positive experience working with a dissertation writing group when I was a graduate student, I have been fortunate to work with a writing partner, film scholar Monika Mehta, throughout my career as a professor. We meet once a week to share our work in progress and offer each other rigorous yet supportive feedback. She has read every word that I have written over the past ten years – not only book chapters and scholarly articles but also syllabi, assignment handouts, and grant applications. Her analyses respond to my ideas, suggest revisions, and raise questions. Because we have worked together for so long, she understands well the central concerns that drive my research and teaching, enabling her to share sharp feedback. After reviewing her suggestions, I hone my arguments, eliminate digressions, and polish my prose. Developing a long term writing partnership like ours may not be practical or desirable for everyone, but consider forging a more limited writing partnership as an experiment. You might ask a colleague at your institution or a student colleague in one of your classes to work with you for one semester. You can begin modestly by each sharing one piece of writing, and then scale up your partnership if you find it to be successful.

### Peer Review

Peer review may be the most familiar form of collaborative writing for students. In her chapter in Part II of this volume, Chiara Grizzaffi discusses her experience writing open access peer reviews of video essays in the online journal *[in]Transition*. The practice of writing peer reviews for publication points to the value of approaching peer review as a rigorous and constructive mode of critical engagement. Most peer reviews will not be published, but approaching them with the same level of care as the editors for *[in]Transition* will be productive both for the writer and the reviewer. The most generative peer reviews include the following phases:

1. *The writer presents the reviewer with a clear explanation of her writing goals*. Like a project abstract or an introduction (discussed in detail in Chapter 4), this explanation should answer the following questions: What? So what? How? You might also opt to draft a letter to your reader.
2. *The writer requests specific feedback*. Consider where you are in your writing process – a tentative first draft or almost-finished near-final draft? – and the forms of feedback your reader is in the best position to offer. Is your reader a specialist in video game studies who might be able to suggest scholarly sources for you to discuss in order to strengthen your argument about a game, or is she a scholar in a different field who might be unfamiliar with video games but able to help you identify the moments when your argument requires additional supporting evidence or a sharper formulation? Ask for feedback that serves your writing goals and that leverages your reviewer's expertise.
3. *The reviewer reads (or watches or listens to) the writer's work with care over time*. One class period may not be sufficient for your reader to review a longer essay (or video or podcast) and write comments. When I am reading drafts – whether from colleagues or from students – I prefer to read in stages – reading the entire draft first without recording any comments so that I can register a general impression of the work, returning to the draft later for a more careful reading during which I record comments, and then reviewing my comments at a later time to make sure that I have communicated my responses clearly and supportively. Give your reviewer sufficient time to review your work and draft a written response. Invite her to jot notes in the margin (or save comments in the margin if she is editing a digital draft) and to write a summary response outlining the parts of your draft that she found most engaging and those that require revision.
4. *The writer and the reviewer meet to discuss the project (in person if possible) after the writer has read the reviewer's written comments*. Thank your reviewer for her time and feedback. Confirm that you fully understand her suggestions, ask any follow-up questions that you might have, and share your plans for revising your draft. Then send her a copy of the final draft of your work, acknowledging formally the value of her suggestions.

## Frame

The writer Anne Lamott urges other writers to keep an empty one-inch picture frame on their desks. She explains that the frame "reminds me that all I have to do is write down as much as I can see through a one-inch picture frame" (17). For Lamott, the frame directs her to think of writing as a series of small, manageable tasks. You do not have to complete an entire writing project in one sitting, just one small element of it.

Framing resonates in multiple ways for writing about screen media. Screens impose frames on our vision and experience. When we study film, television, and other screen media, we analyze framing in relation to cinematography, *mise-en-scène*, and editing (elements of form that will be discussed in detail in Chapter 3). Our analysis may even focus on a single frame from one of those texts. Lamott's advice inspires a classroom exercise that my students use to spark ideas for formal analysis. We project images from the films, television shows, and other media we are discussing onto the screens in our classroom. Then students select empty matte inserts for picture frames of various sizes and use them to frame the image on the screen. By walking toward and away from the screens and exchanging small frames for larger ones, students observe the ways that adjusting their frame impacts the stories they tell. You may adapt this very literal framing exercise for any writing project. Decide how small or big you want your frame to be and where and how you want to position it in relation to the object or objects that you are discussing. What will the format of your writing project be? How long will it be? What do you notice when you change the size of the frame and its orientation? For example, I have written two different book chapters about Netflix – one that considers how professors and students use Netflix in media studies classes and one, co-authored with film scholar Monika Mehta, that investigates Netflix's presentation and promotion of Bombay films and Korean dramas on its website. These chapters both analyze Netflix, but they use very different frames, one considering Netflix in relation to teaching practices and another comparing Netflix to other streaming services such as Drama Fever and Viki as portals for media content from diverse global regions. In each case, the frame shaped the analysis.

Once you have made those preliminary framing decisions, move toward building a critical framework. What are the critical questions that you want to address? What are the existing critical frameworks that might help you to explore those questions? Chapter 1 presents a series of critical frameworks – authorship, representation, transnational media, etc. – engaged by the chapters in Part II of this book. You might position your writing project within one or more of those existing critical frameworks. Making decisions about the critical conversations you want to enter will also guide you toward sources to review as you build a bibliography (or filmography) to engage. The recent book *The Craft of Criticism*, edited by media scholars Michael Kackman and Mary Celeste Kearney, provides a comprehensive collection of different critical frameworks and methodologies that shape contemporary media studies scholarship – an especially useful resource for writers who want to explore a new methodology.

Finally, as you develop your analysis, use the idea of the one-inch frame to remind you to zoom into details. Even if you are producing a project on a grand scale – say, a book – your analysis will benefit from frequently picking up the one-inch frame (so to speak) to examine small details – for example, formal details such as an object visible in the background of a single film frame; or narrative details such as a long break in a voiceover narration during a television episode; or extra-textual details about the ownership history of a media franchise. Keep in mind that concrete details will make your analysis more accessible and more compelling for your readers/viewers/listeners, so incorporate one-inch frame observations into every writing project.

## Curate

You may be asked by an instructor, editor, or colleague to write a review about a specific film or to contribute an essay or blog post about a recent television show. However, your first task as a writer may be selecting the media object or objects you will analyze. In the courses I teach, I offer students progressively more autonomy with their selections as the semester unfolds. Initial assignments invite them to write about one assigned media object, and each subsequent assignment provides more and more curatorial freedom until their final assignment where they have maximal flexibility regarding the media objects they discuss and the critical frameworks they craft. When you choose media objects to write about, think tactically and creatively.

The word "curate" seems to be ubiquitous in contemporary media culture – used to describe everything from Instagram accounts to corporate brand identities to streaming catalogues. Aware of its overuse, I highlight the word "curate" here because it captures the labor of selecting and framing objects to share with an audience. A curator makes tactical decisions about: the objects they deem most important for viewers to encounter, how to place those objects in relation to other similar (or different) objects, what contextual information viewers require, and what argument their project as a whole should make. Framing these decisions in relation to practices of curation reminds us that writing is a social act. Even absent all of the forms of collaboration I advocate earlier in this chapter, writers engage if not with other writers then at the very least with their readers. The language of curation keeps our audience always in view.

Thinking about writing as an act of curating also signals that our decisions to write about specific media objects reflect (and possibly also challenge) media *canons*. In my Introduction to Media and Society class, I introduce students to the concept of a canon by reviewing various media lists – syllabi for classes, tables of contents for books, and lists of "the best" films, television shows, games, etc. produced by various organizations and publications.[1] When you write about a media object that appears on many of these lists, you may be participating in a critical conversation that has spanned decades. If, however, you write about a recent independent film in a language other than English with a limited international release or an amateur video on YouTube that has been viewed very few times, you will enter a different critical conversation. There will be more ground for you to cover – exciting from the perspective that you will not have to worry about the challenge of coming up with an original argument or the responsibility of reviewing and citing scores of sources that focus on the same text but daunting from the perspective that you will have to, in a sense, present the object for the first time to readers. Whether you are writing about a widely discussed media object or a more recent or obscure one, consider the critical contributions you want to make and then curate a selection of other texts that will generate the most engaging comparative analysis possible.

Curation involves juxtaposition or, to think more tactically, collision. What are the ideas, observations, revelations, associations, and provocations that you generate by placing one object next to another? Position widely studied films about which many book-length analyses have been written among new sets of objects, contexts, theories, and points of view. More recent media objects await their first scholarly considerations. Analyze them as individual texts, but also compare them to other texts.

Course syllabi activate these comparisons. For example, in my senior seminar on stardom, we watch the classical Hollywood film *Gentlemen Prefer Blondes* (Howard Hawks, 1953) with the found footage film *Marilyn Times Five* (Bruce Conner, 1973), film scholar Laura Mulvey's video essay "*Gentlemen Prefer Blondes remix*" (2013), Madonna's "Material Girl" music video (Mary Lambert, 1985) – a remake of the "Diamonds are a Girl's Best Friend" sequence from *Gentlemen Prefer Blondes*, and the perfume commercial "J'Adore Dior" (Jean-Jacques Annaud, 2011) which includes digitally edited posthumous images of Monroe. This mix of media texts – a commercial film, an experimental film, a video essay, a music video, and a commercial – sets in motion a lively dialogue about Monroe's star image and its transformations.

Remember that every time you write you are inviting your readers into a critical space that you have designed. Imagine a gallery where you install different media in various static or interactive configurations according to a layout that you have carefully sketched before hanging the first screen. Next imagine filling the room with critical voices – the scholars, critics, fans, and practitioners whose ideas you cite and discuss as you develop your comparative argument about how these texts fit together. Then imagine the readers who will move through that space, following the path of your argument. Design a gallery exhibit that excites and challenges visitors and that provides new perspectives on each object you include.

## Follow (up)

When I return graded projects to students, I give them a detailed grading rubric and a written summary of my assessment of their work. As a next step, I ask students to write a short response to my assessment. Our written exchange of ideas serves as the basis for our conversations during writing conferences. This form of following up – extending the analysis of a project beyond the student's submission of the project and the instructor's initial assessment to a dialogue that unfolds first in writing and then in person – maximizes the opportunities that writers and readers have to reflect on the ideas they are sharing.

In the senior seminar that I teach, the students produce a capstone project – a substantive revision and expansion of an earlier project (and, in some cases, a fusion of multiple projects). This practice of re-visiting and revising earlier work makes visible the ways in which writers develop their ideas and their craft over time. I am always thrilled when students remark to me while working on their final writing projects that "everything connects." This discovery leads them to spend more time considering the best frame for their project – usually one that resists the temptation to include all of the connecting ideas and texts they have excavated in order to focus on the development of a sharp critical argument. Following up through intensive reflection and revision elevates analysis and writing.

Following up extends not only to writing but also to reading and reviewing. Scholars often track the texts and topics that they write about long after they publish their work. Reading widely in the broad field of media criticism – scholarly journals, trade journals, newspapers and magazines, blogs, etc. – will enable you to track many different critical threads and conversations (as discussed in detail in Chapter 5). Setting up news alerts for specific topics makes that process easier since even the most avid reader will be unable to keep up-to-date with the latest issues of every relevant publication. To the extent that writing involves participating in an ongoing critical dialogue (as discussed earlier in this chapter and also in Chapter 4), your participation should not end the moment you publish or submit your writing project. After investing a lot of time and energy on a single writing project, you might, understandably, want to shift your focus. But there is a lot to be gained as a writer from tracking the critical conversations you have entered. So actively look for ways to follow up. If your work is published, monitor its reception and invite direct feedback from colleagues. Whether or not your work is published, continue to follow the critical discussions of the topics you addressed, and seize any opportunities you find to offer constructive feedback to other writers who share your interests.

### In practice

#### Think like a programmer

When you write about a media object, begin by programming the primary text (a film, television show, game, etc.) into a line-up with other related media objects. Not every critical argument must assess a media object in relation to others. As discussed in this chapter, every writing project has a different frame. Your next writing project might involve a very narrow frame, and it may not be necessary to expand the frame to include other texts. However, comparative modes of thinking may enhance even a sharply focused writing project. In my Global Cinema class, I invite students to propose a global film series for our local independent theatre. Working in small groups, students suggest a series of five to six films linked by a shared critical framework – a geographic region, a genre, a theme, etc. – and draft a title and a blurb for the series and for each individual film. (For guidelines about blurb writing, see Leah Shafer's chapter in Part II of this book.) The project begins with students selecting two films from our syllabus and deciding how the connections between those films might generate a critical framework for the film series and lead them to other films.

This approach may apply to any media object. For example, imagine that you are an executive for a major television network planning a prime-time line-up. What shows would you include? How would you market them together?

Projects like these may seed much more ambitious initiatives (for example, turning the film series proposal into a campus event), but they may also function more modestly as brainstorming exercises. Take notes as you plan ways to combine different media objects. What are the elements (formal, narrative, industrial, political, etc.) that link these texts? What differences among the texts does your comparison uncover? How might this comparison sharpen your analysis of the primary text that launched your brainstorming?

### *Think like a director*

Create a storyboard for your ideas. Chapter 4 promotes the value of writing outlines for every writing project. We often associate outlines with traditional writing projects and storyboards with visual media projects, but you can use *both* outlines *and* storyboards for writing projects in any medium and format. Design a storyboard at an early stage in your brainstorming process, when you have some ideas for how to proceed but may not have a sharp thesis statement and may not be ready to commit to an outline (where you should present a thesis, a well-structured argument, detailed examples and other forms of evidence, and a conclusion).

You can find many different storyboard templates online using the simple search terms "storyboard" and "image." For the purposes of prewriting, however, I find that a stack of index cards (or any stack of paper) works just as well. Showcase one image on each card, and then add some basic textual information to accompany each image. By experimenting with different ways of storyboarding your discussion, you may divine the best path for your analysis.

If you are producing a writing project that includes images (for example, a video essay or a written essay with multiple images embedded in the text or included as an appendix), some or all of the images that you include in your storyboard may also be included in the final project. Select the most important images for your project, and remain open to different ways of organizing and presenting those images.

**Think like an editor**

Over 40 scholars contributed chapters for this book. Each chapter provides important guidance, but reading them together generates even more revelations about writing. Editing a collection – soliciting, reviewing, organizing, and introducing the work of other scholars – allows you to bring the perspectives of different scholars together into a (virtual) critical conversation.

The online journal *In Media Res* invites scholars to work independently or collaboratively as editors of "theme weeks:"

> Each weekday, a different scholar curates a 30-second to 3-minute video clip/visual image slideshow accompanied by a 300–350-word impressionistic response. We use the title "curator" because, like a curator in a museum, you are repurposing a media object that already exists and providing context through your commentary, which frames the object in a particular way. The clip/comment combination are intended both to introduce the curator's work to the larger community of scholars (as well as non-academics who frequent the site) and, hopefully, encourage feedback/discussion from that community.
>
> Theme weeks are designed to generate a networked conversation between curators. All the posts for theme weeks thematically overlap and the participating curators each agree to comment on one another's work.
>
> ("About In Media Res")

Contributing a post to a theme week allows you to: analyze a specific (usually very short) media object in relation to other related projects; experiment with an informal scholarly voice; and engage in a critical dialogue with scholars, critics, and (at times) fans and practitioners.

In my Introduction to Media and Society class, I base a collaborative writing project on the *In Media Res* theme week model. Students take turns serving as theme week co-editors – proposing a theme, inviting contributions from student curators, reviewing their posts and suggesting revisions, publishing the posts on our course website, and encouraging other students to share comments online. The individual curators must select a media object (for example, a subtitled still, a music video, a remix video, or a GIF) and write a short essay analyzing the object. Each essay must propose an argument and raise critical questions for discussion.

24  Lisa Patti

> Consider ways to adapt this collaborative exercise on a larger scale (for example, by proposing an official *In Media Res* theme week with a co-editor) or a smaller scale (for example, by writing one post and circulating it, along with the media object you discuss, to a peer reviewer).

## Note

1  For a detailed description of this Introduction to Media and Society assignment – inviting students to curate a set of bonus features for a proposed Criterion Collection DVD release of one of the films on the American Film Institute's "100 Years…100 Movies list," see Patti, 2017.

## References

"About In Media Res." *In Media Res*. http://mediacommons.org/imr/about. Accessed March 1, 2019.

Kackman, Michael and Mary Celeste Kearney, editors. *The Craft of Criticism: Critical Media Studies in Practice*. Routledge, 2018.

Lamott, Anne. *Bird by Bird: Some Instructions on Writing and Life*. Anchor Books, 1995.

Patti, Lisa, "Cinephilia and Paratexts: DVD Pedagogy in the Era of Instant Streaming." *For the Love of Cinema: Teaching Our Passion in and Outside the Classroom*, edited by Rashna Wadia Richards and David T. Johnson, Indiana UP, 2017, pp. 179–194.

# 3 From screen aesthetics to site design
## Analyzing form across screen media

*Lisa Patti*

This chapter focuses on formal analysis – approaching screen media through careful attention to cinematography, sound, editing, and *mise-en-scène*. The chapter opens by discussing screening notes, offering guidelines for preparation before screenings, recording important details during screenings, and reviewing your notes after screenings. The chapter then presents case studies of formal analysis, modeling close readings of visual style across a range of screen media objects. The case studies include multiple screen shots to illustrate key terms central to formal analysis.

## Taking notes

The first question that I ask my students after every class in-screening is "What do you notice?" The formulation of this question is both very broad (you might notice any number of things – from a camera angle to a sound pattern to a text/image relationship) and very specific (because it asks what *you* notice.) The question foregrounds *your* observations, serving as an ideal starting point for discussions and for brainstorming ideas for writing projects. Students prepare to answer this question by taking detailed screening notes, usually during multiple screenings of the same segment.

> **Screening questions**
>
> In order to take screening notes that will prepare you to talk about and write about screen media, approach note-taking as a process that unfolds over multiple stages. Before the screening, create a list of screening questions.
>
> 1 *Take notes before the screening begins.* Whether you are writing about a film, an episode of a television show, a video game, or an Instagram story, prepare for your screening by taking preliminary notes. If you are approaching the media object through the framework of a specific writing assignment, review the assignment prompt. What are the goals of your screening? Are you analyzing the representation of race in a contemporary sitcom? Will you be describing the costume design in a 1960s French

film? Will you be comparing the narrative structure in two music videos? Make a screening checklist that includes all of the relevant details you will need to record in order to answer your central questions.
2   *Read reviews.* Consult a review aggregator website such as Metacritic for reviews of films, television shows, or games. What critical observations or arguments strike you as the most interesting or provocative or confusing? What are the critical questions or positions that you would like to have in mind as you begin the screening?
3   *Research promotional materials.* If relevant to your screening and easily available online, watch one or more trailers or commercials for the media object. How does the trailer ensnare your attention? What does it reveal?
4   *Draft a list of screening questions.* Taking detailed pre-screening notes will position you to formulate questions in advance. Revise your initial list of screening questions to produce a final draft that is manageable (fits on one typed and printed page) and well-organized (presented in a logical order with related questions linked together.)

Supplement your screening questions by noting basic industrial information about the media object: the title; release date; names of directors, producers, writers, and other key personnel; names of actors (and names of the characters they play); studios or networks; etc. Online databases such as the Internet Movie Database (for film, television, and some videos) provide a wealth of generally very reliable information that you can verify later using other industrial and critical sources. Having basic information about the media object at your fingertips will make note-taking much easier. This research, even if it includes reading reviews and other texts that might reveal narrative information about the media object, will not or at least should not ruin your screening experience. On the contrary, this preparation will make it easier for you to incorporate note-taking into your screening experiences. The information that you might want to gather in advance may vary slightly from object to object but the general principle that you should learn as much basic information as possible before your screening applies to most media objects.

I learned to take screening notes in dark rooms (a theatre or a classroom), watching a film for the first time with an audience. I would bring a legal pad and fill page after page with messy, looping script – much larger than my usual handwriting. Over the course of a two-hour long feature film, I might fill 20 to 30 pages with notes, but I would often find when the lights went on that I had scrawled only a few stray observations on each page (since I was writing in haste in roughly a 60-point font!) Next, I transcribed my messy handwritten notes into typewritten notes. During the transcription process, I would flesh out my ideas, transforming a few words into a few sentences. Then I would revise my typewritten notes, not only correcting typos but also filling in gaps and making links between ideas. Finally, I would re-read my original screening questions alongside my screening notes and generate revised screening questions for my next screening experience.

Yes, the *next* screening experience. Whenever possible, writers should aim to screen a film, television show, or other media object as many times as possible. The length of the media object and the conditions of your access to it may determine the number of screenings. I can reasonably expect students to watch a three-minute long music video or an equally short experimental film at least 20 times before they write an essay about it (that is, after all, only one hour of total screening time), but I cannot expect them to watch a long Bollywood or Nollywood film (which may run well over three hours) 20 different times. In cases where a media object is too long or too inaccessible to facilitate multiple screenings, use other strategies to produce close readings. When you write about a media object of any length, you will focus on certain segments. Watch the segment or segments that you will analyze in your writing as many times as possible even if you only watch the whole film or television show two or three times. Whenever possible, create screen shots of the images that are most central for your analysis, or search for screen shots online. These saved images will allow you to extend your close readings beyond the screenings.

## Close readings: case studies

### Lost

In my "Introduction to Media and Society" class, we practice analyzing form through close readings of the television show *Lost*'s pilot episode (J.J. Abrams, 2004). Presenting a complex story about a group of plane crash survivors stranded on an unidentified island and shot on location in Hawaii, *Lost* combines a very "cinematic" visual style with a *serial* narrative. It thus provides an ideal foundation for analyzing both film and television aesthetics.

The *pilot episode* begins with a black title card with the word "LOST" in large white capital letters spinning toward the camera [Figure 3.1] before cutting to the opening *shot* – an *extreme close-up* of the character Jack's closed eye [Figure 3.2a] just before the eye startles us by opening, in tandem with a strange sound effect that sounds like a mechanical pop [Figure 3.2b]. This shot provokes our curiosity. Who is this? Where is this?

*Cut* to the next shot, a *point of view shot* from Jack's point of view, an *extreme low angle shot* revealing the dense tropical tree cover looming over him [Figure 3.3]. After another cut, a *high angle shot* presents our first view of Jack's face, a *medium close-up* that allows us to see not only his face but also the top of the suit he is wearing and the jungle-like ground cover surrounding his body [Figure 3.4a]. The camera *zooms* out to allow us to see gradually more and more of his body and the ground that surrounds it, confirming the visual incongruity hinted at by the previous shots [Figure 3.4b]. Why would a man dressed in a suit be lying on the ground in this jungle environment?

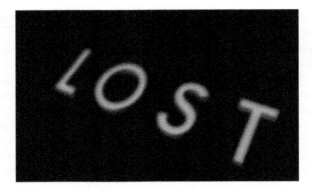

*Figure 3.1* The opening title for the television show *Lost* (2016)

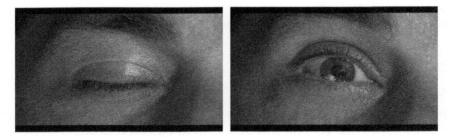

*Figures 3.2a–b* The extreme close-ups at the beginning of the *Lost* pilot episode

*Figure 3.3* An extreme low angle, point of view shot from Jack's perspective in *Lost's* pilot episode

From screen aesthetics to site design    29

*Figures 3.4a–b* High angle shots begin to reveal more information about Jack and his surroundings in *Lost*

*Figures 3.5* Shot that begins a shot/reverse shot sequence in *Lost*

Before we can register any further information about this narrative situation, another cut leads to the next shot – a close-up of Jack's face from the ground level as he turns toward the camera [Figure 3.5]. Then, a point of view shot from Jack's point of view, initiates a series of shots and *reverse shots* that reveal a dog running toward and then away from Jack [Figure 3.6].

Jack stands unsteadily and pulls a small bottle of alcohol – like the ones served on planes – from his jacket pocket. This important detail in the *mise-en-scène* points to the conclusion that he might have been on a plane (and in a plane crash) and also offers a dangling clue about the role of alcohol in Jack's life. In a vertical motion, the camera *tilts* up. Then a long *tracking shot* begins as the camera follows Jack's swift run through the dense trees, pausing briefly to dwell on the eerie presence of a white tennis shoe ominously dangling from a tree branch [Figure 3.7].

Jack emerges from the trees onto a pristine white beach with crystal blue water in the background [Figure 3.8]. The soundtrack slowly fills with the sounds of screams and mechanical grinding and whirring, suggesting an engine or propeller or both. As these sounds increase in number, volume, and intensity, Jack turns toward the source of the sounds. The camera *pans* horizontally only to arrive not

*Figure 3.6* Reverse shot in *Lost*

*Figure 3.7* The camera stops following Jack, pausing instead to invite the viewer to examine the *mise-en-scène*, specifically a white tennis shoe, in *Lost*

*Figure 3.8* The first shot of the beach in *Lost*

on the scene that Jack is witnessing but, strangely, on Jack himself – a shot my students often call a "trick pan" [Figure 3.9]. He then runs toward the site of the plane crash, and the character who has been the sole focus of our attention moves into a chaotic crowd of unknown characters in the immediate aftermath of the crash [Figure 3.10]. Just over two minutes and thirty seconds pass from the beginning of the episode to Jack's arrival at the crash site. We have watched more then 20 shots separated by cuts. The opening scene places us in the middle of an intense drama, not yet knowing the name of the protagonist and not yet having heard a single line of dialogue apart from the screams.

In this short scene – watched over and over, shot by shot, in my classes – we analyze *sound, cinematography, editing,* and *mise-en-scène* to understand the show's style and its structure. We use the following approaches:

1   As I do in the long passage above, describe the scene with two goals – telling an engaging story for your reader and employing precise language to identify key elements of screen aesthetics. To achieve the first

*Figure 3.9* A horizontal pan scans the beach and returns our attention to Jack in *Lost*

*Figure 3.10* A long tracking shot follows Jack in *Lost*

goal, imagine that you are reading the description aloud to a friend, captivating their attention as they wait to hear what you will reveal next. To achieve the second goal, practice using the italicized terms in the passage above and deploying them accurately and in combination with other more familiar terms.

2. Analyze editing rhythms by counting the cuts. In the classroom, we first watch the scene and then describe its rhythm. Is the pace fast or slow? Are the cuts obvious or subtle? I ask students to guess how many cuts there are in the scene. Then we turn the volume off and watch the scene without sound and with a focus only on editing. Each student quietly counts the number of cuts, and then we compare our tallies. Often, we are surprised to find that there are many more cuts than we guessed thanks to the effect of *continuity editing* (also known as *invisible editing*) in which edits that might otherwise seem jarring instead seem very natural to us because we are focused on other elements of storytelling – action, dialogue, etc. Then we re-watch the scene, and I yell "Cut!" every time there is a cut so that we can see just how disruptive it would be if classical storytelling conventions did not allow us to ignore those visual breaks.

3. We then compare sound-image relationships by closing our eyes and listening to the scene without the accompanying images. What sounds do we notice when we turn our attention away from the images? Is the soundtrack dominated by dialogue, *diegetic* music emanating from the narrative world of the show, *non-diegetic* music that was added in post-production, sound effects, silence? In the opening sequence of *Lost*, we have no dialogue to provide exposition and orient us as viewers within the scene. Notice how many other opening scenes in commercial screen media will immediately find a reason to share the central character's name, occupation, location, etc. *Lost* will share this information soon enough, revealing first that Jack is a doctor and later that his name is Jack and only much later (in the series finale at the end of the sixth season, in fact, and no spoilers here) where exactly he is.

4. We similarly learn a lot about images by turning off the sound and focusing on individual *frames*. In a single frame, you may analyze one or more elements of the *mise-en-scène*: *lighting, costume design, props* and *production design, color design, settings* (either locations or sets), *hair and make-up, figure placement*, etc. Analyze each frame as if it were a painting.

5. Compare the show – shot in a *single camera mode of production* – to shows shot in a *multi-camera mode of production* (for example, talk shows, soap operas, some sitcoms). Which features associated with the single camera mode (for example, *realism*, natural lighting, and the use of a hand-held camera) contribute most to *Lost*'s storytelling style?

### Queen Sugar

In Introduction to Media and Society, my students also watch the pilot episode of the television series *Queen Sugar* (Ava DuVernay, 2016). Building on our formal analysis of *Lost*, we analyze *sound, cinematography, editing,* and *mise-en-scène* in the *Queen Sugar* pilot. After completing our close readings of the episode using the methods outlined above, we expand our critical framework to include sources that explore executive producer (and pilot episode director and writer) Ava DuVernay's role as an *auteur*. *Auteur criticism* typically identifies the director as the primary author of a film and the executive producer or "showrunner" as the primary author of a television series. Early auteur critics argued that directors imprinted their films with distinctive authorial signatures (often but not always evident through close readings of each film's *mise-en-scène*), even when their films were made under Hollywood production conditions that limited the director's creative autonomy. More recent theories of media authorship have revised early auteur theory to account for the artistic impact of the many executives, writers, actors, artisans, and others who work together to create a film or television show, especially ones with a large budget. However, scholars, critics, and fans continue to assign authorship to film directors and television showrunners. To illustrate the tensions between different critical approaches to authorship, I usually screen for my students a title sequence that includes a director's authorial claim – for example, "A Spike Lee Joint" – and then screen the end credit sequence for the same film, with its scrolling list of the hundreds of people who participated in the production.

In spite of my ambivalence about auteur criticism, I often use auteur-driven approaches to formal analysis. For analyzing the pilot episode of *Queen Sugar*, a focus on Ava DuVernay as the author of the text directs our attention to two different sets of texts – films directed by DuVernay and interviews and reviews in which DuVernay and film critics discuss her *craft* as a director. To explore DuVernay's filmography in class, we watch two of the films she has written and directed: *Middle of Nowhere* (2012) and *13$^{th}$* (2016). These films share *Queen Sugar*'s narrative concern with mass incarceration's impacts on communities of color – approached through the structures of a romantic drama and a documentary respectively. We compare individual scenes from the three texts, observing the narrative and aesthetic details that comprise DuVernay's authorial signature.

Supporting our textual analysis of the texts she has directed, we read interviews and reviews that focus on DuVernay's style. For example, in a *Vulture* podcast interview with critic Matt Zoller Seitz, DuVernay discusses: shooting *Queen Sugar* on *location* in New Orleans, *lighting* actors of color with different skin tones, assessing *camera distance* (shooting some conversations in a *wide shot* and others in an *extreme close-up*), *blocking* actors, and *framing* shots by using *negative space*, among other formal elements. DuVernay's reflections annotate the episode, allowing listeners to make connections between their formal observations and her strategies and motivations as an artist. DuVernay explicates these decisions clearly and persuasively, relishing the rare opportunity to discuss her craft: "Being a black woman director I very rarely, I can count on one hand and it wouldn't be a full hand the conversations that I've had about craft. Because it's always about

*Figures 3.11a–b* Shots of Ralph Angel and Blue looking directly at each other and at the camera in the pilot episode of *Queen Sugar* (2016)

diversity, about the first this, the first that. No one is asking me about blocking scenes" (Seitz). After listening to the podcast, students re-watch the episode, allowing her observations to guide them through their close readings. For example, she discusses the two consecutive shots in which we see first the character Ralph Angel and then his son Blue, each staring directly at the camera, rare violations of the *90 degree rule* that structures most commercial cinematography [Figures 3.11a and 3.11b.]. DuVernay explains,

> Even though it's not our visual language, it's very moving to me when I cut it. It says so much about what this boy means to him and what the father means to the boy, and I feel like it really does something to the scene, which I really think is a big jewel of this episode, one that's close to my heart. It's this binding together of father and son, and that happens in a really unexpected way by changing those frames.
>
> (Seitz)

DuVernay's explanation connects the scene's visual style to its narrative and emotional impact.

### *Video essays: Kogonada*

The film director and prolific video essayist Kogonada has produced multiple video essays that analyze film form and authorship. In one series of essays, he identifies authorial signatures by presenting similar shots from multiple films in each director's filmography. For example, in *Wes Anderson: Centered* (2014), Kogonada documents Anderson's preference for centered compositions, adding a vertical dotted line through the center of each frame [Figures 3.12a, 3.12b, and 3.12c.] Using a similar strategy, Kogonada assembles *low angle shots* from multiple films directed by Quentin Tarantino in *Quentin Tarantino: From Below* (2012) [Figures 3.13a, 3.13b, and 3.13c]. Presenting a series of similar compositions from multiple films provides compelling evidence of each video essay's claim.[1]

As Chiara Grizzaffi and Jeffrey Middents explain in their chapters in Part II, video essays may use many different methods to develop a formal analysis. For

*Figures 3.12a–c* Centered compositions in Kogonada's video essay *Wes Anderson: Centered* (2014)

*Figures 3.13a–c* Low angle shots in Kogonada's video essay *Quentin Tarantino: From Below* (2012)

example, in *What is neorealism?* (2013), Kogonada employs split-screen comparisons to examine the different editing strategies of two versions of the same film – Vittorio De Sica's *Stazione Termini* (*Terminal Station*, 1953) and the American version of that film, *Indiscretions of an American Wife*, edited by the Hollywood producer David O. Selznick. Presenting each film side by side, Kogonada reveals the American version's emphasis on following its star, cutting quickly from one scene to the next to propel the film's action, contrasting with De Sica's version where each scene lingers even after the protagonist leaves the frame, drawing our attention to the extras she passes [Figures 3.14a, 3.14b,

Figures 3.14a–c Shots from Kogonada's video essay *What is neorealism?* (2013)

and 3.14c]. Comparing these editing styles underscores the differences between Italian neorealism and Hollywood cinema.

## In the Mood for Love

You may also find valuable information about screen aesthetics by examining the material included with physical copies of media objects – DVDs, Blu-ray discs, console game discs, etc. Disc covers, liner notes, and digital bonus features often include relevant information about style and production, including written and audio commentaries from directors, writers, cinematographers, and designers; behind-the-scenes footage; production notes and other artefacts (screenplays, storyboards, etc.); and formal analyses by prominent critics. Online exhibition portals – from studio and network websites to large streaming websites such as Netflix – may also include relevant paratexts, including comments from fans. Analyze each portal's design features:

*Figures 3.15a–b* Menus for the Criterion Collection DVD edition of the film *In the Mood for Love* (2000)

*Figures 3.16a–b* In the Mood for Love director Wong Kar-Wai discussing the film in an interview featured on the Criterion Collection DVD; a subtitled still from Wong's DVD audio commentary for the film

the visual style of the interface, the curation of media texts and paratexts, the navigation options, and the evidence of fan engagement.

Consider, for example, the Criterion Collection DVD edition of Wong Kar-Wai's film *In the Mood for Love* (2000). The DVD menus include a range of bonus features: interviews with the director, a Toronto International Film Festival press conference, a photo gallery, promotional material, and supplemental information about the film's cast, crew, and music [Figures 3.15a and 3.15b]. DVD and Blu-ray editions of films and television shows often emphasize the role of the director and executive producer respectively as authors. As a result, they frequently feature interviews, commentaries, and documentaries that support auteur analyses. For example, the *In the Mood for Love* DVD presents director Wong Kar-Wai's reflections on the film's production history through interview clips and through his audio commentary, allowing the viewer to watch the film from his point of view. These bonus features traverse many topics, but they usually involve at least some consideration of form (and the industrial and cultural factors that may inform screen aesthetics).

Criterion issued a Blu-ray edition of *In the Mood for Love* after the DVD release, and the Criterion website includes other paratexts that engage formal analysis. For example, a short video presents film director Barry Jenkins reflecting on the influence of *In the Mood for Love* and Wong's film *Chungking Express* (1994) on his work. Jenkins both performs formal analysis for the viewer and forges links between Wong's films and his films, such as *Moonlight* (2016) and *If Beale Street Could Talk* (2018), that encourage comparative analysis.

Formal analysis may begin with the close reading of images and sounds from screen media objects, but it should not end there. Seek out supplementary information – interviews, reviews, paratexts, online portals, etc. – to expand, refine, and strengthen your observations of form.

### In practice

#### Curate a digital gallery

Digital galleries allow you to analyze screen form in a media-rich space. Social media platforms such as Instagram invite users to curate images with (short or long) captions. This juxtaposition of image and text provides a helpful model for curating a digital gallery. There are two main strategies for curating images:

**Segmentation**

1. First, if you are writing about a moving image media object such as a television show, select one short scene to analyze. Choose a segment that includes no more than ten shots, and make screen grabs of each shot. Number the shots in the order in which they appear, and then analyze each one carefully, recording detailed hand written notes.
2. Review your notes, and brainstorm ideas that build on your observations. Then develop a working thesis – an argument that you might revise (slightly or significantly) as the process of close reading proceeds.
3. With this thesis as a framework for your ideas, draft a caption for each image. You might experiment with different restrictions for your captions. For example, first write a short paragraph for each caption – in effect, a swift close reading of each image. Then revise each paragraph into a single short sentence that captures the main idea introduced in the paragraph. You might then condense each caption into a single evocative word.
4. Draft a short artist's statement to provide a critical context for your gallery, and then publish the gallery online (on a course website, in a blog, etc.) If the gallery is a means to a critical end rather than the end itself, consider how the images and ideas you have assembled can inform your larger writing project. The gallery – or elements of it – might in that case be a preliminary project (like the sketches that a painter makes before beginning a painting), or it might become an appendix for

your project (for example, in the form of a set of figures that accompany a written essay).

**Iteration**

Identify one important still image to analyze (for example, a single shot from a film, television, show, music video, or game); follow the same guidelines for close reading, note-taking, and thesis development above; and then generate multiple captions for the same image. These captions might point to different directions for your analysis, in effect transforming the various observations recorded in your notes into drafts for different critical approaches to your writing project. The captions generated in this exercise might also form a standalone project because they demonstrate for the viewer the different angles of interpretation a single image might generate. They can also, as with the exercise above, provide a foundation for a larger critical project.

*Make GIFs*

In November 2018, Manohla Dargis, co-chief film critic of *The New York Times* published the essay "What the Movies Taught Me About Being a Woman" in the newspaper's digital edition. She illustrates several of the lessons she shares – Lesson 1: "Women are There to be Kissed."/Lesson 2: "Women Need a Spanking."/Lesson 6: "Women Can Be Dangerous." – with a series of film GIFs (Graphical Interchange Format Files). In one grid of GIFs, we see female characters being hit by male characters in six different films with release dates spanning the period from 1944–2015. This repetitive gallery, with the short sequence in each GIF repeating on an endless loop, intensifies the impact of her argument. These images of casual – and, at times, allegedly comical – assault recur across classical and contemporary examples. The structure of a GIF – the making elastic of a moment or moments from a screen media object – distends our experience, forcing us to reflect on the impact of what we are seeing beyond the fleeting flicker of a single shot or sequence. GIFs themselves may generate comic and/or political effects, and the addition of subtitles may create or underscore those effects.

Dargis' essay demonstrates the critical value of creating and curating GIFs. As media scholar Michael Z. Newman explains,

> GIFs allow us to publish criticism of the moving image using the technology of the moving image, and in a way that is complementary with written language. [...] They are part of a growing cultural commons of image files to use for diverse purposes: in conversation, in expressions of fandom, or in criticism. GIFs can join professional and

academic critics with a wider culture of media appropriation and appreciation.

("GIFs: The Attainable Text")

Generating a GIF does not require extensive expertise. Online GIF generators such as Giphy allow users to enter the URL of an online video, select a specific sequence from the video, and transform the sequence into a GIF.

Either as a complement to a writing project in another format (for example, a traditional scholarly essay or a film review) or as a standalone project, create a GIF or a series of GIFs from the media object or objects you are analyzing. Consider how to frame an argument through GIFs, either with the breadth of your examples (as Dargis does in her illustration of the consistent representations of violence against women) or with the depth of the examples that you mine within a single text. Searching for existing GIFs may also open a window onto the reception of specific texts within fan communities. For each GIF you create, consider whether you want to add a subtitle over the image, a caption beneath the image, or an artist's statement to accompany a gallery of GIFs (easily posted on sites such as Tumblr).

### Record an audio commentary

DVD and Blu-ray editions of films, television shows, and other screen media often include audio commentaries of individual scenes or even an entire film. In her chapter in Part II of this book, Terri Francis discusses her experience recording the audio commentary for the film *Losing Ground* (Kathleen Collins, 1982). Audio commentaries may offer critical perspectives, personal anecdotes, industrial histories, and detailed formal analyses.

Select a short video (such as a music video, commercial, or trailer) or a clip from a longer media object; and record an audio commentary either independently or with one or more collaborators.

1 Identify the short video or clip that you want to analyze.
2 Produce a close reading of the video – through multiple viewings, detailed notes, and background research.
3 Create a storyboard (as you did in the exercise at the end of Chapter 2.) Use the storyboard to outline your ideas by matching them with each shot in clip. In the first drafts of the storyboard, your ideas may take the form of notes. In the final draft, include a detailed script for your commentary. While you might prefer a more improvisational approach to recording your commentary, having a script – even one that you might choose to depart from at certain moments in the recording – will save you a lot of time and will ensure that you present a clear and coherent analysis.

> 4  Analyze the editing rhythm of your clip before you finalize the script commentary, deciding how you want to match your analysis with the shots. Keep in mind that some shots may last for a single second while others last for minutes. If a single shot requires a longer analysis than its duration allows, consider pausing the video to allow your commentary time to unfold (and to allow the viewer time to analyze the shot with the same care that you are lavishing on it.) The most straightforward scene commentary videos allow a clip to screen in real time without any editing (to pause shots, skip shots, reverse the order of shots, etc.). Keep in mind, however, that many screen recording and video editing programs allow for more complicated editing approaches. If you find a more conceptually ambitious approach to recording a scene commentary appealing, you might consider studying the critical methods associated with video essays (as discussed in Part II in the chapters by Chiara Grizzaffi and Jeffrey Middents).

## Note

1  See https://vimeo.com/kogonada for a complete collection of Kogonada's video essays.

## References

Dargis, Manohla. "What the Movies Taught Me About Being a Woman." *The New York Times*. 30 November 2018. www.nytimes.com/interactive/2018/11/30/movies/women-in-movies.html
DuVernay, Ava, director. *13th*. Netflix, 2016.
DuVernay, Ava, director. *Middle of Nowhere*. Lionsgate, 2012.
DuVernay, Ava, director. *Queen Sugar*. Harpo Productions and Warner Horizon Television, 2016.
*In the Mood for Love*. Directed by Wong Kar-Wai. Jet Tone Films Ltd., 2000.
Kogonada. *Quentin Tarantino: From Below*. 2012. https://vimeo.com/37540504
Kogonada. *Wes Anderson: Centered*. 2014. https://vimeo.com/89302848
Kogonada. *What is Neorealism? Sight and Sound*, 2013. www.bfi.org.uk/news-opinion/sight-sound-magazine/comment/video-essay-what-neorealism
*Lost*. Directed by J.J. Abrams. Bad Robot and ABC Studios, 2004.
Newman, Michael Z. "GIFs: The Attainable Text." *Film Criticism*, vol. 40, no. 1, 2016. https://quod.lib.umich.edu/f/fc/13761232.0040.123/--gifs-the-attainable-text?rgn=main;view=fulltext
Seitz, Matt Zoller. "Ava DuVernay on Directing *Queen Sugar*, Properly Lighting Actors of Color, and Why She Used to Be More Brave." *Vulture*, September 6, 2016. www.vulture.com/2016/09/ava-duvernay-directing-queen-sugar.html
"What Wong Kar-Wai Taught Barry Jenkins About Longing." *The Criterion Collection*. 29 November, 2016. www.criterion.com/current/posts/4328-what-wong-kar-wai-taught-barry-jenkins-about-longing

# 4 Entering the conversation
## How and where to develop a critical argument

*Lisa Patti*

This chapter explores the construction of critical arguments across writing formats and platforms. The first section focuses on drafting thesis statements and developing digital arguments in video essays and other digital formats. The subsequent sections – on free writing, outlines, introductions, evidence, and conclusions – review the phases of the writing process and the key components of a writing project. This chapter presents writing guidelines that may apply to a range of writing formats, explaining the ways that traditional writing practices such as writing outlines may be applied to video essays, podcasts, and other projects.

### What is an argument?

Scholarly writing should advance an argument. Different books explain this mandate in different ways. Whether you begin with a research question, a hypothesis, a claim, or – arguably the most common formulation – a thesis statement, scholarly writing should contribute to an ongoing critical conversation. I find the approach presented in the book *They Say, I Say* to be particularly persuasive. In that volume, authors Gerald Graff and Cathy Birkenstein explain,

> Broadly speaking, academic writing is argumentative writing, and we believe that to argue well you need to do more than assert your position. You need to enter a conversation, using what others say (or might say) as a launching pad or sounding board for your own views.
>
> (3)

They suggest that you "write the voices of others into your text" in order to capture this conversation for your readers (3). When we are engaged in a lively conversation with colleagues or friends about screen media, we usually feel comfortable contributing our ideas. When we engage in scholarly dialogues in our writing, we are in effect transporting the principles of a rigorous yet respectful conversation into our prose, acknowledging the points made by previous critics, analyzing them carefully, and then responding to them.

Writing about screen media is the perfect venue for the "they say, I say" template because many writers have extensive experience crafting arguments about screen media if not formally (in institutional settings like classrooms, academic conferences, or film festivals) then informally (in live dialogues in cafés or virtual dialogues on Twitter). We may find it challenging to write about screen media – especially when we are encountering new objects or experimenting with new formats – but we usually have a wealth of conversational experience as a foundation for our work.

Providing a concise and engaging formulation of your argument early in your writing (for example, in one of the opening paragraphs of a traditional written essay or the opening minutes of a podcast episode) extends an invitation to your reader, and you want that invitation to be accepted. I always remind my students that I will read every word that they submit to me with care and diligence whether or not I find the opening sentences, sounds, or images in their projects to be intriguing, but I urge them to craft introductions in an effort to persuade the reluctant reader that their projects deserve attention. When I was an undergraduate student, I was instructed to answer three questions for the reader at the beginning of every essay: What? So what? How? Years later I still use these guiding questions when I am writing introductions.

The importance of presenting an argument applies equally to writing in digital formats. For example, analyzing fan-made remix videos in her article "The Rhetoric of Remix," media scholar Virginia Kuhn (one of the contributors to this volume) explains the term *digital argument*:

> My use of the term *digital argument* is partly strategic; argument is key to academic efforts, and as such, the term holds resonance for the scholarly community. Remix can be a scholarly pursuit: it cites, synthesizes, and juxtaposes its sources. Argument also contains connotations of the dialogic quality of communication that is not anchored to either speech or writing, and so digital argument can extend its features to writing with sound and image in addition to words. It is the embodiment of a speech act. Further, although in common parlance the word *argument* connotes something like polemics, there are many forms of argument; the term is not limiting, and it can help break down the boundaries between fact and fiction.

Kuhn's discussion of digital arguments explains the rhetorical structure of digital writing projects, the forms that digital arguments might take, and the ways that remix videos transform screen media texts into arguments (and evidence.) "Writing" in a digital format does not exempt us from presenting a clear and compelling thesis statement; rather digital projects allow us to rethink how arguments are framed and supported.

For an instructive comparison of the forms of argument available in different modes of writing, consider critic Kevin Lee's review of the film *Transformers: Age of Extinction* (Michael Bay, 2014) in the magazine *Film Comment* paired with his video essay *Transformers: The Premake (a desktop documentary)* (2014). Lee's written introduction to his video essay explains that he edited hundreds of amateur videos of the filming of *Transformers: Age of Extinction* in multiple global locations "into a critical investigation of the global big budget film industry, amateur video making, and the political economy of images." In the traditional review of the film that he wrote after its theatrical release, he concludes with a description of the globetrotting production, referencing his video essay:

> Then there's the matter of "Hong Kong" the location, which in reality is a composite of shots filmed in Chicago, Detroit, and Hong Kong – a pastiche brought forth by competing incentives and stipulations offered by both China and the U.S. cities to attract movie productions. Those like me who have sampled the amateur footage of each location on YouTube will experience the surreal sensation of seeing the Hong Kong action sequences flip between locations literally from one shot to the next, a transformation of space that I find more thrilling than computer-generated shape-shifting robots. This experience of *Age of Extinction* – which posits money as the true protagonist of the movie – was the one I expected to have in the wake of my investigation of the production, and it did deliver levels of subtextual coherence that the film otherwise lacks. Still, amidst all the geopolitical production intrigue, somehow a movie got made, and not an altogether bad one at that.

Lee's written review complements his video essay, re-presenting the thesis that "money [is] the true protagonist of the movie" by emphasizing more familiar forms of textual evidence (for example, discussions of the film's plot, performances, and production values).

## Thinking on the page: free writing

Free writing is one of my staple activities as a writer and a teacher. In almost every class I teach, my students and I spend at least five minutes (and often more time) engaged in free writing every day. I usually distribute a free writing prompt that refers to a passage from a text that we have read or a clip from a media object that we have watched. The aim of the prompt varies – to begin a close reading, to compare two media objects, to apply a critical theory encountered in a scholarly essay to a media object we have screened, to generate a list of research questions, etc. Prompts balance structure with openness, directing students toward a shared set of critical questions while encouraging them to focus on the element of the prompt that most engages their interest. So, for example, if a sample prompt includes a series of three questions, one student might present brief answers to all three, and another might develop a longer answer in response to only one.

Free writing encourages frequent writing as a practice. Students often write over 500 words (roughly the equivalent of two typed double-spaced pages) during 10–15 minutes of free writing. Those pages may not be polished, but they might provide an early version of a thesis statement, concrete examples, and even several well-crafted sentences that will persist into the final draft of a writing project. Free writing reminds writers that they have something to say. My students usually free write at the beginning of class meetings and then refer to their free writing during class discussions. For students who are reluctant to talk, their free writing can be an even more valuable resource than their reading and screening notes. Some students even elect to read their free writing aloud in lieu of sharing more spontaneous comments.

Free writing serves a similar purpose for me as a writer. I view free writing as an important first step of the writing process and devote time to free writing before I draft an outline for a writing project. Free writing allows me to capture my ideas in motion and to discover where my interests lie. I also turn to free writing whenever I reach an impasse in my writing. The blank screen may be most vexing before I have written a single word, but sometimes I find it equally vexing when I cannot move past a particularly difficult section during the later stages of a writing project. In those moments, I find it useful to step away from the screen, grab my pen and notebook, and free write. One of my favorite strategies is to hand write a draft of a letter to my writing partner explaining why I find a particular part of the project difficult to complete (or begin). I generally do not send these letters. Often, I generate my own answers to the questions that I have asked, and sometimes I even write entire sentences or paragraphs in the letter that I can transcribe with only minor revisions into the working draft. In any case, I have accomplished the immediate goal of writing something – anything – and that momentum pushes me back to the writing task at hand with more energy and confidence.

Combining free writing with additional screenings of the media objects you are analyzing may both reenergize your writing and reveal new analytical insights. Sometimes if I am writing about a particular element of a media object, I lose sight of the object as a whole. Re-watching a film or television episode again – not taking detailed notes as you did during the initial screenings but keeping pen and paper nearby – may yield important observations. After the screening, set aside a short amount of time for free writing. You may immediately work through the block that led you to free write, or you may simply sharpen your analysis.

## Structuring your argument: outlines

In every class that I teach, I require students to submit outlines of their writing projects. I have always found it very difficult to persuade students that outlines are a valuable part of the writing process, but by the end of each semester most students agree. I assign multiple pre-writing tasks for each writing project (proposals, thesis statements, introductions, outlines, and drafts) with incremental deadlines leading up to the deadline for the final draft of the project. This method prohibits procrastination (at least to a certain extent). Students can still wait until the last minute to complete each assignment, but each completed phase of the writing process puts them in a stronger position to complete the next phase. Each step in this process is important, but outlines are the key to the process.

### Outlining your argument

- *Do not begin your outline until you have spent time thinking, brainstorming, and free writing and have drafted a strong working thesis statement.* Your outline will be most useful if it provides a structure for the development of your argument. If you do not yet know what your argument will be, spend more time reading, thinking, note-taking, and free writing before you write the first draft of your outline.
- *Do not decide that you do not have time to outline.* No matter how little time you have before your project is due, you always have enough time to outline. But, you say, your project is due in a few hours? You still have time to outline. When I distribute timed essay exams at the beginning of an exam period that lasts anywhere from one to three hours, I instruct students to draft a working outline for each essay. They may have limited time to write, but their outlines will allow them to design essays that respond completely and persuasively to the questions.
- *Organize your main ideas and supporting examples and details in a visual hierarchy.* The relationships of coordination and subordination between and among your ideas should be clear. A reader unfamiliar with your plans for your project should be able to read your outline and answer the questions "What? So what? How?" with accuracy. Different teachers, editors, and style guides advocate specific formats for headings and subheadings. Follow the protocols your writing assignment requires if applicable. If not, choose the format that works best for you, but make sure that the organization of your argument remains consistent and immediately visible.
- *Incorporate evidence and acknowledge your sources in your outline.* If you are noting a specific journal article that you plan to mention as supporting evidence, write the page number where you will find the relevant quote parenthetically. If you plan to discuss a scene from a television show, include the episode number and other relevant details. Your outline should be an information-rich map that you can consult throughout the writing process.

- *Write a one-page outline.* Your project might be sweeping in scope and require a very long and detailed outline to organize your ideas. Even in the case of an outline for a book where you might opt to have a working outline for each chapter that is several (or even many) pages long, aim to have a snapshot outline always on hand. I drafted a one-page outline for the first part of this book that provided an overview of each chapter. I used it to track my progress during the writing process and identify sections that could be moved, cut, or combined with other sections.
- *Revise your outline as you revise your writing project.* An outline loses its value if it is written at the very beginning of your writing process and never updated to reflect changes in your analysis. In fact, the outline itself is a useful tool for revision since it is often easier to notice problems with the structure of your argument when you see it visually represented on a single page rather than sprawling across five or fifty or five hundred pages of your own prose.
- *Incorporate outlines into the peer review process.* Immediately after students write their first draft of a project outline, I invite them to share the draft with a peer reviewer. Reviewers are usually more open to offering substantive criticism at this early stage, and writers are often more open to acting on this criticism because they haven't yet become invested in a particular direction for their project. At a later stage in the writing process, I ask students to give their first drafts of their projects to a different peer reviewer, and I ask that reviewer to write an outline of the project's argument. The writer can then compare the reviewer's outline with their own outline to locate inconsistencies. These differences can help the writer to develop a revision plan for the next draft of the project.

## Setting the scene: introductions

I teach a writing-intensive senior seminar called "Spectral Stardom." In the course, we investigate major theories of screen stardom in tandem with examples of iconic screen stars such as Marilyn Monroe and Beyoncé before turning to an exploration of modes of performance that challenge these models – from stunt performance to performance capture to digitally-produced posthumous performances. One of the case studies we analyze is the BBC America television series *Orphan Black* (2013–2017) in which the actor Tatiana Maslany plays eleven clone characters with the assistance of another actor, Kathryn Alexandre, who operates as her "clone double." Alexandre acts as Maslany's on-set double, participating in a complicated shooting and editing routine that allows Maslany to appear onscreen playing multiple characters simultaneously while Alexandre's performances are digitally erased. After watching the first few episodes of the show, we read media scholar Zoë Shacklock's essay, "Two of a Kind: Revaluing the Work of

Acting Doubles in *Orphan Black*." As the students move toward writing their own scholarly essays about various forms of invisible acting labor such as Alexandre's, we collaboratively perform a close reading of the ways that the opening paragraphs of Shacklock's essay address the central questions of "What? So What? How?" In the annotated version of her essay's introduction printed below, notice the key moves that Shacklock makes to orient you and capture your interest. The annotations, reflecting the observations made by me and the students in our seminar, are printed in bold within brackets.

**Analyzing introductions**

*Zoë Shacklock's "Two of a Kind: Revaluing the Work of Acting Doubles in Orphan Black"*

"Prior to the launch of the second season of *Orphan Black* (2013–), BBC America released a series of promotional posters, each of which featured one of the clones played by Canadian actor Tatiana Maslany. Only the right side of Maslany's face is visible in these posters, with the left superimposed by black fill and the slogan 'One. Of a Kind.'"

[The introduction begins with a very specific reference, orienting the reader to the show the essay will discuss by examining one of the posters used to promote the show. Contrary to the common and, I would argue, misleading advice that scholarly essays should begin with broad claims or contexts before gradually reaching the specific terrain that the essay will cover, many successful essays immediately invite the reader into a clearly defined critical conversation. My students often refer to the opposite approach as the "upside down triangle method." That method may be useful in some scholarly fields and in some critical contexts, but too often I read examples of this approach that have led me to call it the "Star Wars Method" in homage to the scrolling opening credits of the *Star Wars* movies that famously begin "a long time ago in a galaxy far, far away." I have read too many essays that use the terms "media," "society," "history," "culture," and even "mankind" in an attempt to situate very narrow arguments (for example, about the editing patterns in a music video) within a much broader critical context. There is a place for big picture thinking, but beginning with a "close-up" view of your topic is often a more reliable way to invite the reader to join the critical conversation you are entering.]

"As a promotional tool, these posters reflect the basic narrative premise of *Orphan Black*: the story of a group of women who discover they are part of a human cloning experiment."

[The next sentence offers a swift summary of the show's elaborate plot, providing readers with a general impression of the show's narrative structure without delaying the introduction of the essay's central argument with a long narrative exegesis.]

"Yet the posters also have much to tell us about the question of performance in the series. Much of the critical praise lauded upon *Orphan Black* highlights Maslany's extraordinary performance(s), focusing on the skill and effort needed to play multiple protagonists and to act opposite herself. *Gawker's* Michelle Dean calls Maslany 'the thing that takes the show to another level'; Emily Nussbaum's review for the *New Yorker* states that '[i]f it weren't for Tatiana Maslany… *Orphan Black* would be just a likable-enough thriller' […]. The critical consensus seems to be that without Maslany, *Orphan Black* would be largely forgettable."

[The introduction outlines the critical reception of the show through a series of short quotations from reviews, fleshing out the reader's impression of the show by demonstrating how the show was received by critics. This move also brings the reader's attention to the fact that the essay will not rely solely on the show itself for evidence. Rather it will turn to media paratexts (such as the promotional poster) and other critical sources (such as the quoted reviews) for evidence to support the essay's central argument.]

"As the key marker of quality for the series, Maslany's performance in multiple roles is unsurprisingly foregrounded in the program's promotional material. Yet her body is only half-visible in the season 2 posters, suggesting that Maslany is only half of the picture, twinned with something unseen and yet indispensable."

[Shacklock offers a close reading of the poster itself, continuing the formal analysis that she began at the opening of the paragraph. Here we see that formal analysis as a method may be used productively beyond an analysis of the primary text – in this case, the 50 episodes that comprise the television series *Orphan Black* – to include posters and other paratextual material.]

"Indeed, exceptional as it may be, Maslany's work as an actor is not entirely 'one of a kind' but is always underscored and supported by the invisible labor of her body double, Kathryn Alexandre."

[At the end of the first paragraph, Shacklock offers an observation that serves as the first formulation of the essay's argument. This sentence is not a thesis statement, but it sketches the argument that Shacklock will assert more directly in the next two paragraphs.]

"Alexandre acts opposite Maslany in scenes involving two or more clones, wearing the appropriate costume and wig and performing the lines, accents, and physical mannerisms of the clone in question. Once the scene is complete, the two swap, and the scene is performed again. Alexandre's body is then digitally replaced in postproduction. Her work also includes more traditional body doubling, standing in for Maslany when her face is not required to be shown onscreen. Alexandre is usually described as Maslany's 'clone double,' a somewhat awkward tautology that points toward our terminological failure to properly account for her contribution to the series."

[This paragraph summarizes Alexandre's contributions to the show, swiftly explaining a performance dynamic that would be unfamiliar to readers who have not followed the show closely. While the construction of Maslany's performance involves a system of blocking and camera work followed by meticulous post-production editing, Shacklock describes these operations in an accessible way, using short, jargon-free declarative sentences and introducing the key term "clone double" (a term that most readers will be encountering for the first time) with a clear definition so that she can use the term later in the essay without explication.]

"[…] Much like Maslany's missing half in the promotional posters, then, Alexandre's work as an actor is constantly removed, as her face and body are digitally replaced by Maslany in the final broadcast version of the text. This effacement ensures that Alexandre's invisibility extends not simply through the visible frame of the program, but also throughout the attention of critical discourse."

[In the final two sentences of the second paragraph, Shacklock builds on the final sentence of the first paragraph, offering a more fully developed presentation of her essay's critical argument. These two sentences may be labeled together as a thesis statement – Shacklock's clear and compelling answer to the "What?" question – but the following paragraph, the final paragraph of the introductory section of her essay, develops this argument and establishes its critical value.]

"By bringing Alexandre's performative work into focus, I seek to make an overdue intervention into theories of screen acting, which have almost exclusively understood performance as the product of a single individual."

[Shacklock identifies "theories of screen acting" as the broad critical conversation her essay will enter, and this sentence explicitly states what her criticial intervention will be. I encourage students to experiment with using the first person voice in their scholarly writing. In order to distinguish scholarly writing from the personal essay, many writers avoid using the word "I" at all costs, at times creating sentences that read like a rhetorical pretzel, and often opting for the overuse of awkward formulations like "one notices" or "it is evident that." Experimenting with "I", especially formulations such as "I argue," underscores the extent to which the writer is adding their voice to a critical conversation, making an original contribution to the conversation that they have generated through their research and analysis, and presenting that contribution in their own words. As an exercise, I often encourage students to write a draft paragraph in which they use the formulations "I argue," "I contend," or "I demonstrate" to present their argument.]

"I trace Alexandre's impact on the final text of *Orphan Black* through her high visibility in the behind-the-scenes paratexts and through her significant presence in the narratives that Maslany and other cast and crew members tell about their experience as workers on the production. In particular, I link this to the conditions of television production, in which the long-running, fast-paced, and collaborative nature of creating serial television ensures that acting is always a function of the relationships between multiple actors."

[Here Shacklock moves explicitly from answering the "What?" question to answering the "How?" question. The reader now understands fully what her methodology in the essay will be. The long introduction has provided a roadmap for the reader to follow so that she will be able to locate each example within a broader critical framework.]

"To see the double in the work of acting, I argue, is to make a timely discursive and evaluative shift from the individual to the collective, which is increasingly pertinent as acting continues to adapt and evolve within the digital age."

[Finally, the introduction ends with an explicit statement that answers the "So what?" question. While the essay will be of interest to readers who want to learn more about the television show *Orphan Black*, the practices of performance doubling, or the digital editing of performances by doubles, readers with a broader investment in understanding performance labor and the impact of digital technology on both performance and its critical reception will have a stake in Shacklock's essay.]

Please consult the full article to read Shacklock's unedited introduction and her analysis of *Orphan Black*:
   Shacklock, Zoë. "Two of a Kind: Revaluing the Work of Acting Doubles in *Orphan Black*." *Journal of Film and Video*, vol. 68, no. 3–4, 2016, pp.69–82.

The length of an introduction ranges from a single paragraph to multiple paragraphs. When drafting an introduction, consider the length or scope of your project. Developing an introduction over the course of three long paragraphs makes sense for Shacklock because she will explore the argument she introduces over the course of a long article in a scholarly journal. If you are writing a shorter scholarly essay, then draft a shorter introduction. Scale each introduction to suit the length of the writing project. Whether the introduction is short or long, it should answer the three guiding questions "What? So what? How?"

## Telling a story: evidence

The sections above emphasize the importance of presenting and developing a critical argument and devising a sound structure for the logical and persuasive presentation of that argument. Evidence is one of the key building blocks of that structure. Your outlines should include clear references to the pieces of evidence you will marshal in support of your argument. Too often, however, outlines read like dry presentations of bullet points (rather than ideas), referencing information that will be used as evidence without any clear rationale for doing so. Presenting evidence is a key part of the broader process of storytelling. As you are writing, imagine that you are speaking to your reader. Direct forms of person to person communication often activate our capacities as storytellers. Keep that in mind when you prepare to introduce different forms of evidence into your writing projects.

The evidence you introduce may include: quoted passages from books, journal articles, newspapers, magazines, blogs, and other print and digital sources; quoted passages from published or recorded interviews; still or moving images from films, television shows, video games, or other screen media objects; archival documents (including scripts, budgets, or promotional material); sound files from recorded podcasts, live performances, or other audiovisual media; etc. The types of evidence you include will be determined by: the critical frame you build for your writing project; the argument that you want to develop; the format for your project; the audience for your project; and the resources that you can access.

If you are writing a scholarly essay about the critical reception of a television show, read as many reviews of the show as possible. You might begin by consulting a review aggregator such as Metacritic and then read as many of the linked reviews as possible. Take notes as you read the reviews, marking the passages that you find to be most relevant to the argument that you are forming. Then review your notes, locate the observations that are most relevant to your argument, and consider how to incorporate this textual evidence into your project. You might use one or more of the following methods: summarizing the evidence; including short representative passages from multiple sources; or including one or more longer passages from select sources. (In the introduction to her essay on *Orphan Black* analyzed above, Zoë

Shacklock combines these methods effectively.) As you make these decisions, consider the length of your project (a longer written essay will more easily accommodate longer quoted passages) and the format of your project (in a video essay you might opt to include shorter quoted passages as the textual accompaniment to images from the media object or you might incorporate quoted passages into a recorded audio commentary to accompany the video). Take advantage of the opportunities to share evidence (and build the story you are telling) that each writing format affords, and embrace multimodal approaches to storytelling. For example, you can place quoted passages from a scholarly written essay onto an image in a video essay (as Chiara Grizzaffi discusses in her chapter on video essays), you can complement a podcast interview by posting relevant resources on a companion website (as Christine Becker and Kyle Wrather suggest in their chapter on podcasts in this volume), or you can include images to illustrate the arguments in a written essay in print or online versions (as multiple chapters in this book do).

One of the challenges associated with writing about screen media, especially in the traditional format of a printed essay, is that you do not have the opportunity to share clips from the media objects you are discussing. More and more online scholarly journals enable the inclusion of screen media examples (for example, *In Media Res, Flow,* and *Film Criticism*) but many other journals (and many student writing assignments) do not. In those publication and submission contexts, the screen media objects you discuss remain central to your argument, but you need to do more work to describe and contextualize them. When doing so, consider the audience for your writing project. How much information can you reasonably expect them to know about the objects you are discussing? How much information must you then provide to orient your readers?

The feedback of peer reviewers can be vital at this juncture. You might ask your reviewer to note every moment in your project when they lose track of your discussion. Find the right balance – providing enough information to orient your reader without getting bogged down in endless explication. Our assumptions about our readers often inform our decisions about how much exposition to provide. For example, in my Global Cinema course, when students write about films made outside the US and in languages other than English, they usually offer long plot summaries and extensive extratextual information before introducing their arguments. However, when the same students write about the American television show *Friends* in my Introduction to Media and Society class, they offer no plot information at all, assuming that the reader knows as much about the show as they do. Calibrate the amount of descriptive and contextual information that you offer for your imagined readers. Keep in mind that your readers may not share your familiarity (or lack of familiarity) with the media objects you discuss. Even in circumstances that warrant detailed plot summaries and overviews of filmographies, national cinemas, or other subjects, incorporate that information into an engaging story that begins with a clear and original argument.

## Making a last(ing) impression: conclusions

I remember (too) vividly feedback that I received from one of my professors in response to an essay that I had written. "There is no conclusion," she observed, "It just ends." I have always struggled with beginnings and endings, but I have found the task of writing introductions easier to manage over time. Even when I feel that I have made a persuasive argument, I seem to run out of critical and creative energy by the time I reach the conclusion of a writing project. My essays indeed just end, as if I fled the scene of writing in a hurry and forgot to return.

Below I share excerpts from chapters included in the next part of this book that end with engaging conclusions. Each example provides a different model for bringing your argument to a clear conclusion and leaving your reader with an interest in learning more.

In "Making the Absent Present: Writing about Nonextant Media," Allyson Nadia Field introduces a new media object (Cheryl Dunye's 1996 film *The Watermelon Woman*) in order to provide a final – creative – example of engaging nonextant media:

> What I've described are standard tools of historical researchers. However, there are strategies beyond these methods that may be necessary to find, or even create, presence in the absence of surviving history. This can even be based on imaginative but informed speculation about the absent archive. Models for this kind of speculative archival work include not just scholarship but also Cheryl Dunye's *The Watermelon Woman* (1996), the first feature film made by an out Black lesbian filmmaker. The film combines fiction and documentary forms to interrogate the fictional aspect of the non-fiction. Dunye's film is invested in showing the erased labor of Black lesbians in mainstream cultural production, but, unable to retrieve the history she was looking for, she invented an archive of Black queer Hollywood history through fabricated documentary material created by photographer Zoe Leonard. As Dunye's end credits assert, "Sometimes you have to create your own history." While such a model should not replace extrafilmic historical research in scholarly work, it serves as inspiration for generating new creative approaches to resolving archival lacunae.

In "When it All Clicks: Writing About Participatory Media," Lauren S. Berliner offers a swift one-sentence summary of the chapter and then invokes the chapter's title, reminding the reader of the ground that her chapter covered and making a rhetorical link to the first words of the chapter:

> Writing about participatory media can at times feel like a daunting task. You have to analyze: the text itself; the text's social, economic,

infrastructural, technical, and political contexts; and the interpersonal conditions that shape your understanding of any participatory action research you may conduct. But the same characteristics that make this media mode challenging are the ones that make it a rich and fascinating field of research. There are so many pieces to fit together, but at some point, I promise, it all clicks.

In "Feeling Out Social Media," Julie Wilson and Emily Chivers Yochim link the argument in their chapter to broader cultural issues:

> In sum, social media, and digital culture more broadly, are phenomena that, to be understood, must be felt out. For they are profoundly affective media. They work on our individual and shared senses of possibility, shaping in fundamental ways the environments and atmospheres in which we live. Feeling out social media is thus vital cultural work that can help us to tell compelling and new stories about the powers of digital culture – stories that complicate and deepen more prominent accounts of fake news, rampant consumerism, and mass surveillance. Rooting ourselves in everyday media lives via ethnographic methods and attuning to the ordinary affects that swirl and swell promise to help us better understand how people live with social media and, crucially, how they might live, and desire to live, otherwise.

In "'A Very Black Project': A Method for Digital Visual Culture," Lauren McLeod Cramer restates her chapter's thesis and analyzes its critical significance:

> It is not easy to identify our knowledge gaps in order to ask questions about them, but resisting the urge to write answers before questions creates the possibility that our own writing may surprise us. For example, the popular and scholarly discourse on digital image cultures foreground revolutionary connectedness and the possibility of infinite and constant transformation; yet, this chapter's (brief) reading explains how The Very Black Project dynamically visualizes black life and culture using images from various time periods and with different visual styles that can be read discretely or as a network, while its platform remains static. The sense that the project is interactive and multidirectional is actually a function of the project's scaled-up blackness, not its digitality. Thus, The Very Black Project's *very* large image collection wants to create a disruptive "black sociality" (Moten) on Instagram's platform and, in the process, reveals the analogue qualities of contemporary digital image culture. My claim, like any thesis, is certainly debatable, but my interest as a writer in critiquing the technological and racial discourses that tell us Instagram accounts and black popular culture are unworthy of rigorous study is not.

All writing projects – whether their medium is the written word, the recorded voice, a series of still or moving images, a website, or a combination of these – should have a conclusion. A podcast interview might end with the interviewer asking a final question that invites the person being interviewed to reflect on their conversation and offer some final observations or ideas. A video essay might end with audio commentary or text that provides a clear synthesis of the digital argument developed during the video essay. For any writing project in any format, make sure that your writing doesn't just end.

## In practice

### Write an abstract

The abstracts at the beginning of the chapters in Part II summarize each chapter in approximately 100–150 words. Review these abstracts and identify the ways that they answer the central questions addressed in introductions – "What? So what? How?" – in a condensed and engaging form. Then write an abstract for your current work in progress. Design your abstract to entice prospective readers/listeners/viewers. Then share your abstract with a peer reviewer.

### Compare introductions and conclusions

Select a chapter from Part II, and compare the introduction and conclusion. Read the introduction, and then immediately read the conclusion. How does the author bring the critical questions introduced in the opening of the essay to a close? enlist your curiosity about how those critical questions might extend beyond the chapter? tie the conclusion to the introduction without merely repeating it? Then print the introduction and the conclusion for an essay that you are writing on separate pages. Read the two paragraphs and compare them side by side. Your conclusion might point back to the argument that you present in your introduction, but you should not simply repeat your introduction or summarize your project. Revise your conclusion, using the strategies presented in this chapter or modeled in the chapter you selected.

### Write multiple project proposals

The chapters in this collection provide guidance for writing in a wide variety of formats, including scholarly essays, video essays, reviews, podcasts, and blogs. Review the abstract that you wrote in response to the prompt above. Then consider how you would explore the research question for that project in a different writing format. Revise your abstract for a new format. How will your project change if you approach your topic through a video essay rather than a written essay? Does your argument shift? Will you present different

> evidence to support your argument? Will the scope of your project change? As you think about the relationship between writing formats and the critical questions they enable you to explore, decide which format best suits your goals for your current project. Experimenting for the sake of experimenting may be a productive way to learn, but the ultimate goal is to make informed decisions about how specific formats can advance and enliven your research and analysis.

## References

Graff, Gerald, and Cathy Birkenstein. *"They Say/I Say": The Moves That Matter in Academic Writing*. 2nd Edition. W.W. Norton & Company, 2010.

Kuhn, Virginia. "The Rhetoric of Remix." *Transformative Works and Cultures*, no. 9, 2012. https://doi.org/10.3983/twc.2012.0358

Lee, Kevin. "Review: Transformers: Age of Extinction." *Film Comment*, June 27, 2014.

Lee, Kevin. *Transformers: The Premake (a desktop documentary)*. Vimeo, 2014. https://vimeo.com/94101046

Shacklock, Zoë. "Two of a Kind: Revaluing the Work of Acting Doubles in *Orphan Black*." *Journal of Film and Video*, vol. 68, no. 3–4, 2016, pp. 69–82.

# 5 From notebook to network
## When and how to use digital tools

*Lisa Patti*

This chapter offers guidelines for using digital tools to conduct research and to compose and share writing in different formats. Providing an overview of popular digital tools, their utility, and their limitations, this chapter updates well-established writing practices for the digital age. The chapter also presents the current rules from the Modern Language Association (MLA) style guide for in-text citations, notes, and bibliographies, offering sample citations for new media sources such as a Tweet and a YouTube video and providing suggestions for citing sources when working in new media formats such as video essays and podcasts. The chapter concludes by considering fair use policies as they relate to media studies publications.

### Digital resources: reading, watching, writing

*Reading*

The Internet provides a wealth of venues for researching media histories and the media industries. Readers may access material in a variety of databases, from broad research databases such as Academic Search Premier to more specialized databases such as the Film and Television Literature Index. Some databases may only be accessed through an institutional subscription, but other databases are widely available. Below you will find a sample of the online databases that house materials relevant to media studies research.[1]

*Scholarly articles and books:*

Academic Search Premier (EBSCO)
Film and Television Literature Index
JSTOR
Modern Language Association Bibliography
Performing Arts Periodicals Database
Project Muse
Social Sciences Index

60　Lisa Patti

*Data:*

Box Office Mojo
Box Office Mojo International
Business Insights: Essentials
Internet Movie Database
Pew Research Center: Internet and Technology
Statista

*Newspaper and other primary sources:*

Early American Newspapers
Library of Congress Digital Collections and Services
Media History Digital Library
The Internet Archive

*Images:*

Ad*Acess
ARTstor
Life Photo Archive (hosted by Google)
Movie Stills Database
New York Public Library Digital Collections

*Video:*

Academic Video Online
Docuseek2
Kanopy
New World Cinema: Independent Features and Shorts, 1990-present
Silent Film Online
World Newsreels Online: 1929–1966

You may also access some scholarly journals without navigating one of the above databases. Open access online scholarly journals include: *Film Criticism, Film International, Flow, Game Studies: The International Journal of Computer Game Research, In Media Res, Journal of Cinema and Media Studies Teaching Dossier, Journal of Transformative Works, Media Industries Journal,* and *Senses of Cinema.* These journals feature media-rich articles, with images, videos, and hyperlinks allowing readers to explore more fully the media objects that the writers discuss. The Society for Cinema and Media Studies maintains a list of dozens of journals (some with full text articles available for free online and others accessible through individual or institutional subscriptions) on their website.

In addition to these scholarly journals, researchers may also consult media industry trade periodicals, including: *Adweek, Ad Age, Broadcast and Cable, Cynopsis, Deadline, The Hollywood Reporter, Indiewire, Media Post,* and *Variety*. Many popular publications online also cover media and entertainment. The students in my classes often read: *Business Insider, The Los Angeles Times, The New York Times, Vulture (New York Magazine), The Wall Street Journal,* and *Wired*. For the subjects that you are researching for ongoing writing projects, consider subscribing to news alerts through a search engine so that you will receive links via e-mail to relevant stories. Some online publications also offer daily or weekly newsletters with options to customize your newsletter to feature only the topics that most interest you. For example, *Broadcasting & Cable* circulates *B&C Today*, a daily newsletter, as well as daily and weekly newsletters in related fields such as media technology. Your inbox may become very crowded very quickly, so decide whether depth or breadth best suits your current research interests and then customize your reading practice. You may also extend your online "reading" to blogs, podcasts, and video essays.

The suggestions above for online researching – reading, listening, browsing, searching – only scratch the digital surface of the opportunities for critical exploration and interaction available to scholars. *The Arclight Guidebook to Media History and the Digital Humanities* provides a much more expansive analysis of how media studies and digital humanities methodologies and resources impact each other, with individual chapters examining important case studies of digital archives, data analysis, and other relevant issues. Researchers who want to learn more about the most innovative digital research tools and formats may access *The Arclight Guidebook* (http://projectarclight.org/book/) for free online. One key example of digital media research is the Kinomatics project (http://kinomatics.com), led by a team that includes Bronwyn Coate and Deb Verhoeven who co-wrote a chapter on data for this book. Their chapter and their project website demonstrate the affordances of digital humanities research.

Finally, many media scholars rely on various social media platforms for their research. Productive social media research practices include: following other media scholars and practitioners (as well as critics, executives, and other media industry figures) on Twitter; joining Facebook groups that link scholars in media studies subfields; and commenting on the work of other scholars in open access journals. Social media facilitate both the consumption and the circulation of research. Scholars share research questions on Facebook, Twitter, and listservs, provoking critical dialogues and crowdsourcing research.

### Watching

From Netflix to YouTube to the many sites where viewers can download videos illegally, the Internet offers a seemingly endless supply of media "content." (The chapters in this volume by Ramon Lobato, Tijana Mamula, and Fan Yang, to name only a few examples, capture the breadth of online content across global platforms.) While I was writing this book, I was simultaneously working on two other research projects – one on the streaming service Filmstruck (a joint venture of Turner Classic Movies and the Criterion Collection) – a site that marketed critically acclaimed classic and contemporary films to an audience of cinephiles – and another on DramaFever – a site that focused on Korean television dramas. Both sites were owned by Time Warner. When AT&T bought Time Warner, the new media conglomerate decided to close both streaming services (along with several others). DramaFever closed immediately, without warning subscribers. When the closing of Filmstruck was then announced several weeks in advance, I used that time to take as many screenshots of different pages on the site as I could. Since I was studying not only the films that Filmstruck streamed but also the way their online portal presented those films to its subscribers (through the visual design of the site, the interactive architecture of the site's menus, and the curation of supplementary features), the preservation of as many images from the site as possible has enabled me to continue my research after the site disappeared.

Most media objects and events are ephemeral (as discussed at length in multiple chapters in this volume, including the chapters by Glyn Davis, Allyson Nadia Field, Katherine Groo, TreaAndrea M. Russworm and Jennifer Malkowski, and Kirsten Stevens). Access (or lack of access) informs our engagement with both old and new media. As a writer, it is important to keep in mind that whatever access you currently enjoy to the media objects you are studying may not last. So consider creating an archive of your own. Record detailed screening notes. Take screen shots of images, videos, websites, and other online media objects, and organize the image files in folders with clear file names and date stamps so that you can easily locate them later. If you are writing about a media object that you are accessing primarily online, make every effort to secure a physical copy as a supplementary resource if you have the means to do so. Whenever possible, buy films, television shows, and video games in physical formats; ask your library to purchase copies for their media collection; or request a short-term loan through Interlibrary Loan. Keep in mind that an entire streaming site might disappear overnight, and that even stable sites such as Netflix (a company that as of this writing we can reasonably expect to remain in business for some time) offers a very unstable catalog with titles appearing and disappearing every day. Sites that feature user-uploaded content such as YouTube may be valuable resources for finding fan-produced remix videos, trailers, gameplay walkthrough videos, and other media, but as an archive YouTube can be even more unpredictable than Netflix (and copies of YouTube videos in physical formats are unlikely to be available). In the case of YouTube and similar sites, preserving notes, screenshots, and other artefacts of your screening experience will be even more vital for your ongoing research.

You may be familiar with other large commercial streaming platforms such as Hulu (available only in the US) and Amazon, the availability of films and television shows through Apple's iTunes store, and the emergence of many streaming sites launched by individual networks or studios such as HBO GO. You may also be interested in consulting the following streaming services for specialized content: Rakuten Viki (global television with an emphasis on shows produced in Asian countries such as Korea and Thailand), Shout Factory (cult cinema), Mubi (art cinema), Acorn TV (film and television produced in the UK and Australia), Crunchyroll (anime), UbuWeb (avant-garde cinema), and Twitch (games and gameplay). Two additional sites offer very large catalogues for viewers to browse. First, Kanopy makes available all or part its catalogue of over 30,000 films to patrons of public libraries or university libraries. Their streaming catalogue includes films from boutique distributors such as A24 and Women Make Movies along with rarely circulated instructional videos and documentaries. Second, the Internet Archive boasts a sprawling library of films, television shows, videos, radio programs, community event recordings, websites, and other archival material. Users may search and access the material housed through the Internet Archive for free without any formal institutional affiliation.

## *Writing*

You likely already use many of the digital resources available for writers – from word processing programs to online citation tools to bookmarking services for tracking your Internet research. The brief profiles below present three opportunities to extend your engagement with digital resources for writers into platforms and practices that might be new to you:

Scalar (https://scalar.me): The Scalar platform (discussed in detail in Virginia Kuhn's chapter later in this volume) facilitates the publication of layered texts with annotations, visualizations, and other digital tools that enrich the textual elements of online articles and books. On the Scalar website, maintained by the Alliance for Networking Visual Culture, viewers may learn more about the writing possibilities enabled by the platform, browse previous Scalar projects, and register for Scalar webinars that teach participants the various skills necessary for publishing in Scalar. Browse the Scalar site, explore Scalar projects, and consider enrolling in a webinar to develop a new set of writing skills for future online projects.

FemTechNet (https://femtechnet.org): FemTechNet sponsors feminist editing initiatives on Wikipedia. Browse their Wiki Project Feminism page on Wikipedia and review their Open Tasks List. There you will find a list of Wikipedia pages to create, review, and expand using the tools and resources provided by FemTechNet. Consider adding this important form of digital writing to your emerging portfolio of online practices as a writer, ideally in collaboration with students and colleagues. The skills emphasized throughout this volume – writing clear, well-organized, and engaging prose; supporting claims with research and accurately formatted citations; and collaborating with other writers and researchers – all apply to Wikipedia writing and editing.

Rakuten Viki (www.viki.com/community_resources): Rakuten Viki (as noted in the chapter in Part II by Tijana Mamula) invites users to subtitle the content on their streaming platform. You may participate in their subtitling community in several ways – by segmenting videos, by captioning videos (writing titles that replicate, as closely as the space of the frame allows, the lines of dialogue in each segment in the same language as the spoken dialogue), and by subtitling videos (working in the languages in which you are fluent to provide subtitled translations of the spoken dialogue). Participating in the subtitling community provides an opportunity to learn about different industrial practices of translation and connect with an engaged fan community.

## In praise of paper

Debates about whether or not students should be allowed to use laptops in classrooms for note-taking and other academic purposes (research, collaborative projects, etc.) continue to unfold (Supiano). As a teacher, my approach to this question has been mixed. I do not allow students to use laptops to take notes during class discussions (unless they have special permission to do so), but I do invite students to use laptops, tablets, and phones in class for specific class activities.

My approach as a writer is similar. I find the technological resources discussed in the previous section to be indispensable for research and writing. When I write, I often have two screens on my desk – my laptop screen and a larger monitor – with a number of different windows open across the two screens, displaying sections of my work in progress, bookmarked web pages, media images, etc. However, most of the time that I spend "writing" involves shuttling back and forth between the keyboard of my computer and a notebook and pen. I prefer to write on letter-size graph-ruled tablets because the grids on the page facilitate both vertical and horizontal drafting. I take screening notes, reading notes, and writing notes on these pads. As discussed in detail in Chapter 3 and echoed in Part II in Dale Hudson and Patricia R. Zimmermann's chapter, taking notes by hand is part of a longer process that involves transcribing those notes into a word processing file and, as discussed in Chapter 4, eventually using them to develop an outline for your writing project.

Taking notes by hand is also a key element of the final stage of writing – revision. Revising a series of drafts by hand enables you to bring the openness of note-taking and freewriting into the revision process. Do not save hand revisions for the final stages of revision – proofreading – when you might use a pen to correct sentence-level mechanical, grammatical, and syntactical errors. Incorporate hand revisions into your writing of first drafts to identify issues with the structure and development of your argument which may involve moving, adding, or deleting entire paragraphs. Hand revised drafts in these early stages usually include lots of lines and arrows – erasing sentences, indicating where one passage should be cut and then pasted onto a different page, etc. In the intermediate stages of a draft, when the structure of your argument is more well-established, hand revisions can mark places where you need to supply additional evidence, add a figure, check a citation, etc. I recommend saving all of these hand-revised drafts (at least until the final draft of your project has been completed) so that you can refer to them as resources if and when the direction of your project shifts and earlier iterations of your project might be valuable to consult.

Pen and paper-based methods may seem more obviously useful when writing a traditional scholarly essay in written form, but these tools remain valuable even when working in other formats. If you are publishing a written essay in a digital format – for example, a blog post – printing out multiple drafts and revising them by hand will allow you to identify more easily the spots that require additional work. If you are recording a podcast interview, revising your notes and your interview questions by hand will help you to prepare, and taking notes by hand during the interview will allow you to track the arc of your conversation, recording ideas for follow-up questions or subsequent research that you might then include in the introduction that you record. If you are producing a video essay, you might include hand revisions as an element of the editing process, mapping the sequence of the video essay in a storyboard that includes detailed annotations for each shot.

You may take advantage of digital tools for note-taking – for example, a notes app or voice recording app on a phone or tablet – but taking notes with a pen should be part of your note-taking arsenal. Similarly, there are indispensable digital tools for revision – for example, using the track changes or comments functions of word processing programs – but, again, marking revisions by hand should be a part of your revision process. Even in the context of a book that advocates experimenting with new digital formats and platforms for writing, there is room for pen and paper.

## Citation

All of the chapters in this volume follow the style guidelines outlined in the eighth edition of the MLA Handbook (https://style.mla.org). Published in 2016 by the Modern Language Association, this edition of the MLA Handbook explicitly references the challenges of keeping style guidelines consistent and up to date when faced with the rapidly growing number of formats and venues for publication. In her preface to the handbook, Kathleen Fitzpatrick, the Associate Executive Director and Director of Scholarly Communications for the Modern Language Association and one of the book's primary authors, explains the need for crafting a citation style that responds to the mobility both of the various texts we might cite and the texts we might create:

> [W]ith the emergence of each new media platform would come a new query: How do you cite a YouTube video? a blog post? A tweet? With the eighth edition, we shift our focus from a prescriptive list of formats to the overarching purpose of source documentation: enabling readers to participate fully in the conversation between writers and their sources. Such participation requires the presentation of reliable information in a clear, consistent structure.
>
> (xii)

Following this principle, the *MLA Handbook* presents a flexible structure in which writers present the following information (if relevant and available) for each cited source: Author, Title of source, Title of container, Version, Number, Publisher, Publication date, Location. The difference between a source and a container may be illustrated by considering how you would cite a chapter from this book. If you cite a passage from Olivia Khoo's chapter in the second part of this book, your MLA citation in your Works Cited list would appear as follows:

> Khoo, Olivia. "Writing about Transnational Cinema: *Crazy Rich Asians.*" *Writing about Screen Media*, edited by Lisa Patti, Routledge, 2019, pp. 75–78.

This entry offers readers all of the information they need to locate that source and pursue additional research on the topic. Note that the entry does not include every element listed in the template above. This book does not have a Version (as it would if it were printed in multiple editions) or a Number (as it would if it were an issue of a scholarly journal), so those parts of the citation are simply omitted.

For the purpose of writing about screen media, the MLA style allows for the adaptation of this basic citation template for the documentation of many different kinds of media sources. For example, the handbook includes a sample citation for a comment posted on a webpage:

> Jeane. Comment on "The Reading Brain: Differences between Digital and Print." *So Many Books*, 25 Apr. 2013, 10:30pm, somanybooksblog.com/2013/04/25/the-reading-brain-differences-between-digital-and-print/#comment-83030.
>
> (44)

One of many examples of digital media citations in the MLA style, this entry demonstrates how the citation formula allows writers to capture all of the relevant information about a source that might otherwise seem difficult to share.

Specific publication formats and venues may require that you use a different citation style such as Chicago, APA, or Harvard. Within any citation style you use, research the most current guidelines so that you are following models that address new and emerging source types; and make every effort to provide reference information for every source that you cite. Many writers may be most familiar with the process of constructing bibliographies at the end of a written essay, but writers across media formats should cite their sources. In a video essay, you can list all of your sources (for images, text, and audio) in a frame or frames at the end of the video. For some video essays, all of the cited sources may fit within a single frame; other video essays might create scrolling end credit sequences like the ones you would find at the end of a film or television show. In that case, you can combine the presentation of a clearly and consistently formatted list of works cited with more creative elements such as music or additional video images. In a podcast, you can incorporate references to works you have cited in your audio commentary at the end of the podcast. You may also add a more formal written list of works cited to accompany the podcast on a companion website. While citation strategies may vary across media formats and platforms, find the most accurate and accessible way to share key information about the sources you have engaged in critical conversation.

## Fair use

When including copyrighted material in your writing projects – from film stills published in a print publication (like many of the figures included in this book) to video clips incorporated in a video essay – you must consider whether or not your work constitutes a *fair use* of that material. The "Society for Cinema and Media Studies Statement of Fair Use Best Practices for Media Studies Publishing" condenses relevant US copyright law and case histories into two central questions for writers to consider: "(1) Did the user employ copyrighted works with a transformative purpose that differs from the original? (2) Did the user employ only as much as necessary for that transformative purpose?" (181). The SCMS statement provides useful advice for writers and includes a list of frequently asked questions about fair use. Writers will also find many relevant resources on the website for the Center for Media & Social Impact (http://cmsimpact.org/resources/codes/). If you are creating a video essay, Jason Mittell's chapter "But Is Any of this Legal?: Some Notes about Copyright and Fair Use" in the book *The Videographic Essay: Criticism in Sound & Image* provides a detailed overview of the factors video essay producers should consider as well as a bibliography of websites, articles, and books that address copyright concerns. Note that the majority of these sources focus on US copyright law, so writers working in other countries should review relevant laws and policies in their respective countries before publishing work that includes copyrighted material. While writers, especially those with no or little experience publishing work that features copyrighted material, should review these resources, Mittell's concluding advice to video essayists serves as a fitting conclusion here. He writes, "Fair use is a muscle that will atrophy if not exercised – and videographic criticism is some of the most vigorous exercise that scholars can offer their fair use muscles" (60).

## In practice

### Keep a journal

Books about writing abound with advice about the importance of developing a regular writing practice. Specific guidelines about how, when, and where you should write may vary, but I have never encountered a book that suggests waiting until the night before a deadline to write. Whether or not you have any immediate deadlines on the horizon, starting a writing journal will help you to develop ideas and hone writing skills for your next project. Write as often as your schedule allows, tailoring the frequency and length of your journal entries to your writing goals. Use one or all of the following prompts to start your writing practice:

- Write a review of a film, television series, video game, or other screen media object.
- Write a recap of a television or podcast episode.
- Write a guest blog post for a blog you read frequently.
- Write a letter to a friend or colleague describing a writing project that you would like to begin.
- Sketch a storyboard for a video essay.
- Record an audio commentary for a music video.

### Review your queues

Many media critics maintain queues of films and television shows that we plan to watch; wish lists of books, movies, and video games we plan to buy in physical formats; bookmarks for blog posts or newspaper or journal articles we plan to read; or playlists of podcasts we plan to listen to on our next road trip. Review your queues. What do you notice about your lists? What do they reveal about the research questions that interest you? Set aside time to see/read/hear something completely new – a film from a country whose cinema is completely unfamiliar to you, a podcast interview with an independent television producer whose first series you haven't yet seen, a blog launched by an emerging scholar. These new entries in your queue may not launch new research initiatives, but they may expand how you think about contemporary media criticism.

> **Write for a specific venue**
>
> We do not begin every writing project with a specific publishing venue in mind. For some writing projects (especially for students), publication may not even be a final goal. But writing for a specific publication venue has both practical value (for example, allowing you to format your citations according to a specific journal's style) and rhetorical value (allowing you to write for a specific readership). Even if you do not plan to publish your current writing project, work with a specific publication venue in mind. Alternatively, write for presentation rather than publication. Imagine the specific group of people who will gather to hear your presentation – in your classroom, at a conference, etc. – and write for them as your primary audience.

## Note

1 These lists of databases are excerpted from a research guide created by librarian Sara Greenleaf and the staff of the Warren Hunting Smith Library at Hobart and William Smith Colleges. Links to the complete research guide and all listed databases may be found at writingaboutscreenmedia.net

## References

Fitzpatrick, Kathleen. *MLA Handbook*. 8th edition. Modern Language Association, 2016.
Mittell, Jason. "But is Any of this Legal?: Some Notes about Copyright and Fair Use." In *The Videographic Essay: Criticism in Sound & Image*, edited by Christian Keathley and Jason Mittell, caboose, 2016, pp. 53–61.
"Society for Cinema and Media Studies Statement of Fair Use Best Practices for Media Studies Publishing." *Cinema Journal*, vol. 49, no. 4, 2010, pp. 179–185.
Supiano, Beckie. "Should You Allow Laptops in Class? Here's What the Latest Study Adds to That Debate." *The Chronicle of Higher Education*. Vol. 65, no. 2, February 15, 2019.

# Part II
# Writers on writing about screen media

*Objects and events*

# 6 Writing about transnational cinema
## *Crazy Rich Asians*

*Olivia Khoo*

> *Crazy Rich Asians* (2018) is a landmark film, both in terms of its representation (as the first U.S. studio-released film with an all-Asian cast since *The Joy Luck Club* (1993)), and in terms of its popularity (as the highest grossing romantic comedy in a decade). This transnational film – shot in Malaysia, set in Singapore, with a cast and crew from around the world – has been met with divergent responses since its release. How do we write about a film as symbolically significant as *Crazy Rich Asians*? How can we approach the question of ethnic stereotyping in transnational screen media without succumbing to descriptions of racial purity or attempting to avoid stereotypes altogether?

One of the most challenging films I have attempted to write about in recent years has been *Crazy Rich Asians* (Jon M. Chu, 2018), adapted from Kevin Kwan's 2013 bestselling novel of the same name. The film is an entertaining romantic comedy that largely follows the conventions of the genre without challenging its viewers either formally or aesthetically. My difficulty with this film had to do with finding a way to write about it that did not succumb to the polarizing responses that have met its release – from anger and betrayal at the casting choices to deep joy at seeing self-representation on this scale. As the first U.S. studio-released film with an all-Asian cast since *The Joy Luck Club* (Wayne Wang, 1993) 25 years ago, and the highest-grossing romantic comedy in a decade, *Crazy Rich Asians* unavoidably carries the weight of collective representation.[1]

The film centers around a young couple, Rachel Chu (Constance Wu) and Nick Young (Henry Golding), who take a trip to Singapore for the wedding of Nick's best friend and for Rachel to meet Nick's family for the first time. Rachel does not realize that Nick is one of the most eligible bachelors in Singapore, heir to a massive fortune, and has to contend with Nick's overprotective mother, Eleanor (Michelle Yeoh), as well as a slew of jealous women and ex-girlfriends. The decision to cast biracial actor, Henry Golding (of Malaysian Iban and English descent), in the lead role of a Chinese Singaporean actor was highly controversial. Similarly, the casting of Sonoya Mizuno, of Japanese, Argentinian and English ancestry, as another Chinese Singaporean character, Araminta Lee, also drew negative attention.

The challenge in writing about such a landmark film gestures to broader issues of how to approach the question of racial identity and authenticity in transnational screen media without avoiding the topic altogether. Writers who criticize the cast of *Crazy Rich Asians* for not being "Asian enough" are themselves producing stereotypes about who or what an Asian should be. Instead of trying to *avoid* stereotyping, and inevitably falling into this trap, it is important to remain critically aware of cultural and critical contexts when writing about transnational cinema. Below I share some of my strategies for approaching a film like *Crazy Rich Asians*. These are not specific only to writing about this film; they help us navigate the thornier aspects of films that cross boundaries, be they geographical or racial.

In writing about a film that is this symbolically significant – an Asian-led blockbuster and transnational "Hollywood" film – it is understandable that there may be concerns over the stereotyping of characters. How should we deal with this? While stereotypes are usually condemned for being reductive, scholar Rey Chow argues that stereotyping is inevitable and in this way can also be productive:

> The point ... is not simply to repudiate stereotypes and pretend that we can get rid of them but also to recognize in the act of stereotyping ... a fundamental signifying or representational process with real theoretical and political consequences.
>
> (63–64)

Stereotyping is a practice of duplication and imitation; by examining exactly how stereotypes duplicate or imitate, we can question the assumptions on which their negative effects are based (54). That is, instead of simply repeating a stereotype and perpetuating it unquestioningly, or trying to avoid stereotypes altogether, our writing should remain mindful of the operations of this repetition, of stereotypes as a representational device and therefore "a possible tactic of aesthetic and political intervention" (54). Stereotypes need not be devious. For example, *Crazy Rich Asians* plays on stereotypes of Asians as economically successful; while this may represent a (very small) group across contemporary Asia, it is nevertheless a portrayal that is not often seen in mainstream cinema. While other commercial films such as *Crouching Tiger, Hidden Dragon* (Ang Lee, 2000) and *Memoirs of a Geisha* (Rob Marshall, 2005) were successful at the box office, they did not focus on contemporary characters. Finding a U.S. studio-produced film with an all-Asian cast that does not involve martial arts is quite a rarity! The film also debunks gendered stereotypes about the leading man in a romantic comedy, and in particular roles that "feminize" the Asian man. Rather than critiquing the film for its casting or its play on stereotypes, the more productive question would be to ask how these stereotypes allow us to understand the flows and circuits of a successful transnational film, and the ways in which local identity and culture are bound up with the forces of globalization.

While film has always been to some degree transnational, the movement of people, technology, and capital is now greatly accelerated. Transnational films are films that cross national borders and therefore involve an encounter between different national spaces and cultures. The difficulty in writing about transnational cinema is that it involves negotiating (at least two) different national contexts and (often) languages. In thinking about the kind of research methodologies that are most useful in interrogating the transnational dimensions of cinema, film scholar Rosalind Galt reminds us that the prefix "trans" serves as a bridge:

> By shifting our attention to the mode of movement between things, the transnational asks us to look at cinema in terms of processes and transits, rather than objects and states.
>
> (9)

Transnational cinema provides an opportunity for us to make connections between various levels of analysis, be they institutional, industrial, or textual. This may require us to deploy specific methodologies in our research – empirical, sociological, or textual – that allow us to attend to questions of policy, industry, and audience, as well as to questions of narrative and form (Fisher and Smith). In my own approach, this process often unfolds through trial and error – starting out with one theory or method, and finding that I need to supplement or replace with another approach to capture the complexity of a film.

It is worthwhile to note that the producers of *Crazy Rich Asians* turned down a lucrative deal with Netflix (including a greenlighted trilogy) in favor of a theatrical release. The film's producers agreed it was important to the symbolism of the film to have the backing of a major studio, in this case Warner Brothers (Sun and Ford). In making this deal, Kevin Kwan remained as an Executive Producer so that he could retain creative control. While Netflix is emerging as a major producer of screen content, films released on Netflix cannot generate "blockbuster" status because Netflix will not release viewing data. The theatrical release for *Crazy Rich Asians* thus generated multiple revenue streams, blockbuster hype, and a venue for communal viewing among Asian and non-Asian audiences. Taking a media industries approach to the study of transnational films (examining the effects of studios, contracts, and distribution patterns) can provide useful information concerning a film's production and distribution context beyond a textual analysis of characters, narrative, and genre.

By looking critically at the operations of stereotypes, and deploying a flexible raft of methodological tools to attend to the various circuits and flows of transnational cinema, we can celebrate a film like *Crazy Rich Asians* as being symbolically significant and at the same time critique it. Writing about transnational screen media requires us to negotiate different critical approaches. Questions that are useful to ask in deciding on the most suitable approach to take include: Who is this film made for and by? How has it travelled? And what kinds of boundaries (geographical, industrial, and representational) have been crossed? As the film itself reminds us, to "game" a win, you just might have to be prepared to lose (to a stereotype or two).

## Note

1  As of October 2018, the film had grossed over $232 million worldwide (Frater).

## References

Chow, Rey. *The Protestant Ethnic and the Spirit of Capitalism*. Columbia UP, 2002.

Fisher, Austin, and Iain RobertSmith. "Transnational Cinemas: A Critical Roundtable." *Frames Cinema Journal*, vol. 9, 2016, pp. 1–28.

Frater, Patrick. "'Crazy Rich Asians' Sequel to Shoot in China." *Variety*, 29 October, 2018. https://variety.com/2018/film/asia/crazy-rich-asians-sequel-shoot-in-china-1203008180/

Galt, Rosalind. In Fisher, Austin, and Iain RobertSmith. "Transnational Cinemas: A Critical Roundtable. " *Frames Cinema Journal*, vol. 9, 2016, pp. 9–12.

Sun, Rebecca, and Rebecca Ford. "The Stakes are High for 'Crazy Rich Asians' – And that's the Point." *Hollywood Reporter*, 1 August, 2018. www.hollywoodreporter.com/features/crazy-rich-asians-story-behind-rom-com-1130965

# 7 Capturing moments
## Writing about film festivals as events

*Kirsten Stevens*

> This chapter offers up strategies for students and researchers new to the topic to write about film festivals as events. It highlights the challenges that the temporary, experiential and multifaceted nature of festival events pose for approaches to research and writing. In response, it offers strategies connected to ethnography and participant research, archival research and contextual analysis to aid writers in capturing festival moments. While writing about film festivals can take many forms, this chapter presents avenues to begin the process of writing about festival events.

Writing about film festivals presents a challenge for screen media researchers. Film festivals are not clearly defined "texts" that can be read in the same way as a film. Questions of "What *defines* a film festival?" (the films it screens or how it screens them? the people who attend or the experiences they have?) or "What is *part* of a film festival?" (does it include the online ticketing platform that sells the event's passes?) complicate describing such events as discrete texts. Instead, film festivals are complex objects of study that require those writing about them to consider a range of different priorities, participants, agendas, and interactions.

Film festivals are, in many ways, about screen media. Through their programs they are showcases of films, as well as increasingly other forms of screen media, such as television, web film, and virtual reality.[1] Yet, if film festivals are about screening media, they are also about screen culture more broadly: the contexts in which media are consumed, the industries that support them, the places and spaces that house them, the labors that facilitate their presentation, the economies that sustain and are sustained by them, and much more. In a film festival, as film scholar Dina Iordanova notes, "the films remain intrinsic, but they can be any films" (xii). Alongside screen media, then, other elements of film festivals, including award ceremonies, red carpets, audience queues, volunteers, press reviews, gala parties, director Q&As, and professional networking opportunities, are important to discuss when analyzing film festivals as events.

Writing about film festivals requires researchers to engage with the multi-faceted nature of these events. It requires us to look at how these temporary showcases of screen media operate, who they operate for, and the (often contradictory) agendas that drive these events and the different constituencies or publics (filmmakers, industry professionals, cinephiles, general audiences, sponsors, and cities) that they engage. This can complicate the prospect of writing about film festivals; there are many ways to write about these events and many questions that can be asked and answered about how and why they work and the impacts they have. In her introduction to *Film Festivals: History, Theory, Method, Practice*, film festival scholar Marijke de Valck offers novice festival researchers an expanded guide to effective research design and advice on formulating topical research questions about film festivals. In highlighting how topic-driven festival research is, de Valck notes:

> Given the complexity of the film festival world – with octopus arms into the realms of culture, economics, and politics – and the many differences between individual festivals, it really is one's research question that determines what theories to draw upon and which methods to deploy.
>
> (8)

There is more than one way to write about film festivals. The questions you ask will determine how you write – what theories become relevant, what methodologies important. That said, however, some basic strategies underpin much writing about film festivals.

In this chapter, I draw on my own experiences writing about film festivals to offer a toolkit of strategies for writing about film festivals as events. Writing about events is an act of capturing moments. As temporary and often ephemeral occurrences, film festivals offer a unique challenge for writers – how to pin down, research, and convey something that is often fleeting, tied to people and objects doing a particular thing, in a particular place, at a particular time. Reflecting on my own writing process, I offer starting points from which to approach the task of writing about film festivals.

## Writing through experience

Whenever possible, I begin my writing by attending festivals. The experience of a festival reveals much about how it works, who its audience is, how it connects with local, national and regional cultural identities, and what (cultural, political, industrial) purpose it serves. At the festival, I pose a series of questions: What types of films can I see? Who (press, filmmakers, other festival programmers) have accreditation? What motivates them to attend? What do people do between screenings? What kind of atmosphere is created? In writing about a contemporary event, the methodological tools of disciplines such as anthropology – (auto)ethnography, embedded field study, participant observation – as well as forms of in-depth qualitative analysis – interviews, surveys, case studies – form the basis of my approach. Attending events and utilizing these tools to connect with other participants not only allows me to gather information on a particular event, but also helps me better understand the nature of film festivals more broadly. Festivals are not only the sum of their planned elements (such as screenings and award ceremonies) but also the result of unplanned moments, shared rituals, and the coming together of a temporary community. It is through experiencing these environments that I begin my work of writing about them.

## Writing through ephemera

While firsthand access to festivals is useful, it is not always available. When writing about the history of film festivals in Australia, I was interested in long past events. Although interviews offered some of the information I needed, writing about these events mainly meant tracking down archival materials. Festivals may be temporary occurrences, but they also leave traces of their passing. Media anthropologist Daniel Dayan, writing of the 1997 Sundance Film Festival, notes that alongside the audio-visual event there exists another "written festival" (47). This *meta-festival* of printed words – including film reviews, program notes, posters, and press releases – works to caption and transcribe a version of the festival, shaping not only the experience of navigating the event, but producing its record. Writing about past festivals requires us to follow these written traces. However, as festival organizations are often as transient as the events they produce, finding these traces can be difficult. Relatively few festivals keep complete archives, and what is kept will often disappear when events fold. A single poster or advert in a community newspaper can be all that remains, decades later, to mark the existence of an event. Writing about past festivals becomes akin to detective work, then, with researchers needing to reconstruct the record and search through ephemera to write about events.

## Writing through aftershocks

The final strategy that underpins my writing on film festivals incorporates looking beyond the festival to the conditions that mark its existence. Like a seismic event – an earthquake, for instance – film festivals are not confined to a single happening in a specific time and place. They create ripples that cause aftershocks, tsunamis, and tremors felt throughout particular regions. Take, for example, Festival de Cannes excluding films with no French theatrical release from competition in 2018. This decision, made with explicit reference to Netflix and Cannes' particular stakeholders, created ripples which circulated through the global press and signaled potential consequences for the screen industry that extend beyond that one festival's program. Writing about film festivals includes tracing these ripples to explore what impact or influences a specific event has. How does a festival fit within the global hierarchy of major, minor, regional, and specialist events? What impact do they have on the films they screen? How does their location impact their operation? What relevance do they have for broader social, cultural, political or economic concerns? By situating the events you write about within broader systems of exchange, you help to ensure that your writing, and the festivals you write about, holds a wider relevance.

## Between writing and doing

Depending on the topics you choose to write about and the accessibility of the festivals you study, some of these strategies will prove more useful than others. Each, however, should form at least part of your writing process. If you can't experience the event, how can you determine how it went – who attended, how they reacted, what planned or unplanned things happened? If there is no official record, where else might you find traces that tell you that a film festival took place? What impact did the festival have, and on or for whom? Good writing on film festivals responds to these questions, understanding the limitations of festival research they reveal but also working to overcome them. Often the best way to achieve this is to get involved in creating film festivals yourself. There is significant overlap between the community of researchers writing on film festivals and film festival practitioners. Writing on film festivals in Melbourne led me to co-found the Melbourne Women in Film Festival (www.mwff.org.au). My writing on festivals helped me to understand the challenges that such events face, but more significantly, organizing this event helped me to better write about the complexity of these events. Doing, in this sense, becomes another part of writing.

*Figure 7.1* Photograph by Jaklene Vukasinovic, courtesy of Melbourne Women in Film Festival. Festival panel "Making a film on a micro-budget," Australian Centre for the Moving Image, February 2018

## Note

1 Film festivals are not only concerned with films. See, for example, the Toronto International Film Festival "Primetime" TV program (www.tiff.net); Austin Film Festival's "Scripted Digital Series" competition (austinfilmfestival.com); or the VR programs at the Busan (www.biff.kr) and Melbourne International Film Festivals (miff.com.au).

## References

Dayan, Daniel. "In Quest of a Festival." *National Forum*, vol. 77, no. 4, 1997, pp. 41–47.
de Valck, Marijke. "What is a film festival? How to study festivals and why you should." *Film Festivals: History, Theory, Method, Practice*, edited by M. de Valck, B. Kredell, and S. Loist. Routledge, 2016, pp. 1–11.
Iordanova, Dina. "Foreword." *Film Festivals: History, Theory, Method, Practice*, edited by M. de Valck, B. Kredell, and S. Loist. Routledge, 2016, pp. xi–xvii.

# 8 Writing about experimental cinema
## Andy Warhol's *Empire* (1964)

Glyn Davis

> How do you watch, and then write about, a film that tests your patience and endurance? Andy Warhol's *Empire* (1964) is eight hours long and central to the canon of experimental cinema, but it is not easy to source or sit through. When writing about experimental film, this chapter argues, it is not only acceptable but useful to discuss accessing a film, and the physical conditions of watching. The value of sitting diligently all the way through a conceptual piece of cinema is explored, including whether this is necessary in order to be able to write about it. Finally, the chapter asks whether experimental forms of writing are more appropriate to adopt when writing about experimental film.

Andy Warhol's *Empire*, a film of the Empire State Building, lasts for eight hours and five minutes. It was shot over one night in July 1964, looking out of a window of the offices of the Rockefeller Foundation on the 41$^{st}$ floor of the Time-Life Building. Present at the filming was a group of men: Warhol and his assistant Gerard Malanga; the filmmaker, writer and curator Jonas Mekas; Henry Romney, who arranged the shooting; and John Palmer, who is usually credited with coming up with the idea for the film, and as its co-director. Very little happens in the film. The camera stares, without moving, at the building. The sky slowly darkens. Floodlights come on, illuminating the building; towards the end of the film, they are switched off again. *Empire* is a canonical work of avant-garde cinema, notorious for its conceptual simplicity and audacity, and a film that I have repeatedly returned to and wrestled with in my own writing. For our purposes here, it also serves as an illuminating example of the challenges of writing about experimental cinema.

Watching *Empire* is difficult, in more ways than one. First, it is difficult in terms of access. Unlike mainstream cinema, which is widely distributed to audiences across a variety of platforms, options for viewing experimental films can be limited. Of course, many experimental films are available in a variety of formats – on DVD and BluRay, accessible online – and are sometimes screened in cinemas. But many others are not, and the first challenge for the writer can be tracking down the film itself. A financial outlay may be necessary: your access to a specific experimental film might be limited by its location and by whether you have the funds necessary to pay for travel to that place. You may include an account of your quest to find the film in your writing, in a way that you wouldn't if you were talking about, say, a *Transformers* movie. Andy Warhol made hundreds of films between 1963 and 1968. A significant number have been restored and preserved, but many have not. Film theorist Ara Osterweil wrote an essay about one of the latter for the magazine *Little Joe*:

> In October 2013, I drive seven hours from Montréal to New York to see twelve minutes of film. Surely this is one form of insanity. My journey is to see Warhol's film *Three* at the Museum of Modern Art Film Study Center. Made in early 1964, and never publicly screened, the film is slipped from the archive just long enough to catalogue it. After a day or two of careful consideration by a panel of curators and scholars, it is returned to the vault ...
>
> (134)

Here, Osterweil not only engages her readers through setting up a narrative, but provides revelations about the workings of experimental film archives.

Aside from the films stored in collections and archives, many experimental films have been created with particular exhibition strategies in mind that, again, limit access: films may have been made for showing only in specific galleries and/or may require certain screening technologies (for example, 16mm projectors). For the writer, it is necessary to detail the set-up of the space in which the film is screened, and to register the ways in which this affects the work. Readers may not have seen the rare screening, and writing about experimental cinema thus regularly includes information on the venue, its arrangement, and its atmospherics. When an experimental film changes exhibition location, this can have a significant impact on its reception; making a comparison of venues, if possible, can enhance a reader's understanding of the film. To a certain degree, writing about an experimental film involves providing a documentary account of witnessing it, in one or more locations, for readers who have not had the opportunity to do so; this is not required when writing about mainstream films.

The gallery presentation of an experimental film may be the ideal way in which it should be viewed, and the one intended by its creator. However, close readings can be difficult to produce in such circumstances: low levels of lighting and the presence of other viewers can prevent the taking of notes, for instance. Access to a second, supplementary copy of the film – however visually inferior and removed from optimal screening conditions – can be invaluable in enabling analysis. I most recently saw *Empire* in its entirety during an archival trip to the Warhol Museum in Pittsburgh. The digital transfer, accessible through a touch-screen monitor in a small viewing gallery, was removed from the pulse and grain of a film print screening but enabled a level of close personal scrutiny – and an opportunity to skip back and forth through the film – that I had not previously experienced.

Watching *Empire* is also difficult in terms of discomfort. Eight hours is a lengthy running time for a film – though one with resonance, as it is roughly equivalent to the length of the work day, or a good night's sleep. The human body struggles with such an endurance test, needing bathroom breaks, sustenance, movement. Sitting through the entirety of *Empire* is a major challenge, and writing about the film has often acknowledged or drawn attention to this. Art historian Pamela Lee, for example, avoids using the first person but seems to be acknowledging her own discomfort:

> Shifting from side to side, at first quietly and then with increasing impatience, we experience our body as a duration machine. The bones poke through, head lolls on the stem of its neck. With each moment that passes, the eyes play tricks while the mind wanders: we see things that aren't there or perhaps discount what is there. [...] The erect carriage of the committed cineaste gives way to the slouch and sprawl of the tired, the jaded, or the bored.
>
> (287)

Of course, not all experimental films have the distended length of *Empire*. In addition, similar types of discomfort can be experienced watching much shorter experimental films – such as Warhol's Screen Test portrait films, each of which only lasts for several minutes. Lee's comments are useful, however, in making us consider the viewing encounter with experimental cinema, which may often be very different from more mainstream fare. When experimental films are screened in galleries, we may walk into them part-way through; identifying their start and end may not always be simple; seating, when available, may not be the most comfortable. All of these hurdles need to be overcome in order to engage with the film through writing.

How long should one spend with an experimental film to understand it, to be able to write about it? Although the description of *Empire* that I provided in the opening paragraph of this essay provides enough information for you to have a sense of the film, in order to write about experimental cinema – as with all cinema – it is necessary to spend sustained time with the work and to repeatedly re-view it. When you sit through a long film with very little change in content, for instance, your understanding of what amounts to "action" shifts, and minor incidents become of interest. With *Empire*, the turning on and off of the lights on the Empire State Building attains serious dramatic weight. The largely-unchanging image starts to warp before your eyes. As art historian Douglas Crimp writes of the film:

> what I found happened most was that the perspective of the building kept reversing itself, so that instead of a solid contour I seemed to be

looking at a hollowed-out volume, as if I were seeing a cutaway of interior space. When that happened, I would try in vain to turn concave back to convex, to get the building to become a solid exterior again. [...] The image eventually becomes so abstract that you begin to read it like a Rorschach test.

(140)

We start to drift, to read the image poetically. Curator Callie Angell noted that, for her, the building began to resemble "a rocket ship, a hypodermic needle, a heavenly cathedral, or a broad paintbrush;" the "passing light flares, water marks, and other transient phenomena of the medium occur as spectacularly as sunrises and meteor showers in the minimal scenery of Warhol's film" (30). Angell and Crimp demonstrate a key component of much writing on experimental cinema: that, fittingly, it often needs to incorporate stretches or instances of experimental and poetic text. While in theory it would be possible to write poetically about the *Transformers* films, experimental cinema invites such exploratory approaches.

## References

Angell, Callie. "Empire." *Andy Warhol: Motion Pictures*, edited by Klaus Biesenbach. KW Institute for Contemporary Art, 2004, pp. 28–33.
Crimp, Douglas. *"Our Kind of Movie:" The Films of Andy Warhol*. MIT Press, 2012.
Lee, Pamela. *Chronophobia: On Time in the Art of the 1960s*. MIT Press, 2004.
Osterweil, Ara. "Three's Company." *Little Joe*, No. 5, 2015, pp. 132–147.

# 9 From meaning to effect
## Writing about archival footage

*Jaimie Baron*

> This chapter explores the difference between trying to write about the "effect" as opposed to the "meaning" of a text. I argue that we cannot talk about a text as if it were isolated from the viewing experience because the text is co-constituted *in* the viewing experience. Ignoring our own bodily sensations, our own emotional reactions, and our own intellectual activities in our encounter with a film or video in favor of some abstract "meaning" we are supposed to deduce is nonsensical. Looking at "archival footage" as footage producing an "archive effect" for the viewer frees us from thinking primarily about filmmakers' intentions or a film's "meaning" in favor of thinking about archival footage as an experience, which opens up many new avenues of thought.

The first time I saw an experimental found footage film as an undergraduate student, I had no idea how to react. I had never heard of "found footage" before. This being in the era before YouTube and forms like the supercut and the mashup, the idea of reusing existing footage in a new film or video was entirely unfamiliar to me. For the twelve minutes constituting A Movie (1958) by Bruce Conner, I was overstimulated and overwhelmed, entirely uncertain what to make of the barrage of images – of cowboys, animals, car crashes, nuclear bombs, scuba divers – accompanied by a soaring instrumental soundtrack. The images clearly came from many different sources, but Conner – it appeared – had found them and edited them together into a new configuration.

I was intrigued, though I could not say what this film was "about" or what it "meant." When it came to this found footage film, trying to figure out what the filmmaker intended – and therefore what the film meant – seemed fundamentally impossible. Conner had found and edited these images together, but he did not film them. They were not *his*. So how could I possibly locate his intention and, hence, his intended meaning? Although I explored many other avenues of study between my undergraduate years and my Ph.D., my fascination with *A Movie* never left me, partly because I felt I lacked the language

From meaning to effect 89

*Figure 9.1* A found image from A Movie (1958)

to articulate what I had seen and heard in my first encounter with that film. Much later, I published a book called *The Archive Effect: Found Footage and the Experience of History*, which brought me back to the question of what a found footage film is, what it does, and what it might mean.

One of the most difficult challenges I encountered in writing *The Archive Effect* was defining the difference between "found footage" and "archival footage," two terms that are often used interchangeably but have different connotations and are associated with different genres. Why, I wondered, was there so little discussion of the crossovers between the reuse of existing footage in documentary film (associated with "archival footage") and experimental film (associated with "found footage")? What is an "archive" anyway, particularly in an era when filmmakers "find" and appropriate materials from online sites like YouTube as often as from official state or commercial archives? Is YouTube an archive if people are using it like one, despite the absence of an archivist to organize and categorize? What about the Internet as a whole? Is everything suddenly an archive and, if so, has the word "archive" lost its meaning? And if we cannot define "archival footage" as "footage coming from an archive," how can we define it? For me, just articulating these questions was the first step toward a new way of thinking about archival footage, even if I could not initially answer them.

The work of film scholar Vivian Sobchack introduced me to phenomenology and, thereby, to the idea of paying close attention to my own *experiences* and *perceptions* of a media text, to what I actually saw, heard, felt, and thought as I was watching it. In her exceptional essay on nonfiction film, she writes:

> The term *documentary* designates more than a cinematic *object*. Along with the obvious nomination of a film genre characterized historically by certain objective textual features, the term also – and more radically – designates a particular *subjective relation* to an objective cinematic or televisual text. In other words, documentary is less a *thing* than an *experience*.
> 
> (Sobchack 241, emphasis in original)

This passage transformed my understanding of what a documentary – or any text – fundamentally was. I came to recognize that the text does not exist in isolation from the viewing experience; indeed, the text is co-constituted *in* the viewing experience. Ignoring my own bodily sensations, my own emotional reactions, and my own intellectual activities in my encounter with a film – in favor of some abstract "meaning" I was supposed to deduce – made less and less sense to me. By thinking through my own experiences of and reactions to a series of films, both documentary and experimental, I discovered that it made sense to me to define "archival footage" not in terms of where the footage happened to be located before it was appropriated or into what kind of film it was repurposed, but rather in terms of the viewer's experience of the footage. When I started to look at "archival footage" from this perspective – as footage producing an "archive effect" for the viewer – many of my other conceptual problems began to untangle. Indeed, it freed me from thinking primarily about the filmmaker's intention (although I still had to grapple with it) or the film's meaning in favor of thinking about the film's *effects* on the viewer. This shift to effects was, however, extremely difficult because, although I could draw on my own experience, I could not generalize my experience to all viewers. Different viewers will experience a film differently, at least to some degree. However, rather than try to pretend that this was not the case, I found I could write about that fact.

Writing is – or can be – a means of trying to understand the things that confuse us, the things that we do not immediately understand, to "write the problem" as Sobchack (who became my Ph.D. advisor) taught me. In my experience, this means not trying to reduce or simplify the experience of a film but, rather, to start by articulating what is so difficult about expressing how it works. For me, this often begins with a description of the text and my encounter with it. By this, I do not mean summarizing the plot. Indeed, many of the films I write about do not even have a plot. Instead, it means writing down what I actually see, what I actually hear, and how I am making sense of the images and sounds and the relationship between them. For instance, Michael Apted's *Up* series was crucial to the development of my idea of the archive effect. For this series, Apted filmed the same subjects every seven years from the time they were seven years old in *Seven Up!* (1964) until the present – the most recent film being *56 Up* (2012). This film series illustrated my conundrum: the footage from previous films, some part of which reappeared in all of the later films, could not be said to be "found" or "archival" in any traditional sense. Apted himself had produced and saved all of the footage of his subjects. The footage was not stored in an official archive, nor did he have to go "find" it anywhere except his own storage space. And yet, as I watched the films again and again, I could not shake the feeling that, for instance, the footage of the children at seven years old when it appeared in *49 Up* (2005) was "archival."

Slowly, this led me to rethink the idea of the "archival" as an effect produced (in part) by a perception of what I called "temporal disparity." In other words, the archival became, for me, a matter of the *experience* of a

*From meaning to effect* 91

*Figure 9.2* Bruce at seven years old in *Seven Up!* (1964)

given viewer watching a film such as *49 Up* and recognizing the temporal disparity between different images within the same film. Thus, through careful watching and rewatching of *49 Up* and other films I was able to articulate slowly an entirely new way of defining and discussing "archival footage."

This all took a great deal of time – watching a lot of films that reused existing footage, writing detailed descriptions of each film and my experience of it, and then developing a theorization based on those close descriptions. Too often, writers impose an existing theory on a film, whether this means performing an ideological analysis, psychoanalytic assessment, or cultural critique. This is a useful and important exercise, but it is only a beginning. Sobchack taught me that the theory must arise "from the object itself." Of course, one should read what others have written about a film, but the point is not to reiterate what others have already demonstrated or to impose a preexisting framework onto the film. It is to demonstrate something new, something that lies within the film or films themselves (or is constituted in our encounter with them) that is waiting to be revealed through careful observation and precise description. Our initial impulse is often to reduce, to simplify, to contain a film because there is always too much in an audiovisual text for us to account for in written language. Writing about archival footage, however, has taught me the value of close attention to my own experience and the effort to transform that attentiveness into language on the page.

## References

Baron, Jaimie. *The Archive Effect: Found Footage and the Audiovisual Experience of History.* Routledge, 2014.

Sobchack, Vivian. "Toward a Phenomenology of Nonfiction Film Experience." *Collecting Visible Evidence*, edited by Michael Renov and Jane Gaines, University of Minnesota Press, 1999, pp. 241–254.

# 10 Making the absent present
## Writing about nonextant media

*Allyson Nadia Field*

---

> How do scholars write about films and media artifacts that they cannot see? With large percentages of our audio-visual heritage lost or in states of decay, it is incumbent on scholars to find strategies for accounting for these missing pieces of media history. This chapter addresses the reasons for the low survival rates for media objects, reasons for looking past archival absence, and approaches for finding presence in the absence of viewable materials.

As a scholar of cinema and media, and early cinema in particular, it has often struck me as a little absurd to be working in a discipline that has been built around a small minority of surviving exemplars. Because those survivors are often so amazing – from the films of the Lumière brothers and Georges Méliès to those of D.W. Griffith and Mack Sennett – this problem doesn't often arise at a practical level, but it's always there. So, while we don't often think of our work as akin to archaeology, in fact we share a lot with disciplines based on fragmentary evidence of once-robust creative output. With my research, I argue for a centering of the absent majority that comprises our media history.

The numbers are still astounding. The Film Foundation estimates that 50% of American films made before 1950 and more than 90% of American films made before 1929 are lost, likely never to be found. According to the 2013 study by historian and archivist David Pierce on the survival of American silent feature films made between 1912–1929, commissioned by the National Film Preservation Board, about 75% of these are considered lost. As Pierce laments, "There is so little to see" (13).

Rates of survival decrease the further we get from the present and the more removed a work is from mainstream theatrically-released features, but it is a mistake to think that this does not hold with more recent media. I focus here on film, but this discussion could also apply to any media artifact that is no longer available for viewing. With the rapid advancement in technologies, format obsolescence – think of all the floppy disks that once contained media, or VHS tapes, or laserdiscs – can be an obstacle to accessing media works. Further, some formats are simply less stable than others. If properly stored, nitrate film stock is actually remarkably stable in preserving image quality, but it is extremely unstable as a material – it has the disadvantage of being highly combustible and susceptible to decay and fire – if not. Some widely used film stocks, like Kodak's Eastmancolor, were made with unstable dyes that tended to fade, leaving the print looking overwhelmingly magenta. Microsoft Word files from the 1990s are now hard to read.

But the central question here has to do with why so much of film history has been lost. Some of this is due to format. And then there is the perception of value. After their initial release, films were seen to have little to no commercial value and so were not suited for costly storage and preservation. Indeed, because of the highly flammable condition of nitrate, keeping nitrate film could be a major liability. Thus, extant film prints usually survived because of economic incentives. Nearly all American sound films shot on nitrate from the 1930s and 40s survive because, as David Pierce notes, "they had commercial value for television in the 1950s and new copies were made while the negatives were still intact" (5).

The connection of archival efforts to commercial success has produced an especially acute problem for nontheatrical film, marginal cinema practices, amateur media making, and even televised programs. Films produced in regions that have experienced political instability or conflict are disproportionately impacted, as are media kept in under-resourced archives or in regions environmentally inhospitable to preservation. In some cases, entire bodies of work are no longer available for us to view.

For example, despite a robust industry of independent producers and a dedicated audience, *no* films made by African Americans are known to survive prior to 1920 (with the significant exception of two shorts directed by and starring Bert Williams, produced by Biograph in 1916 for a general audience).

Films, of course, can be found, and these finds, however rare they might be, should be celebrated. What I've tried to argue in my work, however, is that film history should not be written just from the standpoint of survivors. If we are serious about studying screen media, we have to confront the issue of loss – not just as incitement to discover more but as a constitutive feature of the media we study. This is especially true for those of us interested in media produced by nonwhite filmmakers, films made for nontheatrical exhibition, or media produced in nonstandard formats. The films are simply not there. Thus, if we are to expand the canon of objects we study, we have to find ways to engage with nonextant works.

So, what does it mean to discuss nonextant film? First, it means acknowledging that the film or media artifact is lost *to you*, to the present, but also recognizing that it was indeed exhibited *to others* at particular places and times. What is now nonextant was once extant. This means that you have to think about the audience that encountered the film (if that's possible to trace), as well as the people and institutions who were involved in the production of the film. In this sense, it means thinking about production, exhibition, and reception of a film as a kind of scaffolding around the now-lost film. The more pieces you can put together surrounding the lost object, the more of a picture you start to get of it. This is what I describe as the effort "to look for the presence in the absence" (Field 25).

Depending on the particular case, there's a wide range of information that we can discover about a film's production, exhibition, and its formal components. Data on a film's length, format, and narrative elements are often more available, whereas aspects of composition, framing, editing, and mise-en-scène are more difficult to discern. If we depend on surviving evidence, inferences regarding questions of form and style must be made with caution (Field 26). The solution is to look adjacently. By marshaling extrafilmic evidence through archival contextualization, we can refine our arguments about how a nonextant media artifact looked, its formal composition, its appeal to particular audiences, and so forth.

Strategies for "looking adjacently" will vary depending on the type of media, the era in which it was produced, and the questions the scholar is interested in addressing. In the case of my book *Uplift Cinema*, my interest in films made by African Americans prior to 1915 led me to investigate a range of ancillary material, including photographs, institutional records, publicity materials, and surviving ephemera. Such materials can tell us about the kinds of rhetorical strategies mobilized for the purpose of African American advancement at the turn of the twentieth century and the following decade. From there, it was possible to get an account of how moving pictures operated in this broader multi-media sphere. To access this history, I looked at materials related to the public discourse around the films, including discussions in the mainstream and African American press (including regional and national newspapers), the trade press (motion picture industry journals), and other accounts of motion picture production and exhibition. Some of this research required trips to archives, but many resources have been digitized and are more readily accessible through newspaper databases such as ProQuest or Newspapers.com or through public projects such as the Library of Congress's Chronicling America. The Media History Digital Library (http://mediahistoryproject.org) is an indispensable resource for accessing books, magazines, journals, catalogs and other material from the histories of film, broadcasting, and recorded sound. Digitally accessible resources comprise a major asset for students and scholars of media, but we should always be cognizant that they represent an incomplete archive. Many sources are harder to access or require visiting specific libraries or archives.

This is, of course, not a problem that is unique to my work. Film scholars Jon Lewis and Eric Smoodin edited an excellent collection of essays, *Looking Past the Screen: Case Studies in American Film History and Method*, that demonstrates how scholarship on film can be augmented by extrafilmic evidence; the essays in this collection can serve as models for approaching nonextant film and the range of methodologies film scholars employ beyond textual analysis. Similarly, film scholar Giuliana Bruno's book *Streetwalking on a Ruined Map* uses fragmentary evidence to composite a cultural history of the filmmaking of Elvira Notari and Italian culture of the early twentieth century, drawing from architecture, art history, and medical discourse, as well as photography, literature and film. Understanding film as a cultural agent produced in and reflective of a particular time and place allows us to approach it through its surrounding context, even in its absence.

What I've described are standard tools of historical researchers. However, there are strategies beyond these methods that may be necessary to find, or even create, presence in the absence of surviving history. This can even be based on imaginative but informed speculation about the absent archive. Models for this kind of speculative archival work include not just scholarship but also Cheryl Dunye's *The Watermelon Woman* (1996), the first feature film made by an out Black lesbian filmmaker. The film combines fiction and documentary forms to interrogate the fictional aspect of the non-fiction. Dunye's film is invested in showing the erased labor of Black lesbians in mainstream cultural production, but, unable to retrieve the history she was looking for, she invented an archive of Black queer Hollywood history through fabricated documentary material created by photographer Zoe Leonard. As Dunye's end credits assert, "Sometimes you have to create your own history." While such a model should not replace extrafilmic historical research in scholarly work, it serves as inspiration for generating new creative approaches to resolving archival lacunae.

## References

Bruno, Giuliana. *Streetwalking on a Ruined Map: Cultural Theory and the City Films of Elvira Notari*. Princeton UP, 1993.

Field, Allyson Nadia. *Uplift Cinema: The Emergence of African American Film and the Possibility of Black Modernity*. Duke UP, 2015.

Lewis, Jon and Eric Smoodin, eds. *Looking Past the Screen: Case Studies in American Film History and Method*. Duke UP, 2007.

Pierce, David. *The Survival of American Silent Feature Films: 1912–1929*. Washington, DC: Council on Library and Information Resources and the Library of Congress, September 2013.

# 11 Expressing race in Brazilian telenovelas

*Jasmine Mitchell*

> Brazilian telenovelas, serial melodramatic narratives, have functioned as a central foundation of Brazilian identity in both national and global imaginations. TV Globo, the leading Brazilian network and producer of telenovelas, captures audiences and reinforces racial myths. With millions of viewers across the globe, Brazilian telenovelas function to disseminate racial ideologies that privilege whiteness and negate racial inequalities. From industry structures to racial representations, this analysis covers some key components and questions to consider when writing about race in telenovelas based on my own experiences and subject position as a U.S. researcher of mixed black ancestry.

A 90-year-old woman knitting in her armchair in Copacabana. Wealthy 20-somethings lazing in gated luxury complexes in São Paulo. Grizzled cowboys swigging beers in a rural Mato Grosso bar. All are glued to the television as the 9pm telenovela (serial melodrama) appears on TV Globo, Brazil's dominant network. Every night, Brazil, across all regions, classes, races, and genders comes to a standstill. Newspaper kiosks tout magazines devoted to discussing the current hit series. These programs shape the national consciousness, launching everything from fashion trends to debates about race, class, sexuality, and gender. Entranced by the unanticipated plot twists, performances from renowned actors, quality writing, and high production values, I realized these were nothing like U.S. soap operas. Far more than any one medium in U.S. culture, they are critical cultural sites. In order to understand the significance of race in telenovelas, I negotiate my presence as a U.S. mixed black female researcher in Brazil and how I interpret multiple racial discourses.

Brazilians telenovelas are sprawling narratives that take on major social issues. Telenovelas have short, defined, intense runs; they typically air almost daily for nine straight months. Millions of viewers in Brazil watch the telenovelas on TV Globo, and 130 countries, including Portugal, Poland, Angola, Mexico, and Turkey, import them as well. The majority of scholarly work written in English on telenovelas analyzes the Mexican equivalent, which are less realistic in terms of settings, dialect, characters, and costumes than Brazilian telenovelas. In Brazil, writers script the episodes according to how audiences react to the storylines in near real time. Focus groups have always been a part of the production; and writers also respond to the popular press, activist organizations, the Brazilian government, and religious institutions (Hamburger 2005, Porto 2012). The high stakes of telenovela representation are integral to how Brazil imagines itself as predominantly white (Araújo 2000, Joyce 2012) and how the world imagines Brazil, particularly with regards to its national identity and racial dynamics. Brazil's reputation as a racially harmonious tropical paradise in which· racism does not exist contrasts with the dominance of white faces in media as well as vast racial inequalities in Brazilian society. Responding to both activist movements and government programs and policies aimed at redressing racial inequality, telenovelas oscillate between acknowledging and discounting Brazilian racism.

It took me some time to realize that television is the primary site of struggles over meanings of race, gender, and nation in Brazil. As part of my dissertation research, I originally thought I should look, as I might in the United States, at film. A Brazilian colleague suggested I examine telenovelas, and at a meeting with the director of Centro dos Estudos da Telenovela at the Universidade de São Paulo she arranged, I immediately saw that telenovelas strongly condition how Brazilians and transnational audiences read race and changed my focus.

While in Buenos Aires, I watched telenovela historical drama reruns of *Xica da Silva* (1996), about a formerly enslaved woman who became the richest woman in Brazil, and better understood how the telenovela elicited transnational responses valuing women of African descent as sexual objects for white pleasure. In Buenos Aires, I was often mistaken for Brazilian, and I experienced the impact of the hypersexualization of brown skinned female bodies in popular media. At the same time, Taís Araújo's performance as Xica was notable as it was the first starring role for a black woman on Brazilian television. While *Xica da Silva* aired on Rede Manchete, a network that would fold in 1999, the telenovela commanded a significant audience. Just a few years later, Araújo became the first black actress to star in a telenovela on TV Globo. She played "Preta" ("Black") in *Da Cor do Pecado (The Color of Sin,* 2004). Preta is a black woman who falls in love with a wealthy white man. The series addresses racism, but also revives colonial tropes by presenting a black woman as a sexual temptation. I was living in São Paulo during the series run, and I regularly debated racial issues and the newly implemented policies of affirmative action with Brazilian friends. *Da Cor do Pecado* and other telenovelas have acted as a lightning rod in struggles over Brazilian identity and the continuing salience of race.

Contending with the Globo media conglomerate is central to grasping telenovela content and production. TV Globo utilizes a vertical production model that facilitates its dominance in terms of audience reach, profits, and the acquisition of talent. TV Globo has produced the vast majority of telenovelas for half a century. Telenovelas and TV Globo are often interchangeable with each other. Globo situates itself as a co-creator in Brazilian identity and articulates its mission to inform, educate, entertain, and improve lives. It is one of the world's largest fictional television exporters, and its telenovelas are a vital site for producing understandings of Brazilian identity in both domestic and transnational imaginations. Although the majority of Brazilians are of African descent, telenovelas are predominantly white even when set in regions that are understood nationally and transnationally as a locus of Afro-Brazilian culture, such as in *Segundo Sol* (2018) which had an almost all white cast for its story set in Bahia. Yet, TV Globo's mission statement claims that reflecting Brazilian cultural diversity is a central facet of the network's identity (Rede Globo 2018). Understanding how a network positions itself across multiple platforms provides further evidence of telenovela conceptualization. It is imperative in analyzing telenovelas to be cognizant of who is invisible as well as the representational power of how nonwhite bodies appear onscreen. Telenovelas are ideological instruments that structure and code racial thought.

Telenovelas reveal the racial contradictions in the Brazilian social order. The disavowal of racism and romanticization of Brazil as a mixed country lie beside the whitening of the face of the nation and the marginalization of black people. Nor is this marginalization confined to actors; a lack of black writers, producers, and directors enables a vision of normalized whiteness. At the same time, there are cracks in this distorted mirror. As a black middle class has arisen as potential targeted consumers for Globo's advertisers, Globo has diversified by developing shows such as *Viver a Vida* (2009) in which Taís Araújo played the first black female protagonist on primetime TV Globo, and other novelas such as *Lado a Lado* (2012) depicting black abolitionist activism, and *Babilônia* (2015) with varied multidimensional ambitious black characters.

In my research on telenovelas, the translation of racial meaning for non-Brazilian audiences poses a challenge. As a researcher, I seek to emphasize the words, cultural meanings, images, and narratives that express race, gender, and sexuality in Brazil. But I am not a native Portuguese speaker. While I generate my own translations of racial meaning, I often talk about my translation in Portuguese with other Brazilian colleagues and friends as racial markers shift and are socially constructed. How do I explain distinct racial terminologies and racially coded slang? Identifying the visual and semantic meanings embedded in Brazilian cultural and social specificities creates numerous challenges of communication and translation.

Researchers who write on the exportation of telenovelas must also look beyond the telenovela as a media text and consider the ideological norms of the receiving culture. How do I as a translator, researcher, and writer convey and capture ideologies of race while transcoding signifiers and norms? For example, *morena* can mean anything from brunette to tan to a polite way to say black. To unpack the multiple ways telenovelas express race, I also take into account how racial terminologies are articulated in different audiences and contexts. White Brazilians have often accused me of projecting a U.S. overreliance on race as a critical focus when studying Brazilian television. Meanwhile, in nonwhite social spaces, I have engaged in colloquial discussions critiquing Brazilian televisual whiteness and the devaluation of blackness. I have had to frame my research questions in a way that does not seem to imply a racial critique when conducting archival research or site visits at TV Globo in order to maintain access to those resources. Awareness of my subject position in writing on telenovelas also allows insight into these strategic negotiations of addressing and denying racism. Due to the exclusion of nonwhite voices in academia and media production, writing on Brazilian telenovelas has forced me to redefine my ideas of who is an expert on media or race as well as to look for perspectives outside of traditional power structures. When writing about Brazilian telenovelas, I use the telenovela as a way to understand political, cultural, and social debates around race and national identity.

## References

Araújo, Joel Zito Almeida de. *A Negação do Brasil: O negro na telenovela brasileira.* Editora Senac, 2000.
Hamburger, Esther. *Brasil antenado: Sociedade da novela.* Zahar, 2005.
Joyce, Samantha Nogueira. *Brazilian Telenovelas and the Myth of Racial Democracy.* Lexington Books, 2012.
Porto, Mauro. *Media Power and Democratization in Brazil: TV Globo and the Dilemmas of Political Accountability.* Routledge, 2012.
Rede Globo. "Social Mission." *Globo Network* website, http://redeglobo.globo.com/Portal/institucional/foldereletronico/ingles/g_rs_missao_social.html2018

# 12 Writing about music video
## Tracing the ephemeral

*Carol Vernallis*

> Remarkably little has been written about the genre of music videos. The paucity of music video scholarship is due in part to the fact that the analyst must feel comfortable with addressing the music, the image (including the moving bodies, cinematography, and editing), the lyrics, and the relation among them. This chapter explains how writers can approach music videos, offering practical strategies for analyzing the formal and narrative elements of music videos and emphasizing the value of collaborative approaches to music video analysis.

I think almost anyone can write skillfully on music video. It just takes a bit of hubris and daring-do. And we might want to write on music video for several reasons. Sometimes music videos can feel like a key driver in our culture: many reach a kind of mathematical-sublime hit count. Luis Fonsi's "Despacito" ft. Daddy Yankee, for example, currently has 5.5 billion views. Music videos on YouTube are how young people most commonly consume popular music today (McIntyre). And the genre's aesthetics are shared with many other forms of moving media, including commercials, YouTube clips, trailers, political ads, and audiovisually intensified segments of post-classical cinema. Understanding music videos may tell us something about ourselves.

Yet remarkably little has been written about the genre. There are few close readings of music videos, or detailed analyses that describe how music, lyrics, and image are placed in relation, or interpretations that consider parameters of sound and image at work in music video's temporal flow. We can imagine why there's been such a paucity of music-video scholarship. It's not only due to, as film scholar Ann Kaplan has observed, the fact that music videos straddle a border between advertising and art, but that the analyst must also feel comfortable with addressing the music, the image (including the moving bodies, cinematography and editing), the lyrics, and the relation among them. (This might include, for example, looking at a dance gesture against a harmonic shift and an edit, and asking how these might relate to one another.) Encouragingly for authors, the field is wide open. Right now on the internet, music videos are most often described with gifs, and what's relayed to us is pretty much what we can see, literally. But music videos are not silent films; they have songs and soundtracks.

I've tried many approaches to writing about music video. Over the form's over 30-year history, I've continued to seek scholarship comparable to what other art forms like painting, poetry, popular music, and film possess. Lately I've been drawn to writing collectively with others (where seven or eight of us will take on different aspects of the clip – choreography, sound, production, thematic interests, and so on). I've come to feel that group writing, alongside friends and colleagues, is the best way to share something about a video and the genre with a larger community. Music videos are open forms, and as each analyst charts her or his path through the video, readers can get a sense of a personal perspective (and readers can then more carefully track their own trajectories as well). When writing a single-authored work, one can still draw on friends and associates to help provide a multiplicity of details and perspectives – for example, musicians, dancers, costume designers, and video makers. And one can also try to wing it and make a best guess, trying to describe phenomena to the best of one's ability. In a dance theory class that I recently took, the students and I aimed to describe dance gestures as neutrally as possible, and I felt we were very successful. A lot about a video and its song can be found through careful internet searching as well. Wikipedia's descriptions of songs can sometimes be quite good, and YouTube piano, guitar, and production tutorials can be helpful. Clips from dance studios that copy a video's choreography, and song covers can also be revealing.

Here's a brief description I wrote about Lady Gaga's "Bad Romance" video in my essay "Beyoncé's Opus; or, the Past and Future of Music Video:"

> Lady Gaga's "Bad Romance" (2009) is a music video in the classic mode. Like director Francis Lawrence's other clips, it does a lot to show off the song. The melody resides primarily in a mid- and low range, and its sonic material is heavily reverberant, and so we have a low-ceilinged space with a long sweep to the back. Historically the harpsichord has been associated with the affluent and cultivated, and there they are. The song's minor key has a flat sixth chord, along with an open fifth that sounds antique; perhaps this harmonic language sparked the idea of the Euro female slave-auction. Gaga's "ra-ras" and the snare-drum sound like chants for ominous swarms of trolls, and we have the crown-capped gremlins. The deedle-dweedle sound effect suggests hard surfaces, which connects with the room's paneling. The song undertakes a sinuous, careful build toward the chorus, so the searchlights take their time checking the space out, and performers emerge slowly from their caskets. The chorus is big, and that's when the phalanxes of dancers appear. The music video also achieves novel effects: while each chorus foregrounds the big communal hook "I want a bad romance," it also subtly pushes forward the narrative. In a later chorus, for example, Gaga will be slipped an elixir and wrapped in a burlap sheet. Puzzles and

conundrums – how much autonomy does Gaga possess? Should she have torched her buyer? – encourage repeat viewings.

I think the more an author has watched and wondered about music video, the stronger the writing will be. Over the years that I've written and taught about this subject, I've become increasingly convinced of music video's own generic modes and constraints. (While YouTube can be thought of as a whoopee cushion, and post-classical cinema as a form that puzzles and pummels the viewer, music video's specialty may lie in conveying a brief state of bliss.) Music video is dependent on ephemeralities of color, movement, and sound. (Aren't some of our most affectively-rich moments tied to music video? How to capture these?) Like popular music, music video possesses motifs, rhythms, grain, and fine details that carry weight.

Here's one quick way of thinking about music video: in the past, as now, music videos are most often short and have to accomplish many things: highlight the star, showcase performances, draw attention to the lyrics, and underscore the music. To teach listeners what's memorable about a song and thereby sell it, the image might emphasize the movement from verse to chorus, or highlight an unusual timbre, melodic contour, or striking rhythm. The visual track might point to one or two musical features at a time, like a tour guide. For while music envelops us, visual features more often momentarily focus our attention, especially if they're working in the service of the song. I've become more willing to believe that music can materially affect the image, and that there is what we might call an "audiovisual contract" among sound, image, and lyrics. Music videos as a form often have odd peculiar entailments: background figures, for example, partly because they are mute (lack lyrics) tend to adopt strange roles.

The best method I've found for writing on music video is the same I've used for other media – songs, films, or YouTube clips. I watch and/or listen to them *a lot*. (My process can involve hundreds of viewings – mercifully music videos are short.) I keep a piece of paper and pen on hand to take notes, and I continually pose questions to the clip – why does this moment move me? Why this color and not another? Why did the video end this way? What if the clip had a different arrangement? There'll be periods where no insights/noticings seem to emerge, and then suddenly many do. During part of the gathering of materials I aim to be systematic, watching just the image, or listening to one aspect of the soundtrack. I focus on how the sound and image seem to be placed in relation. I try to follow where my attention goes, and again, to account for what moves me. I might also try to recall the video as I fall asleep or I'm on a walk. What stays with me the most? After I've gathered a body of material and moved to the writing stage, I choose to emphasize features that I think are important and/or might have been missed by the viewer (and that the viewer might be charmed to discover). I often deploy a temporally-unfolding description as well as one based on parameters.

I think of my work as helping readers find a new path through a video, a way to dance along with it. I also want them to think about this music video's role as a conveyor of culture, of values and ideologies along lines such as ethnicity, race, class, gender, sexuality, and disability. I like to think of myself as someone who belongs within the artistic practice of making this video, and who is entering into the process at one of the last stages (that might have first begun with a songwriter and/or producer, a musician, and then a musician working with an industry head and director, and then a choreographer, costume designer, cinematographer, and editor, and so on). Wonderfully, after the color timer, I come in. Music video directors like to say that there is no one right setting for a song—there are many possibilities. I, and now hopefully you, can help the viewer discover one more way to experience a song and a music video.

## References

McIntyre, Hugh. "Report: YouTube Is The Most Popular Site For On-Demand Music Streaming," *Forbes*, September 27, 2017. www.forbes.com/sites/hughmcintyre/2017/09/27/the-numbers-prove-it-the-world-is-listening-to-the-music-it-loves-on-youtube/#75b20c871614

Vernallis, Carol. "Beyoncé's Opus; or, the Past and Future of Music Video." *Film Criticism*, vol. 41, no. 1, 2017. https://quod.lib.umich.edu/f/fc/13761232.0041.105/–beyonce-s-overwhelming-opus-or-the-past-and-future-of-music?rgn=main;view=fulltext

# 13 Writing across divides
## Locating power in K-pop music videos

S. Heijin Lee

> Using South Korean rapper PSY's 2012 viral hit, "Gangnam Style" as a case study, this chapter argues that an analysis of the uneven power dynamics and historical relationship between the US and South Korea and how these have shaped South Korea's music industry offers a rich methodology for thinking and writing about the transnational music videos K-pop produces. Devoid of an analysis that tracks the genealogies of power that shape cultural forms, analyses of music videos, and the stars that produce them, fall flat, often relying on stereotypes or generalized assumptions without centering the music itself and how imperial histories have produced hybridized global forms of music.

In the Fall of 2013, I attended the American Studies Association of Korea conference where multiple presentations responded to the singular query: Why "Gangnam Style?" Korean scholars of American studies were referring to the hit song that had just the year before set a world record for "Most Liked YouTube Video" with over 4 million "likes" and 1.5 billion views worldwide. They were perplexed, not that a Korean cultural product had crossed over so spectacularly, but that it was PSY – a comedic rapper seemingly antithetical to the sleek pop star aesthetic – who had achieved such global notoriety. One panelist even conjectured that Americans were drawn to PSY's horsey dance because it was reminiscent of the movements of the cowboys that symbolize the U.S.'s frontier past and thus, triggered subconscious associations with "the West" for American viewers. Americans, on the other hand, were equally as fascinated with PSY's success. One journalist, for example, explained it as such: "PSY is the 'Asian man who makes it' because he fits neatly into our pop cultural milieu wherein Asian men are either kung-fu fighters, Confucius-quoting clairvoyants, or the biggest geeks in high school" (Pan).

These attempts not only to situate but to explain the popularity of PSY's "Gangnam Style" point to the challenges of writing about transnational music videos. At the most basic level, how do we read a cultural product produced in a culturally foreign context? How do we understand its reception elsewhere? This chapter argues that we cannot answer either of these questions without an exploration of the historical relationship between the two, that is, between the context that produced the video and the country that receives it – in this case, South Korea and the U.S. Without understanding the power dynamics that shape this relationship and how that power pervades even the production and pleasure of music, analyses of transnational music videos and other forms of entertainment are reduced to stereotypes. Moreover, the instantaneousness of the digital platforms on which these forms travel, where a cultural product is just a post, share, or click away from being viral and global, requires that we pay ever more attention to the historical entanglements and power differentials that produce these cultural forms, the industries that generate them, and the cross-cultural collaborations upon which they are founded. In other words, our highly digitized and globalized worlds belie the historical processes that make these cultural products possible.

In both instances laid out above, the Korean scholar and the American journalist take for granted the inherent foreignness or otherness of PSY's music and music video in relation to American cultural products. Starting there, each seeks to find an explanatory framework through which an American consumer might possibly relate, one settling on frontier subtexts and the other on racist stereotypes. In both cases, however, the music is overlooked as that point of relation. I would like to suggest that writing creatively about transnational music videos requires us to undo this very assumption and to instead seek to understand how the music and the pleasure it induces are underwritten by imperial histories. Doing so helps to overcome the impulse to emphasize differences as in the two instances cited above.

These musical entanglements are perhaps best illuminated in PSY's performance with MC Hammer at the 2013 Billboard Music Awards, which was precisely orchestrated to underscore how the two artists inhabit the same genre. After rapping the initial two verses of the song, PSY pauses as the lights go down and says, "Stop, Hammer Time," MC Hammer's signature phrase. The lights come back up to reveal MC Hammer, and the two (along with an

*Figure 13.1* PSY's performance with MC Hammer at the 2013 Billboard Music Awards

army of background dancers) dance to a mash up of "Gangnam Style" and MC Hammer's 1990s hit, "2 Legit to Quit." Not only do the two songs mash together harmoniously but Hammer's 90s dance moves flow seamlessly into, out of, and then back through PSY's Korean horsey inspired choreography. As American studies scholar Crystal Anderson argues, this evidences how "Korean artists create authentic music in the tradition of black musical culture because they employ black musical aesthetics that reflect the same musical meanings as music produced by black artists" (294). American audiences as well as audiences worldwide have thus responded to Korean popular music like PSY's because "audiences recognize those aesthetics and meanings" (Anderson 294).

PSY characterized the pairing as both natural and nostalgic: "I practiced his moves 20 years ago so I've done that for 20 years" ("Psy, MC Hammer American Music Awards"). Here, PSY refers to the fact that he became familiar with American codes of rap and dance while studying in the US. From 1996–2000, PSY studied abroad for a secondary education, initially in business administration, at Boston University. As PSY tells the story, he tricked his parents and used his tuition to attend instead the Berklee School of Music ("[tvN]Paik Jiyeon's People Inside – Psy"). During this time living in Boston, PSY decided to become a rapper. While listening to rap on the radio he realized he could combine his comedic talents with his musical ones vis-à-vis the particularly American genre of music. Despite the fact that PSY made the specific decision to enter into the genre of comedy hip-hop, "commentators do not connect his viral hit 'Gangnam Style' to the comic hip-hop genre" (Anderson 297).

Indeed, when viewed through this lens, it becomes clear how, in the "Gangnam Style" video, PSY employs comedy to satirize South Korean materialism through a defiance of visual expectations. The first scene, for instance, features him lying out on a beach being fanned by a beautiful woman ("Psy – Gangnam Style"). When the camera pans out, however, the viewer realizes he is lying in the middle of an unglamorous children's park. In another scene, PSY appears to be dancing in a club and once again when

*Figure 13.2* PSY on a tour bus in the "Gangnam Style" music video

the camera pans out, the viewer realizes that he is dancing on a tour bus with middle-aged ladies rather than the beautiful young women epitomizing Gangnam's standards of beauty. By producing one comic reveal after another such as these, PSY subtly references the failures of "Gangnam style" as well as aspirations to achieve it, as attested to by the fact that the average South Korean carries credit card debt worth 155% of their household income (Yoo). PSY uses the music video genre to bring into sharp focus the ubiquitous desire of Koreans today to "keep up with the Joneses" or in this case, "the Kims." Thus, in keeping with hip-hop's roots, PSY's video provides entertainment and social commentary.

While PSY's personal journey studying in the US and then becoming a rapper might seem like a unique story, such transnationally informed artistic shapings are the consequences of US neocolonialism in South Korea. Studying abroad is simply the most contemporary way in which Koreans are exposed to American culture. Since the signing of the armistice, one can see the imprint of US military presence and political and social influence in Korea across a multiplicity of cultural forms. For example, watching the American television shows and films aired on The Armed Forces Korea Network (AFKN-TV) shaped the cinematic thinking of contemporary Korean film directors like Bong Joon-ho (Klein 22). Similarly, US military presence in South Korea brought with it American pop music through U.S. Armed Forces Radio including rock and black musical traditions such as rhythm and blues. Often US military bases were the only places where Korean artists could go to make a living playing music; and, since they were playing for US military soldiers, they played American songs and styles (Shin and Kim). Korean affinity for black music intensified in the late 1980s and early 1990s with the political shifts represented by the change from the Park Chung Hee regime to the more tolerant Kim Young Sam administration. Furthermore, Koreans began to travel to the US bringing back with them Americanized musical sensibilities. It is in this context that we see the birth of Korean hip-hop with the advent of Seo Taiji and Boys in 1992 (Maliangkay). These entangled histories of power and music have shaped the Korean music industry. When we track this imperial history as part of our analyses of transnational cultural forms, we are better able to recognize K-pop's hybrid formation and the genealogy that created it rather than characterizing it as merely a copy, a stereotype, or an inauthentic rendition.

Music is a nexus for empire building and soft power. While this chapter has shown how US imperial legacies are reflected in the formation of Korean pop music as well as in the personal histories of artists like PSY, such an analysis of power is critical precisely because today, South Korea popular music boasts over 35.5 million fans in 86 countries as a result of a decidedly pointed campaign to increase its soft power and international profile (Kim). As such, whether the receiving country of South Korea's hits is the US or elsewhere, a just analysis of transnational music videos must place Korean popular music within a larger constellation of power. In doing so, we might paint a bigger picture in which Korean artists can be much more than "kung-fu fighters, Confucius-quoting clairvoyants, or the biggest geeks in high school" (Pan).

## References

Anderson, Crystal. "Hybrid Hallyu: The African American Music Tradition in K-Pop," *Global Asian American Popular Cultures*, edited by Shilpa Dave, Leilani Nishime, and Tasha Oren, New York University Press, 2016, pp. 290–303.

Klein, Christina. "The AFKN nexus: US military broadcasting and New Korean Cinema," *Transnational Cinemas*, vol. 3, no. 1, 2012, pp. 19–39.

Kim, Steven. "Korea's Cultural Juggernaut is a Cultural Strategy Worth Copying," *The National Interest*, August 4, 2016, https://nationalinterest.org/feature/koreas-cultural-juggernaut-soft-power-strategy-worth-copying-17246 Accessed January 7, 2019.

Maliangkay, Roald, *The Popularity of Individualism: The Seo Taiji Phenomenon in the 1990s*, edited by Kyung Hyun Kim, Duke UP, 2014, pp. 296–313.

Pan, Deanna. "Is 'Gangnam Style' a Hit because of our Asian Stereotypes?" *Mother Jones*, September 24, 2012, www.motherjones.com/mixed-media/2012/09/gangnam-style-asian-masculinity%20 Accessed September 25, 2012.

"Psy – Gangnam Style (강남스타일) M/V," *YouTube*, 2012, www.youtube.com/watch?v=9bZkp7q19f0

"Psy, MC Hammer American Music Awards Moment Courtesy of Bieber Braun," *YouTube*, 2012, www.youtube.com/watch?v=kMo44FNpSPM

Shin, Hyunjoon and Kim, Pil Ho. "Birth, Death, and Resurrection of Group Sound Rock," *The Korean Pop Culture Reader*, edited by Kyung Hyun Kim and Youngmin Choe, Duke UP, pp. 275–296.

"[tvN]Paik Jiyeon's People Inside – Psy (ENG SUB)," YouTube, 2012, www.youtube.com/watch?v=5KmG8Gnzbxc

Yoo, Choonsik. "Analysis: South Korea's reckless consumers edge towards debt," 2011, www.reuters.com/article/2011/08/25/us-korea-economy-debt-idUSTRE77O4JU20110825 Accessed January 30, 2016.

# 14 Playing to write
## Analyzing video games

*TreaAndrea M. Russworm and Jennifer Malkowski*

> This chapter prompts readers to consider the unique opportunities and challenges of writing about video games, from the conceptual recognition of medium specificity and how analyzing video games is different from, say, analyzing films or novels to logistical challenges like accessing playable versions of the games one is writing about. The authors also reflect on the importance of situating oneself as a writer in relation to the game (integrating the human with the computational) and on how one's personal relationship with the medium changes when it becomes a topic of scholarly examination. The chapter also points readers to additional resources for learning game studies terminology and for accessing older video games.

Although there are many ways to approach the task of writing about video games, we both begin with a seemingly basic directive: the goal of "playing to write." That is, just as you would presumably read a novel or watch a film before commencing to write about it, so too do we value gaining first-hand knowledge of game worlds, mechanics, avatars, and stories by actually playing the games before we write about them. It is our strong preference to play the games we write about in their entirety (and more than once for shorter games). Playing a game gives us the chance to: experience the game and its attempts at creating immersive play on its own terms; grapple with all of the overt features of video games, such as interfaces and character representations; and experience some of a game's unanticipated moments and realities, like glitches and instances of player agency.

Perhaps it seems a strange and obvious starting point to advise playing the game one is writing about, but there are unique challenges to doing so in video game studies. Our own skill levels come into play when we are writing about games that are notoriously difficult to complete, such as *Dark Souls* (2011, FromSoftware) or *The Binding of Isaac* (2011, Edmund McMillen). There are also other factors that may prohibit us from playing a game to completion or even playing a game at all. These include: time investment (as in the hundreds of hours it might take to complete or replay a difficult or long game); player expertise, physical comfort, and visceral predispositions (can you write about a virtual reality game if the camera perspective makes you nauseous?); and access to the appropriate hardware or software (imagine you are interested in a game that can no longer be played, or that requires prohibitively expensive hardware or software). Regrettably, there are occasions where the only way a writer can experience a game at all is by drawing on indirect methods: second-hand accounts like written blogs and video walkthroughs of other players completing the game posted to sites like YouTube. The potentially prohibitive factor of access to the games is sometimes more difficult to solve, however. For example, due to the ephemeral nature of technology, some games that were once readily playable can no longer be found in their original or even *any* form, thus further troubling the goal of playing to write. This means that while you might have great difficulty in tracking down an original version of a classic game like *Pong* (1972, Atari) to play, even more recent games like *Afro Samurai 2* (2015, Redacted Studios) or *The Walking Dead: Season 4* (2018, Telltale Games) may suddenly disappear from retail markets in ways that render the original games either unplayable or incomplete.[1]

If it can be tricky for writers to access the hardware and software needed to research a video game, similar challenges carry over to readers, too. When we write about a commercial film or television show, we often do so with the knowledge that many readers will be familiar with our case studies already or will be able to stream them easily online if our writing inspires them to do so. But in our writing on video games, we are less likely to find an audience who has pre-existing experience with our game case studies or easy access to them (except, perhaps, in the case of mobile phone games). In fact, when we write for a broad public or for colleagues and students outside the small field of video game studies, we understand that some of our readers may not only be unfamiliar with the specific game we're discussing – they may have little to no experience with gaming as a whole.

For these reasons, writers need to be more generous in explaining the basics about their texts when writing about video games. An essay on *World of Warcraft* (2004–present, Blizzard Entertainment), for example, can't launch right into analysis of phasing's narrative integration in the *Cataclysm* (2010) installment. It needs first to devote significant word count to explaining how a MMORPG (massively multiplayer online role-playing game) like *WoW* works at the most basic level and what the texture of this specific MMORPG feels like. How do players access the game? What relationship do they have to on-screen characters in the game? What actions can they take while playing and what goals do they pursue? How do they interact with other players and what is the dominant culture of interaction among players of this game? How long is the game and how does it end (or, why can we not apply the concepts of a set duration or ending to this game)? And what the heck is "phasing," for that matter?

A good way to approach this task is to step back and consider the broader *medium specificity* of video games. On a fundamental level, what makes a video game different from another kind of text one might write about? We explain this to students by having them think back to their high school literature classes where they analyzed novels and wrote about plots, characters, themes, dialogue, and so on. To evolve from writing about a novel to writing about a film, they would need to attend to an additional audiovisual layer, adding elements like cinematography, sound, or editing to their previous analytical concerns. To progress into video game analysis, they would need to further consider the computational nature of video games, which usually have all of the familiar elements – plots, characters, themes, dialogue, cinematography, sound, editing – and also player actions, machine actions, game mechanics, controller configurations, informational interfaces, code, and so on.[2] This awareness of medium specificity can then contribute to argument-based writing that pays attention to form and also indicates the writer's positionally. By writing about games in this way we also try to keep the both the computational form and our experiences as people who engage these works always in view.[3]

Video games today are a major site of commerce, ideology, culture, education, and art, and the world needs many more sharp thinkers writing analytically about the medium. But video games also remain a site of pure fun. That is, perhaps, until you start writing about them. Both of us have seen our relationship to the medium drastically change as we moved into video game studies. Since writing about a game often involves a good deal of time and focus, there are times when the motivation to play games that we are not writing about is low. If one of us is writing about *Grand Theft Auto V* (2013, Rockstar North) and player agency, for instance, that person may resist the impulse to play other games purely for fun out of fear that playing the other games will siphon precious research time from the game being written about. We also have to fight against our own styles of gameplay and genre preferences in order to position ourselves best to encounter new objects for research. Where one of us might prefer to bask in obsessively completing 100+ hour open world games, that person might now engage but not finish those games so as to make room in the finite amount of available gaming time to sample other games that might spark research ideas.

Such feelings of loss will be familiar to many scholars of literature, art, and theater who have also turned leisure pursuits into work pursuits. But what makes the feeling more acute, perhaps, in game studies is that video games function more purely as play in most people's lives – as the kind of fun that can still be joyful, exuberant, and yes even "mindless," at times. Since we both entered game studies as scholars who were first fans of the medium, we have also both had to grapple with the consequences of turning our hobbies and leisure space into work and productivity that can be measured and accounted for. Although overall the pleasure we gain from writing about video games typically outweighs the sense of loss as play metastasizes into work, we end here with a note of caution about "playing to write," as those newly working on video game studies may also feel like they're writing away their play.

## Notes

1 *The Walking Dead: Season 4* was canceled, disappeared from retailers, and then was eventually completed by another studio in 2019. There are a few resources that may be useful in locating difficult to find games. For researching arcade-era and early home console games, The Internet Archive hosts an invaluable collection of emulated versions of those games now playable on internet browsers (arcade: https://archive.org/details/internetarcade, console: https://archive.org/details/consolelivingroom). While an emulated experience is not a perfect substitute for playing the original (think, for example, about how using a mouse vs. a joystick would change the feel of a game), it is sometimes the only practical approach to playing games from this era. Visiting retro barcades – for those who live near one – can be another (more fun) strategy! For those able to fund research travel, collections like those at the Strong Museum of Play in Rochester, NY are also excellent resources.
2 There are many great resources for learning the basic terminology and concepts of video game studies. A few that we recommend are listed in our works cited section (Wolf and Perron; Payne and Huntemann; Galloway).
3 For examples of this approach from us and a number of other contributors, see the works cited entry for Malkowski and Russworm.

## References

Galloway, Alexander. "Gamic Action. Four Moments." *Gaming: Essays on Algorithmic Culture*. U of Minnesota Press, 2006, pp. 1–38.

Malkowski, Jennifer and TreaAndrea M. Russworm, editors. *Gaming Representation: Race, Gender, and Sexuality in Video Games*. Indiana UP, 2017.

Payne, Matthew and Nina Huntemann, editors. *How to Play Video Games*. New York University Press, 2019.

Wolf, Mark J.P. and Bernard Perron, editors. *The Routledge Companion to Video Game Studies*. Routledge, 2014.

# 15 When it all clicks
## Writing about participatory media

*Lauren S. Berliner*

> This chapter shares critical insights gleaned from researching and writing about queer youth media producers and the media they've created. The chapter provides advice for pre-writing considerations, such as ethical frameworks and project scope, as well as suggestions for creating clear and convincing analysis.

Some people will tell you that writing about participatory media is just like writing about any other kind of media, but trust me, it isn't. Sure, there is form and content to consider, a specific medium and a context; but there are also crucial differences that must be addressed in any good analysis.

My work with digital media content creators has taught me that the production and distribution contexts are integral to understanding the meaning being produced through the content of the artifact itself. "Participatory media" by definition suggests that multiple parties outside the scope of traditional media industries have been involved in the production and circulation of the object (Jenkins 2009). It is therefore incumbent on the researcher to take stock of those processes while also attending to the semiotics at play in an ethical and precise way. *How* to take stock will look different for each person, depending on the themes and context in question. In this chapter, I will share a few of my experiences with different participatory media research projects, highlighting some of the specific challenges I encountered as a researcher and writer and the lessons I learned.

My first foray into academic research on participatory media began with my involvement in a digital audiovisual media production program I created and facilitated with queer teens in San Diego. The experience of working with this group using participatory action research methods (Mills 2010) became the foundation for my book, *Producing Queer Youth: The Paradox of Digital Media Empowerment* (2018). The book presents one discrete case, in which the group was tasked by our parent organization to create an anti-bullying public service announcement for wider circulation. Homing in on one particularly vexed moment enabled me to consider the concentric circles of assumptions and expectations surrounding youth digital media production so that I could attend to the nuances of the group's choices and experiences with more granularity. Deciding on one slice of time to write about was not an easy task. I had worked with the youth for three years and had developed meaningful relationships with several of them. We had made many kinds of media together, and there were several shifting logistical details that were difficult to address. I therefore had to figure out what my key research questions were and how my experiences would help me to provide context and depth for readers who were unfamiliar with the project. I had to think carefully about which moments of our work together could best exemplify the types of experiences I wished to highlight, as well as what other online media I would examine. Ultimately, I spent an entire chapter discussing what had been just a few days among several years of collaboration.

## Narrowing the focus

I wish I could say that the process of narrowing the focus happened quickly. It didn't. I wrote a lot that I later discarded. What helped was paying attention to connections between what exactly the youth in the workshop were producing, and what they were doing and saying while they were making it. What felt like coincidences at the time – such as the suicide of 15-year-old Jamey Rodemeyer after making an uplifting personal video for the *It Gets Better Project* online video campaign (2011) – turned out to be clues leading me back to my observations in the workshop. I now understand how important it was for me to pay close attention to the context around the workshop in order to locate the ways the media we produced were already situated within and responding to existing discourses and practices. The more I sensed trends and patterns, the more it became clear that I needed to focus specifically, and primarily, on the production of the PSA video that the group made and let my claims emerge from there. Midway through writing, I knew I needed to focus in on the ways that discourses of participatory media as inherently empowering risk masking the support needs of queer youth.

## Ethical considerations

If you are doing any kind of research with participatory media, you will likely first be required to complete an application to the Human Subjects Review board at your institution, which will require you to consider and adhere to an ethical framework of how you will record and represent your work with the subjects included in your study. But, as you will quickly learn when filling out the paperwork, the IRB was not designed for media research. Its strength is protecting vulnerable subjects of medical studies. The kinds of requirements you will need to meet in order to have your IRB approved are not necessarily representative of the full range of ethical considerations you will want to pursue. It will be useful to draw upon any knowledge you have of visual culture and documentary theory when creating your own rubrics for what details and forms of representation are appropriate to include in your writing. In other words, what values will guide what you write about and how you write it? Ask yourself questions such as, what matters most to the people I am writing about? How might they be impacted by my writing about them? Where and how will they have input into the writing? What are the opportunities for exchange to take place? And finally, and most importantly, how am I situated in this work, and where and how does my identity factor into the analysis?

For me this meant engaging in ongoing conversations with the youth I was working with to learn more about their needs and desires. It meant being transparent with them about what I planned to write about and sharing thoughts and ideas with them. It meant participating in forms of reciprocity, such as helping them with college applications and job recommendations. In other words, despite the fact that I myself identify as queer, it was imperative that in my writing I was clear about the ways that differences were also in play. Reflexivity is key to any ethical research engagement (and arguably, *any* kind of interaction). Where are *you* situated in your research? As anthropologist Sarah Pink (2001) argues, you are never outside of your own perspective, so it is critical to account for it.

## Getting down to writing

I have found these questions to be even more challenging when conducting textual analysis of YouTube videos (as opposed to analysis of the media production process). When fair use laws and IRB guidelines have not (yet) been designed to protect those who have posted self-produced media, and you don't know the makers or subjects personally, you may feel like there is little holding you to the same methodological standards as ethnographic or participatory action research. But how you handle this ethical gray area is a test of your methodological strengths. Just because you *can* write about a video, doesn't mean you should. How vulnerable are your subjects? And in what ways? If you do choose to write about it, make sure to do so as if the person who made the media at hand will one day read what you wrote. Here I am not suggesting that you necessarily soften your argument or adjust your claims; rather, I am advocating for empathy to guide your choices, and a kind of writerly precision that will buttress your argument with evidence from (and indexed by) the text.

When performing textual analysis on an artifact of participatory media, first begin by providing *context*. Where and how did you encounter the media? Who made it? When? Where? How? What do you know about how and with whom it has circulated? Next, clearly detail what you see/hear/experience as objectively as possible. In other words, *describe* rather than analyze at this point. This important first step in any visual/audio analysis will help ground your reader in seeing and hearing through your eyes, as well as provide crucial descriptive information that they will need should they not have access to the full media that you are analyzing. Finally, you can start to *synthesize* what you know about the context with what you've observed about the text to begin to make claims. As you note the maker's production choices, be sure to always tie back to the context of production and circulation. When possible, *continue to track* the life of the media you are analyzing for as long as you can, noting changes in viewership, comments, perceptions, and re-circulation through other media platforms.

Writing about participatory media can at times feel like a daunting task. You have to analyze: the text itself; the text's social, economic, infrastructural, technical, and political contexts; and the interpersonal conditions that shape your understanding of any participatory action research you may conduct. But the same characteristics that make this media mode challenging are the ones that make it a rich and fascinating field of research. There are so many pieces to fit together, but at some point, I promise, it all clicks.

## References

Berliner, Lauren. *Producing Queer Youth: The Paradox of Digital Media Empowerment*. Routledge, 2018.
Jenkins, Henry, Ravi Purushomota, Margaret Weigel, Katie Clinton, and Alice J. Robinson. *Confronting the Challenges of Participatory Culture: Media Education in the 21st Century*. MIT Press, 2009.
Mills, Geoffrey E., ed. *Action Research: A Guide for the Teacher Researcher*. Pearson Publishing, 2010.
Pink, Sarah. "Interdisciplinary agendas in visual research: re-situating visual anthropology." *Visual Studies*, vol. 18, no. 2, 2010, pp. 179–192.
Rodemeyer, Jamey. "It Gets Better, I Promise!" *YouTube*, 2:04. Posted as xgothemo99xx, May 4, 2011, www.youtube.com/watch?v=-Pb1CaGMdWk

# 16 Feeling out social media

*Julie Wilson and Emily Chivers Yochim*

---

> This chapter suggests that exploring and understanding the powers of social media and digital culture more broadly require "feeling out" what's actually happening in everyday lives. It argues that digital media are largely affective phenomena and offers an approach for studying them as such. More specifically, drawing heavily on their own research and writing about mothers' everyday lives with digital media, the authors reflect on how traditional ethnographic methods, including long interviews and participant observation, coupled with engagement with emerging theories of affect, can help media scholars and makers better understand the complex and often highly mundane ways that digital media are shaping everyday experiences and sensibilities and thus our broader social worlds.

---

We spent much of 2012 in long, hard conversations with twenty-nine moms, all of whom had children ten years and younger, and most of whom were in heterosexual partnerships. We talked, sometimes for hours, about the slogging days of motherhood, its endless and multiplying labors, and the heavy, heart-stopping experience of loving children in precarious times. We were stunned by the women's candor. In our offices, their homes, coffee shops, and bars, we invited them to "tell us about you, your kids, and your everyday life," and their stories poured out. The women talked animatedly about managing schedules and sometimes quivered with anger about husbands' frank disregard for their needs. They cried a lot. They shared feelings of invisibility, deep and abiding fears, a strong desire for more control over their lives amidst job losses and potential health threats, and a staggering need to protect. They loved their kids, but motherhood? It felt impossible, brutal.

As media scholars, we embarked on these interviews in an attempt to work out how women in our rural Rust Belt towns were encountering mothering media. We knew that media were swirling with contradictory and weighty messages. The "Mommy Wars" were on, and they weren't only pitting working moms against stay-at-home moms. Women were also being inundated with debates: breast vs. bottle, attachment parenting, tiger moms, helicopter parents, cry-it-out vs. co-sleeping. Celebrity moms were everywhere. Photos of happy families were flooding Facebook and Pinterest. How were moms navigating these competing and relentless messages, we wondered? What kind of meaning were they making in this contradictory and exhausting atmosphere?

But when we turned toward media in our interviews, our conversations with mothers lost their charge. They told us about logging onto Facebook to feel connected to far-away friends, checking recipe blogs for dinner ideas, Googling questions about kids' development, and using apps to manage family chores. Managing screen time felt stressful, sometimes, but it also gave busy moms moments of respite. Some of them talked about crowdsourcing advice about mothering, and most all of them shared photos of their kids on social media. Media suffused their lives, but we weren't sure what we were learning from these stories. A laundry-list of media uses, yes, but what meaning were the women making?

What we didn't quite have our heads around at the time of our interviews was what we ended up calling the *digital mundane* in our book, *Mothering through Precarity: Women's Work and Digital Media*. The digital mundane refers to the banal yet intense ways digital media are threaded through everyday lives. As we found in our study of mothers, the digital mundane cannot be reduced to particular texts (for example, individual posts), platforms (for example, Pinterest), and/or practices (for example, sharing family photos). It is at once all of these and none of these, as it is constantly taking shape in ongoing interplays of digital media and everyday lives. Indeed, as mothers moved through the hard and heavy work of holding things together for their families, the digital mundane provided a crucial though taken-for-granted foundation for getting by. Ever-present possibilities of dipping into social media for a quick dose of adult interaction, scrolling through Pinterest feeds for party ideas, or Googling health conditions undergirded most of their so-called "women's work" (Wilson and Yochim 2017 15–16).

While many media scholars and critics suggest that our interactive, always-on, networked culture is collapsing boundaries between media and lived experience, digital anthropologist Tom Boellstorff argues that there remains a socially constitutive gap between the two (41). Just because digital media underpin and enable everyday lives does not mean simply that all of life is now inseparable from digital media. Rather, the gap is a space of situated and contingent encounters between flows of media communication (for example, streams of party ideas or health advice) and movements of everyday lives (for example, a child's upcoming birthday or a concerning behavior noted by a teacher). If we want to understand the impacts and implications of social media, we have to understand what's happening in this gap.

Ethnographic methods provide invaluable and necessary tools for *accessing* the digital mundane and the encounters between media and everyday life that happen there. Long interviews like those we conducted teach us about how particular everyday lives are mediated and help us to understand how different groups make sense of their experiences. Still, it's tough to appreciate the gap –

and in particular the hard-to-articulate feelings that linger in that gap – in interviews alone. As Boellstorff reminds us, interviews relay the meaning that's been made, but they're less able to reveal the mundane movements that happen in the gap. Participant observation is necessary for producing rich and responsible ethnographic accounts of social media and digital culture (53). For example, in our own research, we could hear in the women's words the intensity of their feelings about mothering, and their accounts of mundane engagements with digital culture revealed the sheer everydayness of their media lives. We immersed ourselves in these engagements, following mothering blogs and social media accounts. While we did conduct observations in a local mothering group, in hindsight, we wonder what we might have seen and what other stories we might have been able to tell had we undertaken more committed participant observation in women's homes, spending time with mothers as they moved through their everyday lives.

While ethnographic methods can immerse us in the digital mundane, we have found theories of affect incredibly generative when it comes to *interpreting* what's happening there. Affect is most often defined as "a body's *capacity* to affect and be affected" (Gregg and Seigworth 2). It names baseline orientations to and capacities for life that, for example, enable one to get out-of-bed in the morning (or not), or to engage in a relationship (or not). As a theoretical lens, affect helps us to see and consider feelings, emotions, and senses of possibility, as well as how these are structured and shaped by broader forces.

Affect theory enabled us to shift our attention away from ideological analysis of mothering media – for digital feeds ceaselessly deliver profoundly contradictory messages to moms – and instead tune into the realm of what anthropologist Kathleen Stewart calls *ordinary affects*. According to Stewart, ordinary affects are those "varied, surging capacities to affect and be affected" that give everyday life its tenor and texture, and "catch people up in something that feels like *something*" (2–3). Ordinary affects happen in the mundane flows of living; they are what, where, and how things come to matter as they do. They animate how folks experience, move through, and inhabit their daily routines. During our research and writing, we found that mothers' engagements with and experiences of social media were deeply entangled with ordinary affects. The constant churn of mothering communication and information was shaping their affects in profound ways: producing fears and desires; shutting down and opening up horizons and possibilities; moving them to frustration, inadequacy, competition, joy, connection, mental breakdown; making life feel variously do-able and impossible. Within media and cultural studies, there is a growing body of literature on affect and social media. For scholars interested in exploring this exciting new research, we recommend the books *Affect and Social Media: Emotion, Mediation, Anxiety, and Contagion* and *Networked Affect*, both edited collections that present a wide range of case studies and approaches.

Early on in our work together, we developed our own shorthand for thinking about these interactions of digital media and ordinary affects: packets and pockets. In our essay, "Pinning Happiness: Affect, Social Media, and the Work of Mothering," we argued that digital culture could be understood as a "pulsating sea of packets" (Wilson and Yochim 2015 237). A packet is a bit of digital communication: for example, an online coupon or a comment on a Facebook post, or a birthday party idea pinned to Pinterest. Digital culture is energized and continuously shaped by flows and movements of packets. Likewise, everyday life can be understood in terms of pockets. A pocket, Stewart argues, is a moment in the course of life where "a space opens up" – a "pocket" – where it feels like something is going to happen, come to matter. As we put it, "Digital packets come into contact with and work to develop pockets, opening up space where one feels like something significant is happening. Packets may offer information about that thing; provide images of that thing happening; suggest what to do to avoid that thing or how to manage that thing; and so on" (Wilson and Yochim 2015 237–238). In digital culture, packets are constantly circulating, and, occasionally, they enter into and open up pockets in everyday life. In this way, the cultural power of social media is often experienced as an affective punch or charge in the course of daily living (Wilson and Yochim 2017 107–115).

How should researchers enter into this churning affective world? While audience studies, that rich body of ethnographic and interview-based work in media studies, most frequently begins with questions about either a particular audience or a particular media text, we propose that researchers orient their questions toward the mundane contours of daily life. Rather than thinking of research subjects as audiences, which presumes a common media experience, we might start with a community, seeking folks who are connected through a place or a practice, and ask about what it feels like to be them. What are their typical days like? For what and whom are they responsible? When do they feel appreciated, or not? What do they worry about? When do they use technology in their lives, and what do they think about that? Questions like these, paired with participant observation, can help researchers to discern how social media are folded into the work of everyday life.

To really see the intersections and interactions of digital packets and daily pockets, researchers must decenter media content in their questions and analysis. That pulsating sea of packets in social media – and online more generally – is profoundly contradictory, always moving, and unpredictable, and lives become entangled with digital media in ways that variously mobilize and short-circuit everyday encounters. Our questions and observations, consequently, should zero in on what scholar Jasbir Puar calls "affective intensification" of digital junctures (61). In other words, rather than focusing solely on media's ideological impact, this work should ask, how do digital packets underpin ordinary affects? How do they orient folks' daily lives? When do they beckon, and when do they repulse? How are they charging up life with expectations, fears, and desires? When do they weigh down, and when do they lighten the load?

Discerning and making sense of these digital junctures – these moments of opening up or shutting down, charging or short-circuiting – can be a messy and complicated practice that yields few clear answers. It's critical that researchers stay open to letting the ethnographic process work, so that the story can emerge from interviews and observations. We have found the book *Writing Ethnographic Fieldnotes* to be an invaluable text for learning how to analyze ethnographic data, for it describes an iterative process of research and analysis that is both theoretically rich and grounded in daily life. As scholars move through this process, feeling out social media and attuning to ordinary affects and everyday media life, a fully cohesive story might not emerge. Instead, though, we might begin to see patterns of encounters, moments of commonality in a profoundly fractured media world.

In sum, social media, and digital culture more broadly, are phenomena that, to be understood, must be felt out. For they are profoundly affective media. They work on our individual and shared senses of possibility, shaping in fundamental ways the environments and atmospheres in which we live. Feeling out social media is thus vital cultural work that can help us to tell compelling and new stories about the powers of digital culture – stories that complicate and deepen more prominent accounts of fake news, rampant consumerism, and mass surveillance. Rooting ourselves in everyday media lives via ethnographic methods and attuning to the ordinary affects that swirl and swell promise to help us better understand how people live with social media and, crucially, how they might live, and desire to live, otherwise.

## References

Boellstorff, Tom. "Rethinking Digital Anthropology," *Digital Anthropology*, edited by Heather A. Horst and Daniel Miller, Bloomsbury, 2012, pp. 39–60.

Emerson, Robert M., Rachel I. Fretz, and Linda L. Shaw. *Writing Ethnographic Fieldnotes*, 2$^{nd}$ ed. U of Chicago Press, 2011.

Gregg, Melissa and Gregory Seigworth. *The Affect Theory Reader*. Duke UP, 2010.

Hills, Ken, Susanna Paasonen and Michael Pettit, editors. *Networked Affect*, MIT Press, 2015.

Puar, Jasbir. "'I Would Rather Be a Cyborg Than a Goddess': Becoming Intersectional in Assemblage Theory," *philoSOPHIA*, vol. 2, no. 1, 2012, pp. 49–66.

Sampson, Tony, Stephen Maddison, and Darren Ellis, editors. *Affect and Social Media: Emotion, Mediation, Anxiety, and Contagion*, Rowman and Littlefield International, 2018.

Stewart, Kathleen. *Ordinary Affects*, Duke UP, 2007.

Wilson, Julie and Emily Chivers Yochim. *Mothering through Precarity: Women's Work and Digital Media*, Duke UP, 2017.

Wilson, Julie and Emily Chivers Yochim. "Pinning Happiness: Affect, Social Media, and the Work of Mothers," *Cupcakes, Pinterest, and Ladyporn: Feminized Popular Culture in the Early Twenty-First Century*, edited by Elana Levine, U of Illinois Press, 2015, pp. 223–248.

# 17 "A Very Black Project"
## A method for digital visual culture

*Lauren McLeod Cramer*

> Regular social media users are familiar with the ways image and video sharing platforms like Instagram allow users to curate dynamic online identities and how social media has dramatically changed the culture of commerce and information sharing. Our familiarity with these digital spaces can make it difficult to identify knowledge gaps and articulate new research questions that enrich our understanding of the images we make, view, and share daily. Through an analysis of the Instagram account "The Very Black Project," (@theveryblackproject), this chapter offers strategies for writing about online image repositories like Instagram and focuses specifically on the work of developing research questions and methods that not only reveal new information about contemporary screen media, but also reflect our ethical and ideological investments as writers.

The one billion people who use Instagram, the video and image sharing platform that was launched in 2010 and purchased by Facebook two years later, are well versed in the cultural significance and stylistic tendencies of the app and its users; that familiarity, paradoxically, poses a major challenge for writing on contemporary digital images. We already know that the application allows users to curate online identities and represents dramatic changes in the culture of commerce and information sharing. Moreover, unlike other objects discussed in this volume that are difficult to access, like found footage films, digital image cultures are distinguished by their readiness and availability. So, what is left to ask about the images we make, view, and share daily? Questioning Instagram in spite of its apparent obviousness articulates a fundamental thesis of visual culture studies. As theorist W.J.T. Mitchell explains, "visual culture is not limited to the study of images or media, but extends to everyday practices of seeing and showing, especially those that we take to be immediate or unmediated. It is less concerned with the meaning of images than with their lives and loves" (Mitchell 2002 91). Visual culture scholars look inside and outside the frame to understand an image's desires and relationships. For example, Instagram is a highly-referential visual economy that wants to consume our time and attention. Thus, this *social* media also visualizes images with a *social* life. When Mitchell famously asked, "what do pictures really want?" he encouraged us to begin the writing process by identifying an image's demands of us, instead of demanding to know how an image represents us (Mitchell 1996 71).

The Very Black Project (@theveryblackproject) is an Instagram account that was created by two artists, Justin Fulton and André D. Singleton, who wanted to use social media to promote celebratory messages about black life and art. Despite the unambiguous title, the account includes a wide variety of images that appear only tangentially related to the artists' stated intention. For instance, the account placed a short time-lapse video of a caterpillar entering the pupal stage directly between a screenshot of the dictionary entry for the word "affable" and archival footage of a performance by gospel singer Carrie Robinson. It makes sense to ask, "what is *very black* about this collection of images?" We could search for posts with specific racial meaning or connect reoccurring themes to grand narratives about race, but what happens when ten new images are posted the next day? These approaches leave us with an unsustainable number of images to interpret and, more importantly, a set of explanations that only reveal our prior assumptions about blackness. Writing about screen media requires we make these objects, even something as explicit as a very black project, strange. This chapter offers strategies for writing about online image repositories like Instagram and focuses specifically on the work of turning the social life of images, their *lives* and *loves*, into research questions and methods for developing new conclusions about our visual culture.

A research question is the beginning of an evolving exchange between question, methodology, and discipline (Clement). Together, Visual Culture Studies and Black Studies address The Very Black Project's use of everyday image technologies to construct blackness in digital space. The former encourages us to identify the connections between a social media account and the other images we encounter every day, including famed works of art and the most mundane and utilitarian design objects. Visual Culture Studies scholars ask what the relationships between images make visible. For example, what can be seen in the graphic and rhythmic resemblance between the stuttering movement of a chrysalis rapidly transforming and a gospel singer's dancing? What is the significance of the grid as an organizational aesthetic that connects objects as disparate as the interfaces of Instagram and YouTube, modern architecture, and digital spreadsheets? (Cramer) We can also ask, what is obscured when these images come together? Black Studies is a field of inquiry that explicitly critiques anti-blackness by imagining "a sizable archive of social, political, and cultural alternatives" (Weheliye 6). In other words, this set of theories does not take the fact of The Very Black Project's blackness for granted. Instead, Black Studies raises important questions about the sociopolitical process of creating racial difference: what are the shifting cultural and aesthetic structures that make the project's blackness visible? Does the project offer an alternative organization of racializing assemblages? How does the project critique the structure of racial hierarchies (Weheliye 6)?

These examples demonstrate how our objects of study require certain disciplinary frameworks that, in turn, determine the kinds of questions we ask. In this case, theoretical tools emphasize the issue of scale as we explore the relationships between vast image collections and the many ways blackness can be expressed. Perhaps the operative word in The Very Black Project is not "black," but "very." Initially, we tried to recognize blackness in this seemingly random project; now, with the help of these critical tools, we are encouraged to consider the possibility and implications of the project's visualizing of blackness in new and unfamiliar ways. Thus, we arrive at a new research question: how do images that want a *social life* that exceeds beyond their frames affect the racial frames designed to organize visual information and people into distinct categories?

Our revised research question required critical distance to construct; yet, evaluating the appropriateness of any line of inquiry is deeply personal because the questions and the methods we use reveal our ethical and ideological investments as writers. My decision to shift the emphasis from a singular definition of "black" to the plurality of "very" is situated in my fields of research and my refusal to further marginalize blackness by asking essentializing questions. In other words, in the face of racial discourses that attempt to restrain black life and art, I have selected a question that considers the possibility of black images forming new relationships and blackness being visualized in new ways.

The analytic tools used in this study are equally entrenched in value systems our work can reaffirm or reject. My study will use formal analysis — close readings of style and form — because I want my questions and answers to emerge from my object of study in hopes of avoiding the logical fallacy of constructing an argument first and seeking visual confirmation second. I am particularly wary of this circular thinking's effects on black expressive culture, which has been historically overdetermined by racial politics. Similarly, I want to ask questions about The Very Black Project's intentionally derivative aesthetics without judgement. Performing formal analysis without identifying the provenance of each post is an explicit dismissal of exclusionary fine art values and even the legacies of artists and auteurs that were vital to the development of Art History and Film Studies. I am interested in the project's creators, but I also want to show consideration for their marked absence from the site and to recognize a privilege that black artists are rarely afforded – the ability to exist separately from their art (Raengo).

As we explore the social life of the images in The Very Black Project, by closely analyzing the connections and disconnections within the project, information and relationships that exceed the frame become visible. For example, we can only recognize the project as disjunctive if we note the dramatic differences in the content and style of the posts. Similarly, the project's constant change is only apparent if we consider its daily accumulation. A close reading of the collection should also include the tense relationship between the account and Instagram's platform. The Very Black Project tends toward low-resolution archival footage and the warmth of these images, both the nostalgic sepia tone and the brown skin tones, exists in stark opposition to the clean white lines of Instagram's grid. There is also opposition between the project's varied posts, which include almost every digital image genre (stills, video, text, memes, etc.), and the grid's tidy organization that make each post the same size and shape. Finally, Instagram's Stories function allows users to post full-screen vertical content in a linear order that resembles a short film; as a result, it introduces the forced perspective of traditional cinema into a seemingly open digital space and, thus, directly opposes the project's loose narrative logic and assorted compositions. The social, political, and cultural complexity of blackness cannot be captured in any one image, even an image from The Very Black Project; instead, blackness is rendered as the unlikely connection between the project's varied content. The account uses its unwieldy scale to visualize blackness alternatively as evasive, undisciplined, dynamic, and capable of making complex and unexpected connections that are disruptive to the structures around it.

It is not easy to identify our knowledge gaps in order to ask questions about them, but resisting the urge to write answers before questions creates the possibility that our own writing may surprise us. For example, the popular and scholarly discourse on digital image cultures foreground revolutionary connectedness and the possibility of infinite and constant transformation; yet, this chapter's (brief) reading explains how The Very Black Project dynamically visualizes black life and culture using images from various time periods and with different visual styles that can be read discretely or as a network, while its platform remains static. The sense that the project is interactive and multidirectional is actually a function of the project's scaled-up blackness, not its digitality. Thus, The Very Black Project's *very* large image collection wants to create a disruptive "black sociality" (Moten) on Instagram's platform and, in the process, reveals the analogue qualities of contemporary digital image culture. My claim, like any thesis, is certainly debatable, but my interest as a writer in critiquing the technological and racial discourses that tell us Instagram accounts and black popular culture are unworthy of rigorous study is not.

## References

Clement, Tanya. "Where Is Methodology in Digital Humanities?" *Debates in the Digital Humanities*, edited by Matt Gold and Lauren Klein, Minnesota UP, 2016, pp. 153–175.
Cramer, Lauren M. "Race at the Interface: Rendering Blackness on WorldStarHipHop.com," *Film Criticism*, vol. 40, no. 2, 2016.
Mitchell, W. J. T. "Showing Seeing: A Critique of Visual Culture," *The Visual Culture Reader*, 2nd edn, edited by Nicholas Mirzoeff, Routledge, 2002, pp. 86–101.
Mitchell, W. J. T. "What Do Pictures 'Really' Want?" *October*, vol. 77, 1996, pp. 71–82.
Moten, Fred. "The Case of Blackness," *Criticism*, vol. 50, no. 2, 2008, pp. 177–218.
Raengo, Alessandra. "In the Shadow," *Camera Obscura*, vol. 28, no. 2, 2013, pp. 1–43.
Weheliye, Alexander G. "Introduction: Black Studies and Black Life," *The Black Scholar*, vol. 44, no. 2, 2014, pp. 5–10.

# 18 Writing about transnational media
## From representation to materiality

*Fan Yang*

> This chapter argues that critical screen studies in transnational contexts can benefit from a rethinking of media not just as textual artifacts but also *material* objects. The implications of this re-conception for writing about transnational screen cultures are three-fold. First, it involves approaching media as events rather than preformed artifacts. Second, it entails attending to the more explicit roles played by audiences today in shaping the configuration of transnational media objects. Third, it requires recognizing ourselves not only as "writers" who study screen cultures from a distance but also as participant observers who take part in the production, circulation, and consumption of our objects of analysis. Drawing on my experience of writing about *Under the Dome* (2015), a transnationally circulated documentary on smog in China, I suggest these ways of probing into the multifaceted processes of mediation can help us better engage the discourse and reality of "rising China."

Cultural studies of transnational media have long been concerned with the question of representation. In early critiques of cultural imperialism, for instance, American media products are said to represent US ideologies in such a way as to exert significant impact on non-US audiences (see, for example, Dorfman and Mattelart). Such ideas of Americanization or cultural invasion, which erroneously presume the purity of national culture and dupability of audiences, are now largely discounted (see, for example, Morris). Yet screen studies in transnational contexts remain preoccupied with the production, circulation, and consumption of media as *texts*.

To be sure, the uneven power relations between dominant and subordinate social groups still oftentimes manifest themselves through the modes and means of representation. Hollywood's hegemonic grammar of storytelling and perpetual Othering of people of color, among other representational issues, deserve continuous critical attention. However, as digital media's ubiquitous presence in everyday life becomes a lived reality for many across the world, screen artifacts and their transnational circulation can no longer (if they ever could) be studied as textual representations alone. Indeed, attending to their *materiality* can illuminate more dynamic processes of meaning making that help shape the ways in which these screen artifacts are made and made legible.

In 2015, a video about air pollution in China called *Under the Dome* (Chai Jing) went viral on the Chinese internet. Within 12 hours of its release, it garnered six million hits. When the viewership hit 200 million, the central Publicity Department ordered major Chinese outlets to remove the video and its coverage from the spotlight. Yet the video continued to circulate beyond China's national borders. For Chinese nationals living overseas, the video was first shared on WeChat before becoming available on YouTube, the former being the most popular social media app in the Chinese-speaking world and the latter only accessible outside China. With English subtitles provided by fan-sub groups as well as Chinese-speaking activists from abroad, the video went on to become one of the most talked about environmental events in China. Its significance is considered to be on par with that of Al Gore's 2006 documentary, *An Inconvenient Truth* and Rachel Carson's 1962 book, *Silent Spring*.

I decided to write about *Under the Dome* not long after it disappeared from the Chinese web. Much of the discussion at the time quickly shifted from a celebration of the video's format – reminiscent of an Apple product launch – toward a routine critique about China's censorship practices. The prevailing assumption was that the video had sparked a national conversation (see, for example, Lee and Turner) about air quality in China - a conversation that unfortunately could not continue due to the workings of the repressive state apparatus. Observations like this, of course, failed to consider that most people in China experience smog on a daily basis, and environmental issues have been on the radar of many politicians and activists alike.

As I looked further into the transnational discourses generated by the video, I became intrigued by a central contradiction. On the one hand, a lot of attention was paid to its status as a screen artifact that seeks to *represent* Chinese pollution. On the other, viewers appeared to be more fascinated by its sleek packaging of information – in the form of elegant Keynote slides

*Figure 18.1* The sleek packaging of information in *Under the Dome*
Source: Jonathan Papish, Part 3 of 8 "Under The Dome" Documentary on China's Pollution by Chai Jing (Best English Subtitles), available at www.youtube.com/watch?v=BXMZpF0K1ME

consisting of 332 data sources and 51 figures – and instantaneous spread via mobile platforms.

Amid the celebration of the speed and scope of the video's virality, what is represented became secondary to *how* the information is delivered and by whom. The sheer number of views and social media comments generated was cited as evidence that the video had exerted significant impact in raising awareness among the Chinese public.

In the resulting journal article, I argue that the fascination with the video's virality is symptomatic of a long-standing global environmental discourse that privileges technological solutions over structural change. The fetishization of its information delivery and dissemination overlooks the fact that a key contributing factor to China's smog problem is its status as a major manufacturing site of media devices – among other consumer goods – for the global market. The discussion surrounding the video thus precludes a different dialogue about the materiality of media, which involves the geological formation of earth metals to be extracted as raw materials for the production of digital gadgets, the health hazards inflicted upon the laboring bodies who assemble these products, and the accelerated generation of e-waste due to sped-up cycles of planned obsolescence championed by companies like Apple (Yang). And China, of course, figures prominently in each of these material processes.

My turn from media representation to media materiality, upon reflection, consists of three primary shifts in observing, conceptualizing, and writing about screen objects. The first is what I would call a shift from media artifact to media event. When writing about *Under the Dome*, my central object of analysis is not the media text – that is, the video as a preformed and self-contained entity. Rather, I followed the event as it unfolded on Chinese-language social media, observing the ways in which audiences were activated to re-post the video (released online only) and use their mobile devices as means to remedy environmental problems. This process helped me establish the connections between the air pollution discussed in *Under the Dome* and China as a manufacturing site of digital devices and the recycling of e-waste.

My data collection, so to speak, then relates to the second shift – the blurring of production and reception in the age of user-generated content. The timing of *Under the Dome*'s release is an integral part of the producers' plan to recruit audiences as promoters. The video first appeared online the weekend before two of China's most highly publicized media events – the 12th National People's Congress and the 12th Chinese People's Political Consultative Conference. The choice of the timeframe is also significant because it was the first weekend after a week-long Chinese New Year vacation for many urban residents. Audiences as distributors, in other words, already informed the making of the video as a media event. This blurring of production and reception prompts us to rethink the meaning of textual analysis, as what counts as a text now often more directly involves the work of audiences.

The third shift, therefore, concerns our own engagement with contemporary media events as scholars of screen culture. Increasingly, becoming a participant observer appears to be necessary even for those of us who may not explicitly conduct ethnographic research. To me this heightens the *temporal* dimension of studying media events. If I were to start gathering information about *Under the Dome* now, I would not have been able to trace some of the social media posts that were generated at the time of the video's viral spread; they now exist as screenshots on my computer. My research process, therefore, involves an active construction of archival information not unlike the recording of interviews and interactions with informants during anthropological fieldwork.

In this light, our own role as users of media who participate in the generation and distribution of media content warrants closer attention. In the book *Life after New Media*, media scholars Sarah Kember and Joanna Zylinska rethink media as mediation – "a complex and hybrid process" by which the "nonhuman entities" of media objects and the "biological and social lives" of humans become entangled and inseparable from one another (xv). From this perspective, humans and non-human technologies are co-constitutive and always engaged in what feminist theorist Karen Barad calls "intra-action" rather than interaction (ix). Perhaps for anthropologists and cultural critics alike, doing research is always already "doing media," as we insert our bodies in the specific space-time of the field. We are never outside of media, and approaching media as material objects is one way in which we can exercise our reflexivity as knowledge producers who partake in the meaning-making processes that help construct our objects.

The discourse and reality of "rising China" are increasingly shaping the contours of transnational media, whether in terms of Hollywood's box office or the production of personal electronics. Re-orienting our understanding of media as material *as well as* textual artifacts, then, is a helpful step toward a more critical engagement with this enormous object – itself a product of both government and corporate actions and the representational apparatus of transnational media. Probing into the multifaceted processes of mediation increasingly entails a re-thinking of media as events rather than preformed texts or artifacts. This re-conception, in turn, demands that we attend to the oftentimes more explicit roles played by audiences today in shaping the configuration of transnational media objects. It also requires the recognition of ourselves not only as "writers" who study screen cultures from a distance but also as participant observers who take part in the production, circulation, and consumption of our objects of analysis. In doing so, we may be in a better position to reflect upon the persisting unevenness within transnational media culture so as to re-envision the economic, political, cultural, and ecological futures of media globalization.

# References

Barad, Karen Michelle. *Meeting the Universe Halfway: Quantum Physics and the Entanglement of Matter and Meaning*. Duke UP, 2007.

Chai, Jing. Under the Dome. 2015. *YouTube*, www.youtube.com/watch?v=V5bHb3ljjbc.

Dorfman, Ariel, and Armand Mattelart. "Introduction: Instructions on How to Become a General in the Disneyland Club." *Media and Cultural Studies: Keyworks*, edited by Meenakshi Gigi Durham and Douglas Kellner, Blackwell, 2006, pp. 122–129.

Kember, Sarah, and Joanna Zylinska. *Life after New Media: Mediation as a Vital Process*. MIT Press, 2012.

Lee, Andrew, and Jennifer Turner. "'Under the Dome' Confronts China's Dire Air Pollution Crisis." *CBC Radio-Canada*, 2015, www.cbc.ca/radio/thecurrent/the-current-for-march-4-2015-1.2981015/under-the-dome-confronts-china-s-dire-air-pollution-crisis-1.2981025

Morris, Nancy. "The Myth of Unadulterated Culture Meets the Threat of Imported Media." *Media, Culture & Society*, vol. 24, no. 2, 2002, pp. 278–289.

Yang, Fan. "Under the Dome: 'Chinese' Smog as a Viral Media Event." *Critical Studies in Media Communication*, vol. 33, no. 3, 2016, pp. 232–244.

# 19 Writing about digital and interactive media

*Dale Hudson and Patricia R. Zimmermann*

> Digital and interactive media require rethinking the research and analysis process. These new forms open up disruptions in user access and modifications. They transition from linearity to modularity in navigable databases across transmedia platforms. This chapter guides writers through a process of how to think and write about these new forms. It suggests architecture, navigation, interface, automation, design, data, structures, and patterns as key analytical modes. It offers a writing system: use the 90/10 workflow, immerse deeply, handwrite notes, specify, research context and compare, interpret significance, make connections, outline by word count, read out loud, revise, and copyedit.

Access to the internet changed how we communicate, find information, and access and exhibit media. Digital cameras, editing software, streaming platforms, and website hosting allowed nonprofessionals to produce and distribute media without film's high costs or coding's expertise.

Today critics invent terms: browser art, counter-games, interactive media, internet art, multimedia, and new media. Indigenous media-makers create videos that reject professional production values for political reasons. Artists make mods (modifications of videogames) by altering hardware (consoles, controllers) and software (game engines) to generate critiques about technology and society. Shot inside videogames with humans controlling avatars, machinima reimagines animation. Other makers design web-browser plug-ins that automatically replace images of unpopular politicians with cats or disrupt mass surveillance software that scans our emails for key words. Linearity transitioned to modularity in navigable databases across transmedia platforms. Both media and the possible roles and relationships between makers and users changed.

We have collaborated on digital and interactive media, producing exhibitions, presenting conference papers, and publishing articles and books since 2004. Our collaboration emerged in an ecological way when Ithaca College, where we taught, assumed full sponsorship of the Finger Lakes Environmental Film Festival (FLEFF; www.ithaca.edu/fleff/). We learned that writing about digital and interactive media projects moves beyond film and television studies' emphasis on form and content. Projects exceed questions of identification and spectatorship. Writing about websites and apps requires thinking about much more. It requires considering how our very understanding of media is shaped by design allowing multiple ways to navigate form and content, by platforms constantly updating data from other sources, and devices allowing us to access media in the palm of our hands as we move through physical space. These projects sometimes resonate with analog film screened in a purpose-built cinema or broadcast on television, but they also require moving beyond these spaces to consider other kinds of media architectures.

## Architecture and navigation

Architecture refers to how projects organize open or closed pathways with user-generated or designed content through their systems. EngageMedia, for example, operates as an open portal to aggregate user-generated, NGO-produced, experimental, activist, and advocacy videos from the Asia Pacific. It tags by country, genre, language, and topic. Users navigate content on biotechnology, human and animal rights, and water/food security. In another example, Molleindustria's *McDonald's Video Game* invites users to role-play as a corporation. They raze forests, evict indigenous populations, underpay employees, and maintain customer satisfaction. Winning involves toggling between multiple game levels to avoid bankruptcy.

When you analyze digital and interactive media, consider how architecture facilitates navigation. What user acts are required? Do you select from menus

*Figure 19.1* Design of home page to navigate media and other information
Source: Engage Media, Indonesia/Australia

or click on images or icons? Do links open to embedded content, advance a larger narrative, or offer a more complicated argument? How does the project organize multiple pathways of knowledge production by participants? Are these pathways structured by qualitative analysis, quantitative data, subjective perspectives, or some other material for knowledge production? Do they rely on affect and emotion, archival documents, visual information, or some combination to communicate this knowledge? What do these multiple pathways offer? Do users contribute comments, images, videos?

*Interface and automation*

Digital and interactive media involve tactile engagement with hardware or embodied experiences with mobile or wearable devices. Consider where humans and machines meet. GUI (graphical user interface) and API (application program interface) should not be overlooked. By clicking a copy icon, you inaugurate computer operations that clone a series of instructions. By clicking the print icon, you initiate communication between computer programs. Most human-machine interfaces are tactile – clicking a mouse, tapping a keyboard, touching a screen. Others operate by motion sensors or by face- or voice-recognition software. How do human-machine encounters function?

Digital media frequently involve automated acts. AI (artificial intelligence or bots) is software that makes its own decisions. Robert Spahr's *Distress Cruft (my fellow americans)* scraped security photos from a tourist attraction's database at predetermined intervals. He designed software to composite photos with images of a US flag in distress position to underscore complicity with surveillance. Souvenir photos are security photos. Paolo Cirio and Alessandro Ludovico's *Face to Facebook* scraped Facebook public profile photos, sorted them with visual recognition software, and uploaded them to a fake dating website called Lovely-Faces. These projects interface with public and private databases and document how we gift our data for free services. When writing about digital and interactive media, consider whether the meaning-maker is human, machine, or both.

*Design and data*

Data are images, numbers, texts, or videos organized in databases. Selecting data allows users to produce knowledge by comparing or sequencing. Many projects do not make deductive arguments. Instead, they design routes toward knowledge production and feature multiple voices. Rejecting linearity, these projects open multiple pathways into complex problems such as politically polarizing situations or pollution. Consider how the design allows or disallows knowledge production by organizing data.

The design of mobile apps expand documentary practice. They are open-ended because new data can be uploaded. They allow users to move through physical space to witness present locations while learning about the past. *The Green Book of South Carolina* mobile app, for example, documents African American history that conventional tourist guides erase. Users produce different knowledge on-site than they might at home.

### *Structures and patterns*

Media forms involve a structure, whether argument, composition, or story. It might be linear (beginning, middle, end) and determined by the maker. It might be modular (loops, variations) and determined by software in response to user acts. Look for patterns such as color, graphic elements, image resolution, and volume. Interpret the frequency and duration of repetitions and variations. Is the project structured with user options? Can users customize or contribute original content? How does the structure contribute to understanding context?

## Research and writing process

Adopt journalism's adage of 90/10. 90% of your time should be devoted to thinking, reading, immersing, analyzing, and researching historical and cultural context. The remaining 10% of your time should focus on writing from an outline.

### *Immerse deeply*

Ground your thinking in the projects themselves. Start with deep immersion. Explore projects repeatedly – consider how form, content, context, and interface intersect. Elizabeth Miller's interactive documentary *The Shore Line* includes short videos and interactive maps within a storybook design. Too vast to scan quickly, users need to explore the project and stream videos on different community responses to rising sea levels and increasingly violent storms. You need to see data visualizations of common concerns in noncontiguous places, such as Bangladesh and Panama. You need to download the action guides that assist people to rewrite active responses to climate change. Streaming the videos in sequence is insufficient to understand the variety of ways users can access the stories.

### *Take notes by hand*

Online and mobile media entice and seduce. It is easy to get lost. To stay anchored to content and context, slow down. In a media-saturated world infused with rampant multitasking and rapid editing, slower is always better. Dedicate a notebook to your essay. Handwrite notes. Handwriting physicalizes ideas. It forces us to slow down because it takes longer to write than to type a sentence.

## Be specific

We can't stress enough the importance of providing specific concrete examples from the project. Don't be seduced by theory. Clear arguments require evidence to support claims. When in doubt, specify. Then interpret, explaining how and why.

## Research context

Situate projects within their cultural, historical, political, and social contexts. For example, it would be difficult to analyze Dorit Naaman's *Jerusalem, We Are Here*, a virtual tour of a formerly multiethnic and multi-religious neighborhood in old Jerusalem without understanding the dispossession of indigenous Palestinians in the 1948 *Nakba*. The project recovers Armenian, Greek, and Palestinian – that is, Christian and Muslim – history to contradict Israel's erasure of non-Jewish presence. Users select between three tours by clicking on photographs, text, and videos added to a base map. Unlike conventional documentaries with a single story or unified argument, *Jerusalem, We Are Here* suggests history as multiple and dis-unified. Under state surveillance, consider context such as the risk for certain populations to upload content to the project.

## Compare

Compare projects. We caution against thinking about only one project even when you are only analyzing one. Without comparisons, writing can default into formalist analysis that misses the significance of generative, iterative, and constantly reforming projects which foreground *process* (how) over *product* (what). What is similar or different? *The Shore Line* and EngageMedia aggregate short videos. The former collaborates with producers to make new videos; the latter works with existing activist-generated videos.

## Interpret significance

Essays explain why projects are significant for their innovative or effective approach, subject, or strategy. Projects can make interventions into unresolved debates (for example, environmental justice or territorial disputes), unsettle unproductive assumptions (for example, black/white or cisgender/transgender binaries), or innovate design and function (for example, animated data visualizations or real-time messaging features).

## Make connections

Conclusions show readers the argument's journey in ways that seem self-evident but are the product of careful analysis. Identify connections between different points in your argument. Explain how these connections support your thesis.

### *Outline by word count*

Make an outline on a grid. Break the argument into topic sentences, evidence, analysis, and interpretations that support a thesis. Assign word counts for description and analysis of each point.

### Seven steps

1   Spend more time researching and engaging with the media than writing about it.
2   Slow down, take notes, immerse.
3   Work from the project, not from presumptions. Ask questions about everything.
4   Outline your argument and assign word counts.
5   Your first revision should focus on structure. Identify where definitions, explanations, and transitions are needed. Replace vague assertions and overstatements with specific examples.
6   Your second revision should focus on style. Read your essay out loud. Vary sentence structure. Use active voice and action verbs.
7   Use a style guide for proper endnotes and correct grammar.

### References

*Distress Cruft (my fellow americans)*: www.robertspahr.com/work/distress/
*EngageMedia*: www.engagemedia.org/
*The Green Book of South Carolina* (app): https://greenbookofsc.com
*Face to Facebook* (video): www.youtube.com/watch?v=eQI1vYoXaqE
*Jerusalem, We Are Here*: https://jerusalemwearehere.com/
*McDonald's Video Game*: www.mcvideogame.com/
*The Shore Line*: http://theshorelineproject.org

# 20 (Un)limited mobilities

*Rahul Mukherjee*

> This chapter reflects on how to write about the imaginaries of freedom and mobility that are enabled by the contemporary mobile phone, which as a medium marked by rapid convergence of technologies has broken all limits to move from basic cellular mobile telephony to become a complex assemblage of a range of mediascapes. Mobile media companies promise frictionless mobility and tout the boundless capabilities of mobile media through faster download speeds, "seamless" streaming services, and a plethora of apps. However, the use of the word "unlimited" by telecom corporations and app developers to characterize their offered services itself suggests that they brush up against "limits" all the time, whether it is resolving bottlenecks of storage and bandwidth or the challenge of introducing new apps and technologies on mobile phone networks. Finally, the concept of "(un)limited mobilities" should help us examine how lived experiences of social space and time have changed with mobile media technologies.

In 2007, media studies scholars would write about the mobile phone as mobile phone and not mobile media. Soon enough, the mobile phone ceased to be just an extension of the landline telephone as a range of locative, social, and networked media converged into it. Now, once the camera took the picture, the photograph contained metadata about the location where it was captured. And then there was the Instagram app with its range of color filters to provide a nostalgic tint to the captured image which could then be uploaded and shared on social media as the mobile phone already had an internet connection. Media scholars Larissa Hjorth, Jean Burgess, and Ingrid Richardson among others have argued that these changes present new challenges and opportunities for scholars belonging to diverse disciplines (Internet Studies, Visual Culture Studies, New Media Studies, Video Game Studies) who approach phones as mobile media through varied conceptual and methodological routes.

Mobile media are a complex assemblage of ideas, cultures, and material practices. Mobile media produce numerous affordances for sharing and fostering a sense of community, but those affordances could lead to promoting individualistic competition as well. In writing about mobile media as part of modern technocultures, one needs to be cognizant of socio-economic contexts and different cultures of modernities – western, non-western, and others. Mobile media emerge with immense potential for egalitarianism. At the same time, the technological modernity shaped by and shaping mobile media development can lead to furthering social exclusions.

In the discussion that follows, I shall reflect on some of the moments of technological shifts, changes in socio-cultural usage patterns, and infrastructural limits with regard to cellular phones and telecom networks with examples from India. In doing so, I will address questions and concerns about "digital divide" and "differential access" as well as the affordances and pleasures of mobile media and cellular infrastructures. My teacher Lisa Parks, a media infrastructure studies scholar, often told us to write vivid stories of infrastructures so that scholars will attend to the often invisible infrastructural systems that lay the foundation for mobile communication. With this in mind, I write below in the form of anecdotes drawn from my personal encounters with mobile media and advertisements and my fieldwork in India.

In December 2017, a Russian tourist in the beach town of *Varkala* (Kerala, India) told me that he was surprised that Indian telecom companies could continue to promote their mobile internet service offers as "unlimited" when they give a finite quantity of daily data usage – 2GB. While agreeing with him that cellular operators in India are prone to hyperbole, I had to explain that for a large number of Indian mobile phone consumers 2GB was indeed "unlimited." "Unlimited" is a cherished word for telecom companies, and they use it liberally to advertise for "unlimited calls," "unlimited streaming," and "unlimited talk time." In June 2018, I took this picture of Indian cellular operator Airtel promising "unlimited incoming and 3GB data" in the Delhi airport (see Figure 20.1) on my way to New York City, and I was greeted with a few more such ads after landing in the JFK airport.

So much of the discourse of telecom companies in the United States and India (among other places) has been about promising frictionless mobility, about transcending previously set limits. This tendency to tout continuously the breaking of barriers and limitations is not something restricted to mobile phone companies but extends further to the wider discourse around technological growth and unfettered capitalism. Perhaps the smartphone equipped with powers of omniscience and mobility is the latest manifestation of the expansive logic of capitalism. However, the use of the word "unlimited" itself suggests that mobile media companies brush up against "limits" all the time, whether resolving bottlenecks of storage and bandwidth or introducing new apps and technologies on mobile phone networks. Since 1995, when mobile phones were first introduced in India, I have been writing about technological shifts (from 2G to 3G to 4G wireless technologies) and advertisements announcing new mobile networks, platforms, and apps. Each moment of negotiating a limitation was framed as a moment of joy, anticipation, anxiety, and uncertainty.

(Un)limited mobilities 139

*Figure 20.1* Airtel ad promising unlimited calls and data at New Delhi airport
Source: Photo by Author

While studying these media shifts, I have been aware that mobile phone services are subject to infrastructural limits of inadequate spectrum and/or lack of cell towers in a particular coverage area. I have realized that notwithstanding the tall promises of the telecom industry, wireless access or mobile Internet is going to be contingent and negotiated and not easy and seamless. Indeed, attention to behind-the-scenes infrastructure and the labor that go toward maintaining the cellular phone services offers a perspective of limits to/against the discourse of unbounded mobilities propagated by telecom companies. This awareness of infrastructural limits has been key to my writing about mobile media as I have continued to witness the flagrant growth of the cellular services in the last three decades.

In a Vodafone/Hutch ad released in India in 2005, Bollywood actor Irfan Khan posits a situation where a lover needs to patch things up with his girlfriend on the phone, but has no talk-time left. Hoping that a simple "I love you" will suffice, he can opt for a 10 rupee *"chota recharge"* (small recharge). Mobile phone conversations involve intimacies and expressions, but these intimacies and expressions have to be budgeted, rationed, and calculated. Capitalism modulates affections ("Hutch – chota recharge"). Vodafone ads of 2005 emphasized economizing talk times and budgeting streaming videos, but this discourse was completely transformed by the arrival of Reliance Jio in 2016. Jio promised free talk time and boundless data connectivity at affordable prices. Jio customers did not have to count how many times they were downloading a Bollywood film song or streaming a cricket video. The Jio ad ends by showing a woman with outstretched hands in a lush field with the sun's radiant light on her as Bollywood film star Amitabh Bachchan's inimitable baritone voice offers the coda: *"Ab Ginh ke nahi, khul ke jio"* *(Now, do not count and live, just live openly)* ("Happy New Year offer ad").

While Jio, indeed, has revolutionized the Indian telecom landscape, stories of lived experiences suggest a more complex interplay of differential access and infrastructural limits. In the summer of June 2017, a friend and I were waiting for Uber in central Delhi. From the Uber GPS map, the car seemed to go around in circles (instead of reaching us) even though we had clearly marked our destination on the map. When the Uber driver finally arrived, he blamed Uber's GPS app saying that "the map had 'frozen'." My friend surmised that the driver's mobile phone connection was not able to support data usage by Uber. The driver had a dual-SIM card, which was presently operating on a Jio connection. While making the switch to Airtel, the driver told me that he had shifted from one SIM card to another based on the proximity of towers on a number of prior occasions. Upon switching to Airtel, the GPS within the Uber platform started working again (Mukherjee).

This vignette captures the everyday encounters with mobile phones and mobile phone towers that one observes on the streets of India. Our Uber driver had a dual SIM card smartphone, not uncommon in India among people who want to get the benefits of two different cellular services. He had taken the Reliance Jio connection to utilize the large amount of data (1 GB per day) the operator provided so as to watch several videos on his phone screen. Whenever he wants better data speeds and quality phone calls, he switches to the Airtel SIM. There are regional fluctuations in infrastructural investment and network coverage by different operators. The location of Airtel's headquarters in Delhi helps it provide stronger coverage in India's capital while Jio provides better services in Mumbai where the company's head office is located.

I have briefly discussed what infrastructural limits are attached to "(un)limited mobilities," but it is not difficult to imagine that this concept should help us examine how lived experiences of social space and time have changed with media mobile technologies, which in turn have a bearing on shifting considerations about privacy, decency, gender-religion-and-caste dynamics, intimacy, and public-private boundaries. While I would not like to generalize, it does at times happen that advertising about media objects or telecom services is often too visible and telecom infrastructures tend to be less visible or, even if visible, somewhat inconspicuous. That is why media scholars have a special responsibility to write about media advertising and media infrastructures together because in such a juxtaposition might lie a way to critique media capitalism both discursively and materially.

## References

"Happy New Year offer ad," *Reliance Jio ad*, 2016. www.youtube.com/watch?v=TlgbZM6O06U Accessed 4 July 2017.

Hjorth, Larissa, Jean Burgess, and Ingrid Richardson, "Studying the Mobile: Locating the Field." *Studying Mobile Media: Cultural Technologies, Mobile Communication, and the iPhone*. Routledge, 2012.

"Hutch chota recharge," *Hutch/Vodafone recharge ad*, 2005. www.youtube.com/watch?v=ARz0YKTVSWM&spfreload=1 Accessed 4 July 2017.

Mukherjee, Rahul. "Jio sparks Disruption 2.0: Infrastructural Imaginaries and Platform Ecosystems in 'Digital India.'" *Media Culture & Society*, vol. 41, no. 2, 2019, pp. 175–195.

# 21 Context is key

## How (and why) you should write about outdoor advertising

*Beth Corzo-Duchardt*

> Context is important to consider when writing about any medium. But it's especially important in the case of outdoor advertising because each time we view an outdoor advertisement, we see something different. This chapter lays out three guidelines for taking in the context of outdoor advertisements: limiting yourself to one specific ad in one specific location, observing and recording objects and images that coexist in the visual field surrounding your advertisement, and considering unintended viewing positions in addition to intended ones. Additionally, it provides some research tips for accessing images and descriptions of outdoor advertisements in their contexts so you are not limited to writing about those that you can physically access.

Outdoor advertising is a broad term that describes a diverse field of media objects including billboards, signs, posters, and screens that adorn the facades of urban buildings, face drivers on highways, confront shoppers in stores and malls, barrage travelers in airports and transit stations, and confront fans at sports arenas, music venues, and theaters. Most of us encounter these media multiple times a day, although we rarely consciously register the messages they send. But this is the precise reason we need to analyze and write about outdoor advertisements: so that we can become consciously aware of the meaning and impact of these ubiquitous media.

Unlike television, film, or computer screens, outdoor advertisements do not demand or even encourage undivided attention. Because of this, the meanings they deliver are profoundly impacted by nearby objects, which are distinct in each location. The same advertisement that you see on a digital billboard amid a cityscape takes on a different meaning when viewed against the backdrop of a rural landscape or on a kiosk in an airport. In addition to considering the impact of surrounding objects and spaces, we must also attend to the specificity of the platforms on which outdoor advertisements appear, which range from bus shelters to building facades, vehicles to telephone poles. These platforms vary in size and aspect ratio, and there is no standard distance from which outdoor advertisements are viewed. Furthermore, the materials that constitute these media objects range from paint and paper to LCD screens. This is the challenge and the opportunity that we face when writing about outdoor advertising: we must attend to the unique material features and contextual details surrounding each instance, and interpret the content of the advertisement in relation to these features and details. What follows are some practical guidelines for analyzing outdoor advertisements in their specific contexts.

First, begin with one specific advertisement in one specific site. Even if your goal is to write about several ads, such as a series of billboards along a stretch of highway, assess them initially one at a time. This will enable to you to observe everything that shares the visual field with your advertisement and record your observations. Taking photographs and short videos of the advertisement in context is helpful, but taking detailed written notes works too. Video recordings are useful if the advertisement is on a moving vehicle (for example, a transit wrap), if it's typically viewed by vehicles moving at high speeds (for example. a billboard along a highway), or if the advertisement consists of moving images (for example, a digital billboard that cycles through a set of still images or plays short videos on a loop). Be sure to take wide shots (or position yourself so that you can take in wide views) that record adjacent objects and images, such as landscapes, the architectural details of nearby buildings, and other advertisements. These details will play an important role in your analysis.

Scholar Ann Cronin's book *Advertising, Commercial Spaces and the Urban*, provides many detailed analyses of singular outdoor advertisements in juxtaposition with their surroundings. In one section, she presents and interprets a photograph of a specific advertising "wrap" (an enormous piece of material wrapped around a building) on an abandoned nineteenth-century mill in Manchester, England (137). Despite being four stories tall, the advertisement in question, which promotes Cadbury's chocolate, takes up very little space in Cronin's photograph. Cronin interprets the meaning of the ad's content in relation to its context, writing: "The advertising wrap creates a disjuncture between its referent in contemporary capitalist society and the nineteenth century embodied in the mill...this is both a temporal collage and a direct display of change" (140). She comes to this understanding through analyzing the formal elements and textual content of the Cadbury advertisement together with the architectural details of the building. More examples of analyses of how contemporary outdoor advertisements transform the spaces they occupy can be found in the edited collection *Ambient Screens and Transnational Public Spaces* (Papastergiadis).

You do not need to have physical access to analyze outdoor advertisements, but you should carefully select sources that provide as many contextual details as possible. While a Google image search for "billboard" or "outdoor advertisement" will reveal countless results, few will be accompanied by crucial contextual information about the date and location of the advertisement. Instead, go directly to websites and databases that you know will contain this information. For recent material, consult the websites of outdoor advertising companies such as JCDecaux, Clear Channel Outdoor, and websites for organizations like the Outdoor Advertising Association of America, F.E.P.E. International (International Federation of Outdoor Adverting), and Digital Signage Connection. While their home pages tend to feature images of billboards taken out of context, if you do a little digging, you will find other pages on these sites that contain videos, photographs, and case studies that provide detailed information about specific campaigns including the date and location. If you are interested in older advertisements, start your search on digital archives hosted by libraries, archives, historical societies, and universities located in a region of interest. These institutions keep meticulous records, and you can be sure their photos will be accompanied by detailed information about their date and location of origin. Two excellent resources for photos of outdoor advertising are The Library of Congress' digital archive of photographs of "Roadside America" taken by John Morgolies between 1969 and 2008 and Duke University's "Resource of Outdoor Advertising Descriptions (R.O.A.D.) 2.0," a digital database with descriptions and links to photographs of American outdoor advertisements from the 1880s through the 1990s. Historian Catherine Gudis makes extensive use of the latter resource in her book *Buyways: Billboards, Automobiles, and the American Landscape*.

In addition to photographs, verbal descriptions and illustrators' renderings of historic outdoor advertisements in old newspapers, journals, or archival documents are useful documents. I rely on these types of sources in my own historical research. For example, I was inspired to write my article "Paper Girls" after finding an 1898 newspaper article in which an illustrator depicted a circus poster that had been partially covered over in a censorship effort by police in Webster City, Iowa. Apparently, they had pasted huge sheets of white paper over the sections of the poster depicting the bare legs of female (but not male) trapeze artists. The illustration showed how the already haphazardly-placed additions to the poster were peeling off from the surface. This detail, along with the rhetoric used by the poster's enemies led me to investigate how the materiality of early outdoor advertisements – the ephemerality and fragility of the wood-pulp based paper on which images of scantily clad women were mechanically reproduced on a mass scale – contributed to their objectionable status. Later, I found a digitized image of a similar poster that provided a useful visual reference, but my analysis hinged on the visual details of the specific poster in Webster City that had been altered by police (Corzo-Duchardt).

Whether you are writing about current or historic advertisements, be sure to consider what the advertisement looks like from all likely viewing positions, even those that are unintended. Don't limit yourself to a direct frontal view. Consider what the advertisement (and the structure on which it is located) looks like from above, below, and behind. Eventually you will have to limit yourself to a few points of view, but consider all likely possibilities before making the obvious choice.

Context is key    145

*Figure 21.1* A newspaper illustration depicting how policemen covered objectionable poster content with large sheets of white paper. Note how the illustrator uses shading to demonstrate how the censors' paper is coming up at the edges.
*Source*: From "Couldn't Stand the Posters: Webster City People Drape Pictures of Scantily-Dressed Women," clipping from unknown newspaper, ca. 1898, scrapbook, p. 41, box HI5, courtesy of the Outdoor Advertising Association of America Archives, David M. Rubenstein Rare Book & Manuscript Library, Duke University.

For example, you might consider what a particular billboard looks like to the high-rise apartment dwellers whose windows lie behind them, such as in the film *True Romance* (Tony Scott, 1993), whose protagonist, Clarence, lives in a building adorned with a billboard. Although it was not designed to be viewed by Clarence, it occupies his field of vision. The spotlights that illuminate the billboard seep into his bedroom at night. The advertisement features an image with text that aligns car ownership with power and freedom. The location and material features of the billboard are, by themselves, manifestations of the value American culture places on car travel and consumerism. Leasing space to a billboard company is, for Clarence's landlord, obviously worth any decrease to the value of the apartment itself. And Clarence might enjoy a free balcony that provides easy outdoor access and some city views, despite the cost of nightly light pollution and frequent disturbances to his privacy. In short, his experience of the billboard is full of the ambivalence that characterizes many Americans' experiences with consumer culture.

Context is important to consider when writing about any media form. Film historians have long understood that the experience of watching a film in a ramshackle nickelodeon theater in an urban community in 1907 differed vastly from watching that same film 100 years later in a purpose-built movie theater surrounded by silent cinema enthusiasts. And television scholars understand that a person watching a show on a large screen in their living room will take in different meanings than if they were watching it on their phone while riding a commuter train. But context is especially important in the case of outdoor advertising because unlike films and television shows, the content of outdoor advertisements is not designed to command our undivided attention. Most of the time they occupy our peripheral vision, and even when they are central, they are often juxtaposed within and among other sights. Nonetheless, the strategies I have laid out here provide useful lessons that can be adapted for writing about the contexts of other media as well.

# References

Corzo-Duchardt, Beth. "Paper Girls: Gender and Materiality in Turn-of-the-Century Outdoor Advertising." *Feminist Media Histories*, vol. 1, no. 3, 2015, pp. 38–65.
Cronin, A. M. *Advertising, Commercial Spaces and the Urban*. Palgrave Macmillan, 2010.
Gudis, Catherine. "Buyways: Billboards, Automobiles, and the American Landscape." *Cultural Spaces*. Routledge, 2004.
Papastergiadis, Nikos, editor. *Ambient Screens and Transnational Public Spaces*. Hong Kong UP, 2016.

*Methods and locations*

# 22 How sound helps tell a story

## Sound, music, and narrative in Vishal Bhardwaj's *Omkara*

*Nilanjana Bhattacharjya*

> Within many popular Indian films, the narrative is often interrupted by a series of song sequences with varying relationships, if any, to the narrative. During a song sequence, spoken dialogue mostly disappears and gives way to music. Within the 2006 film *Omkara*, the relationships between the narrative and the film's music are especially rich because its director, Vishal Bhardwaj, also composed the film's songs. The song, "Nainon Ki Mat Suniyon Re (Do Not Listen To Your Eyes)" reveals how multiple layers of meaning in aural and visual texts interact. The sound of a voiceover and song lyrics interrupt, reorder, and question the visual text's depiction of romance and intimacy and also serve to foreshadow the film's violent conclusion. The tensions between the aural and visual texts lead us to question who the narrators in this sequence are, whether they tell the truth, and whom they intend to address.

Within many popular Indian films, the narrative is often interrupted by a series of song sequences, during which spoken dialogue mostly disappears and gives way to music. Audiences and critics have long debated the extent to which these song sequences relate to the narrative — in many cases, whether they relate at all. In some films, the songs may seem like unwelcome intrusions upon an otherwise coherent narrative, but in other films, these interruptions can structure the narrative. Examining song sequences as integral parts of a film as opposed to extraneous, supplemental afterthoughts can reveal new ways to understand how a film's narrative works as a whole. Film scholar Lalitha Gopalan notes that the space of the song sequence can define different senses of time and space, where music and sound may serve to bridge otherwise unrelated settings; to compress the passage of time; and to portray a diegetic performance of an event occurring in real time (129–136). Within the 2006 film *Omkara*, the relationships between the narrative and the film's music are especially rich because its director, Vishal Bhardwaj, also composed the film's songs.

The song sequences in *Omkara* punctuate significant dramatic points in the narrative, which sets Shakespeare's tragedy *Othello* in contemporary rural northern India where gangs of outlaws collaborate with local politicians to enforce order and security. In the film, a midlevel gang member, Langda, starts to resent his superior, the "half-caste" Omkara after Omkara chooses another person as his successor. Seeking revenge, Langda insinuates that Omkara's wife Dolly has been unfaithful, and Omkara's rage and jealousy grow until he murders Dolly. The eight song sequences in this film include: a song that helps introduce Omkara's character as a leader; a love duet between Omkara and Dolly that proves the depth of their love; another song that conveys Dolly's growing sense of doom about her own fate; two diegetic song and dance performances by a local courtesan during which the tensions among respective onlookers erupt into physical violence; two iterations of a lullaby that convey first, Omkara's love for Dolly, and later, his sadness after he murders her; and the first song, a flashback that narrates how Dolly and Omkara's relationship began, which we will focus on here.

This first song, "Nainon ki mat suniyon re (Do not listen to your eyes)" reveals how aural and visual texts contain multiple layers of meaning, all of which interact. Within this sequence, the visual narrative – what we see onscreen – compresses and reorders time to offer a believable series of events culminating in Omkara and Dolly's relationship. The song lyrics we hear in the aural text over that visual narrative, however, warn us to not trust what we see. Just after Dolly, having eloped with Omkara, confesses to her father that she loves Omkara, the first shot of the sequence flashes back to an injured Omkara appearing at Dolly's door one rainy evening and then collapsing into her arms. As viewers, we seem to be revisiting Dolly's memories as the sequence begins. Listeners familiar with Hindi film and musical traditions will recognize the distinctive timbre and ornamentation of Rahet Fateh Ali Khan's male vocals, but they clash against the apparently female point of view.

Khan's singing evokes the Sufi devotional style of *qawwali*, a genre associated with Muslims in India – a minority invisible within the film's immediate narrative, but closely associated with the Urdu poetic tradition from which the lyricist Gulzar's lyrics originate, as well as the history of the city of Lucknow where some of the film occurs. Although Hindi and Urdu's conversational language is mutually intelligible, Urdu's poetic register is more influenced by Persian and Arabic. Films, and especially film songs, have long featured Urdu since many of the earliest lyricists and screenplay writers in Bombay were Urdu poets. In other songs in this film, Gulzar adopts alternate local inflections. As Khan sings in Urdu, "Don't pay any attention to your eyes, don't listen to them," he warns us not to trust what we see – to not *listen to our eyes*.[1] Although the sequence seems to begin from within Dolly's memories, we must consider whether the lyrics' warning, sung by a male voice, also comes from Dolly – or whether it comes from an external omniscient persona somewhere in the future that warns us about what Dolly herself cannot see, even from hindsight in a flashback. This omniscient persona is evident within the visual narrative through shot/

reverse shots during which the camera peers over Dolly's shoulder at Omkara, and over Omkara's shoulder at Dolly, and later, a montage of shots of the couple together as well as in isolation. The opening montage compresses the span of a few days to reveal how Dolly grows increasingly close to Omkara as she nurses him.

In this song, Bhardwaj manipulates our sense of continuity within the montage's conventional compression of time by interspersing scenes outside the series of events, an offscreen voiceover narration, and as previously stated, the sound of lyrics from an unidentified speaker that question the truth of what we see. Midway through the sequence, during an extreme close-up of Dolly's face illuminated in darkness, she opens her closed eyes and breaks the fourth wall to look directly at the viewer, and even if her mouth doesn't move, we then hear Dolly's spoken voice (in Hindi) address the viewer over the music: "God knows how I lost my heart to Omkara."

During the next shot where Dolly and Omkara stroll past Lucknow's historical architectural landmarks, she continues, "I was in love, but it was too late." Khan's singing then returns to the foreground in a montage of scenes that depict Dolly's engagement party to another man, and some days later, a tea party during which while preparing tea, Dolly secretly drops her engagement ring into one of the teacups for Omkara to find. During these scenes of the engagement and the tea party, Khan sings, "Eyes don't differentiate between good and bad, loved ones and strangers. They just love to sting." In the next part of the sequence, one shot breaks from the montage to depict Dolly in darkness from above sprawled on a bed as if dead, and her voice once again speaks over Khan's singing: "I remember

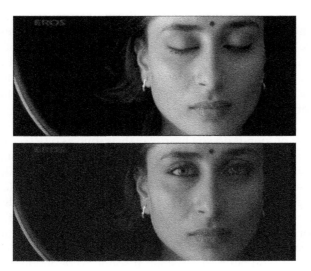

*Figures 22.1a–b* Extreme close-ups of Dolly's face in *Omkara* (Vishal Bhardwaj, 2006)

feeling like a blind bird plunging into darkness." The progression of time resumes as she then rides in a cycle rickshaw through Lucknow traffic and speaks, "Everything seemed hopeless," before the next shot returns to the chronological beginning of the relationship as Dolly touches her sleeve stained with Omkara's blood from when he first collapses into her arms, against which Khan sings, "Their [eyes'] poison is intoxicating."

The last shots include Dolly's voiceover shifting from narrating the past to her reading out loud a letter addressed to Omkara. We see Dolly writing a letter at her house, delivering the letter to a friend at college, and finally, Omkara's reading the letter as she speaks: "And then I decided I'd end my wretched life.... But then there was no point in it when whom I was dying for didn't even know why.... [To Omkara:] Since you won't in this lifetime, let me confess. I'm yours and yours only. Put me down in your list of slain. Love, D." Against her voice, Khan sings, "Your eyes will sow rainbows in clouds and make it rain till morning. They'll show you rainbows and drive you mad."

This sequence's aural texts, including Dolly's own framing of the text as well as Khan's lyrics, interrupt, reorder, and question the visual text's depiction of romance and intimacy and also serve to foreshadow the violent conclusion to their relationship. After the song ends, the next shots return to the scene where Dolly tells her father about her love for Omkara. It's unlikely that she has shared all the visual details of her intimacy with her father. But given that not all of the details depicted represent her point of view, we must question the identity of the potential narrators, whether they are telling the truth, and whom they intend to address.

When writing on music's role onscreen, remember that sound can often reinforce the visual text's version of narrative but sometimes may go against it – especially when it fails to connect directly to any sense of space and location within the visual text. In this instance, the sound serves to contain the sequence's manipulation of time through its reordering of events and foreshadowing. When analyzing sound on screen, you may find it helpful to consider the following questions to determine the relationships between what you see and what you hear, and how those relationships in turn affect your sense of time and space.

1   What type of sounds do you hear? Are their sources offscreen or onscreen? Do those sounds occur within the same time as those events onscreen?
2   If you hear song lyrics or spoken language, who is the speaker? Can the speaker see everything the viewer sees? Describe the persona(e) who speak(s) or sing(s) the lyrics, and how they relate to the framing of the visual text.
3   How do the director's choices (composition, movement of the camera, length of shots, rhythm of cuts, relation of the cuts' rhythm to that of the music itself, etc.) correlate with sound events?
4   What would you fail to understand if sound were omitted altogether?

Although many writers have written on how sound functions to accentuate other significant elements in film, addressing instead how sound itself defines those elements often leads to more compelling conclusions.

## Note

1 The translations here are partly taken from the subtitles on my personal DVD of the film and partly from my own translation. In addition, subtitling can be arbitrary during song sequences, if subtitles appear at all. Songs' lyrics are almost always posted online, and functional translations of these often convey more than the brief subtitles onscreen.

## References

Gopalan, Lalitha. *Cinema of Interruptions: Action Genres in Contemporary Indian Cinema*. British Film Institute, 2002.

*Omkara*. Directed by Vishal Bhardwaj, performances by Ajay Devgan, Saif Ali Khan, and Kareena Kapoor, Eros Entertainment, 2006.

# 23 Writing outside the text
## A cultural approach to exhibition and moviegoing

*Jasmine Nadua Trice*

> Grounded in studies of exhibition and moviegoing, this chapter discusses ethnographic approaches to public film consumption. It is drawn from the author's research on film circulation and consumption in Manila, Philippines. Questions it examines include: How do we define the parameters of an object, when the event of cinema consumption is fleeting? How do we capture the significance of a particular screening event or venue? What kinds of theoretical frameworks should we draw from, in order to unpack our observations? What can our observations tell us about how cinema – as a text or a social practice – becomes meaningful within particular historical, cultural settings? The chapter examines three, interrelated objects for writing about exhibition and moviegoing from a cultural perspective: *spaces*, *discourses*, and *performances*.

Whether we watch them at home or in a public space, the act of consuming a movie is a live event, happening in a particular time and place. This isn't always how we think about films when we write about them, but it *is* how we experience films in our everyday lives. In much of American moviegoing culture, for example, we go to the cinema at the multiplex, sometimes alone, more often with friends. We purchase a ticket, maybe some food and drink. We sit down in an air-conditioned room, in comfortable, cushioned seats, to watch a few advertisements, trailers, and finally, a feature film, which we consume from beginning to end. This is fairly standard operating procedure, a set of protocols that has been naturalized for many viewers. We only notice these norms if there is some disruption – faulty air-conditioning, a patron entering the theater after the film has started, someone talking to a seatmate during a quiet moment on screen. But such norms are not neutral; they promote a certain kind of relationship between viewer and screen and among the viewers gathered in that screening space. Moreover, these moviegoing norms are not universal. Indian cinemas are arranged according to ticket price and social class, and audiences are encouraged to speak amongst themselves as they react to what's happening on screen (Gunckel 2015; Serna 2014; Srinivas 2017). Even within the U.S., cinemas that cater to particular communities have welcomed more participation from viewers at different points in history (Stewart 2005; Thissen 2012). Different social practices situate the event of moviegoing within a particular socio-cultural and historical context.

What do these social protocols tell us about the film as a text, and what does it mean to write about the object of exhibition and moviegoing?[1] If we write about a particular screen text – a film, television program, or videogame – the boundaries of that object are somewhat straightforward. We might analyze the text itself, or its production history. We might consider its reception with a particular audience – how British women remember Hollywood stars, or how African-American women respond to the film *The Color Purple* (Steven Spielberg, 1985), for example (Bobo 1988; Stacey 1994). But writing about the circumstances of that text's circulation and consumption is a bit trickier. How do we define the parameters of an object when the event of cinema consumption is fleeting? How do we capture the significance of a particular screening event or venue? What kinds of theoretical frameworks should we draw from, in order to unpack our observations? What can our observations tell us about how cinema – as a text or a social practice – becomes meaningful within particular historical, cultural settings?

My research on film exhibition in Manila, Philippines raised many of these questions. The Philippines was an especially rich site for studying film, as the country has a long history of film production and consumption, and cinema was once called the national pastime. More recently, experimental and independent films have flourished on the international festival circuit, while finding few venues for exhibition at home. I had arrived in the country at a time of transition (2006), when cinema's relationship to ideas of nation was being heavily debated, and the infrastructures of cinema production and circulation were in formation. I analyzed these debates about cinema, its audiences, and its modes of circulation in my writing. Because cinema was taking shape as a politically charged object of public discourse, I wanted to allow the theoretical frameworks I employed to emerge from the raw materials of the research – the multifaceted objects of study that would come to constitute "the cinema" for my project. So, I decided to emphasize cinema's socio-cultural meaning, in addition to its industrial and institutional structure. I settled upon three, interrelated objects that helped me write about exhibition and moviegoing from a cultural perspective: *spaces*, *discourses*, and *performances*.

First, I focused on the *spaces* of film circulation and consumption. This included the spaces where films were distributed, screened, and consumed, such as movie theaters or alternative screening venues. It also included attention to where those spaces were situated within particular urban settings. For example, when I wrote about the informal DVD district of Quiapo, a neighborhood in the old city, I visited the site on a regular basis, recording my observations of the space in a loose variation of what anthropologists call fieldnotes. Fieldnotes are detailed, reflective descriptions of what was observed during a particular site visit. They involve decisions about what to include and what to leave out, and researchers reference them as they write their analysis. Sometimes, seemingly random or unimportant observations become significant as the analysis develops. For instance, Quiapo is primarily a working-class neighborhood, and middle-class visitors like me stood out. Once, I noted a young man who carried a digital SLR camera with him. He hovered around a DVD stall, training his lens on the vendor and the act of exchange. This was noticeable not just because of class difference, but because his camera seemed expensive, and my local friends had warned me that the area was known for street crime (one had been pickpocketed). I didn't think much of it until later, when I began to consider how the district's DVD market incarnation had become an object of the middle-class, cinephile imagination. Plainly displaying how viewer and viewed were divided along class lines, the glimpse of the photographer encapsulated some of the power dynamics involved in this process.

In addition, the history of the space became integral to its more recent incarnation as a hub for gray market DVDs. Public discourse about Quiapo appeared in many forms in early-2000s Manila, forming a rich archive of materials for analysis. Heritage discourses found in organizational documents, books, and popular media became one means of understanding how the space had come to be seen as the "heart of Manila" and the "crossroads of the country." These ideas were rooted in the district's role as a hub for the archipelago's diverse cultures. Intranational migrants came from the highlands, creating a market for Animist charms around the perimeter of the district's Catholic cathedral. Muslim migrants came from the war-torn south, and soon became leaders in the DVD trade. Middle-class cinephiles who now frequented Quiapo's markets as they hunted for more unusual DVDs often took up this discourse of multiculturalism, in blog posts and in online message boards that emerged to help discerning consumers find particular titles. Films became another resource for analysis. Alternative filmmakers set scenes in Quiapo in their films, and their emphasis on the district's overwhelming abundance of DVDs created another facet of analysis. At the same time, the state's Optical Media Board, a regulatory body, linked piracy to terrorism. Discourses around heritage, art cinemas, and ethnicized criminality worked in tension with one another to create a version of a new Manila film culture, predicated on cultural difference. My analysis tracked these tensions across this wide range of discourses, found in various media.

A student-led study of contemporary film consumption practices might combine interviews, discourse analysis, and participant-observation.[2] These research practices are often associated with ethnography, a method used most often in the discipline of anthropology. Broadly, the term describes a research practice that seeks to understand the everyday lives of human beings, analyzing various kinds of evidence – observations at a particular site, interviews with participants, public discourse, visual materials – in order to understand a particular cultural practice. As with all research projects, media ethnography begins with research questions. What might this particular media circulation site/film consumption practice/production culture tell us about the relationship between local film communities and larger industrial infrastructures? How do proprietors of an exhibition site or organizers of a screening event construct these projects' roles in social life? The ethnographer aims to understand media practices in their social context, from the perspective of community members themselves. For example, if you were to attend a film screening during which people interacted with the screen or talked with one another throughout the film, you would want to be aware of whether this was a social protocol associated with that particular viewing community. At the same time, ethnographers are reflexive about the practice of their research, recognizing their own role in constructing the research and its outcomes. Unlike journalism, which is usually expected to be an objective report of what transpired, an ethnography is an interpretation, and it is important that the writing acknowledges that. Media ethnographers take copious notes during events, transcribe interviews with key participants, and review documents (publicly available documents, such as advertisements, online message boards, news coverage, and annual reports or internal documents, such as budgets and correspondences). They look for patterns within this data, noting anything that might stand out, and considering what questions it raises. Do people often frame a particular small-town art cinema as a link to broader, cosmopolitan culture? Do teens consider the local multiplex a site for illicit meetings? If you want to make an argument about a pattern in one form of evidence (say, interviews), see whether other forms of evidence also substantiate this claim.

As students write up their studies, they will want to think about how theory might help them analyze their work. Studying cinema as an event that takes place in time and space means being open to a wide range of theoretical tools, some from outside the discipline of cinema and media studies. For instance, the field of performance studies offers ways for thinking about how performances affect the city space. The field of urban studies brings models for thinking about class, culture, and neighborhood change. Though they may seem removed from media studies, these dynamics all inform how cinema and media take shape in the public imagination. Spaces, discourses, and performances become windows into screen media's interface with public culture.

## Notes

1 For more on this growing area of study, see: Allen 2006; Maltby, et al. 2011; and Moran 2013.
2 I focus here on contemporary practices. For historical methods, see: Hallam and Roberts 2013; Horowitz and Comiskey 2014. For an overview of media ethnography in anthropology, see Ginsberg, Abu-Lughod and Larkin 2002.

## References

Allen, Robert C. "Relocating American Film History; The 'problem' of the empirical." *Cultural Studies*, vol. 20, no. 1, 2006, pp. 48–88.

Bobo, Jacqueline. "Black women's responses to The Color Purple." *Jump Cut: A Review of Contemporary Media*, vol. 33, no. 3, 1988, pp. 43–51, www.ejumpcut.org/archive/onlinessays/JC33folder/ClPurpleBobo.html

Ginsberg, Faye, Lila Abu-Lughod, and Brian Larkin, editors. *Media Worlds: Anthropology on New Terrain*. U of California Press, 2002.

Gunckel, Colin. *Mexico on Main Street: Transnational Film Culture in Los Angeles Before World War II*. Rutgers U Press, 2015.

Horwitz, Jonah and Andrea Comiskey. "Case Studies of Local Film Exhibition: An Undergraduate Research Assignment," *Cinema Journal Teaching Dossier*, vol. 2, no. 3, 2014, www.teachingmedia.org/category/assignments/writing-research-papers-assignments/

Hallam, Julia and Les Roberts. *Locating the Moving Image: New Approaches to Film and Place*. Indiana UP, 2013.

Maltby, Richard, Daniel Biltereyst, and Philippe Meers, editors. *Explorations in New Cinema History: Approaches and Case Studies*. Wiley-Blackwell, 2011.

Moran, Albert editor. *Watching Films: New Perspectives on Movie-Going, Exhibition and Reception*. Intellect, 2013.

Serna, Laura Isabel. *Making Cinelandia: American Films and Mexican Film Culture before the Golden Age*. Duke UP, 2014.

Srinivas, Lakshmi. *House Full: Indian Cinema and the Active Audience*. U of Chicago Press, 2017.

Stacey, Jackie. *Star Gazing: Hollywood Cinema and Female Spectatorship*. Routledge, 1994.

Stewart, Jacqueline. *Migrating to the Movies: Cinema and Black Urban Modernity*. U of California Press, 2005.

Thissen, Judith. "Beyond the Nickelodeon: Cinemagoing, Everyday Life and Identity Politics." *Audiences: Defining and Researching Screen Entertainment Reception*, edited by Ian Christie, Amsterdam UP, 2012, pp. 45–65.

# 24 Writing about streaming portals
The drama of distribution

*Ramon Lobato*

> While the discipline of screen studies has traditionally focused on the analysis of texts, screen distribution can also be a fruitful area for critical writing and analysis. This chapter offers some reflections on how (and why) to write about distribution, using Netflix as an example.

Streaming portals such as Netflix, Hulu, iPlayer and iQiyi are integral to film and television distribution in many nations. For screen scholars, these portals represent an interesting challenge because they are simultaneously cultural, technical, and logistical in nature. This means that the topic of streaming can be approached from many different angles simultaneously, and written about in diverse ways.

What writing styles and techniques are available to students approaching this task for the first time? How can we delve imaginatively into the range of issues that streaming portals present – from catalog curation and algorithmic recommendation to frame rates, freezing and pixellation? In this chapter, I want to suggest that streaming portals, as technologies of distribution, present rich possibilities for interpretation and critique: they invite us to tell interesting stories about how movies and TV shows reach their audiences (or do not reach them, as the case may be).

The first step in the process is to decide on your angle. What do you find most interesting about a given portal? Is it the range of movies, TV shows, and other texts in its catalog? Or are you more interested in the user communities that congregate there? Perhaps even the portal's institutional or regulatory history? Each of these approaches lends itself to a particular analytic approach, from content analysis to audience studies to regulatory/policy studies. Reading across the literature by media scholars will reveal how these approaches can be used, and the diversity of ideas and theories that can be applied in your analysis – from Amanda Lotz's analysis of streaming business models and affordances, through to Ghislain Thibault's media-archaeological analyses of streaming metaphors.

One can also look outside the academic literature for ideas. For example, technology websites – *Wired*, *The Verge*, *Ars Technica* – contain valuable information, reportage, and product reviews about streaming services. The best technology journalists combine business and cultural analysis in a way that seems effortless, but is actually very hard to pull off. Consider, for example, Alexis Madrigal's famous 2014 article in *The Atlantic*, "How Netflix Reverse Engineered Hollywood," which blended ground-breaking reporting into Netflix's genre classification system with the writer's personal reflections about how Netflix works from a user perspective. Using scraping experiments and other online detective work to dig into the Netflix system, Madrigal produced a memorable piece of journalism that mixed big data analysis, industry reportage, and cultural criticism.

Business and trade press publications such as *Variety* and *The Financial Times* are also useful sources to consult, and may provide some ideas for writing techniques. The best business journalists write in a way that goes beyond mere financial reporting and tells a larger story about power struggles in the media industries, explaining what is at stake for governments, investors, audiences, and producers. Sometimes business reporting offers its own implicit theories. For example, journalist Michael Wolff's inimitable book *Television is the New Television* – a collection of short essays with provocative titles like "The Netflix Unrevolution" and "Consolidating Consolovision" – is a memorable example, combining business commentary with media history and theory.

As these examples show, there is no single way to write about streaming services, and writers need to find their own approach and their own voice in this endeavor. I speak from experience here, having spent the last four years writing (and wrestling with) my own book about Netflix's internationalization (Lobato). Writing about Netflix was a more challenging task than I initially realized, and I learned a few things along the way about how to reconcile the fast-changing world of digital media within the slow-moving world of academic publishing. I was also fortunate to learn from scholars around the world – all fellow members of the Global Internet TV Consortium (globalinternet-tv.com), our research network dedicated to comparative study of multi-territory streaming services – who were grappling with similar challenges. Based on this experience, I offer four simple suggestions:

## Take a long-range view

When writing about digital media, it is tempting to try and keep pace with every new development, from new app features to today's stock price. Consequently, much writing about streaming is very "present-ist." In my view, the best writing on this topic is engaged with longer-range questions about the history and future of the moving image. My advice, then, is to historicize wherever possible: while attending to the dynamic nature of the portal you're describing, also try to keep an eye on the bigger issues, and look for the continuities as well as the changes. (This is easier said than done, of course.)

### Focus on links between technology and culture

Streaming services are highly technical, and it is easy to get lost in the minutiae of codecs, bit rates, and file sizes. For humanities students writing in a critical mode, this technical aspect can be daunting. The best approach may be to focus on the connections *between* culture and technology. For example, what does the shift to 4K streaming mean for the availability of older and classic movies in streaming catalogs? What might future developments in artificial intelligence (AI) mean for film archives, cultures, and appreciation? There are fascinating cultural angles to any given technical phenomenon, so seek them out and see where they lead you.

### Look beyond the hype

A third suggestion is to take industry rhetoric with a grain of salt – especially trade sources, which are full of spin and product placement. For example, much of the best-known trade reportage around Netflix has been produced by embedded journalists (in other words, journalists whose access to the company has been arranged and approved by senior management). One never knows the back-story of a trade article, so it is essential to read these sources critically.

### Consider the experiential specificity of streaming

Finally, try wherever possible to account for the distinct viewing and production protocols associated with streaming, as opposed to broadcast or cable/satellite television. Binge-watching a Netflix original is obviously different from watching a series on broadcast television, one weekly episode at a time; and as many commentators have noted, the shift to streaming is also reconfiguring production practices (especially in scriptwriting, where longer narrative arcs and complex storylines are becoming more common).

One consequence of all this is that we often need to adjust our analytical paradigms – for example, presumptions about audience agency, spectatorial engagement, or attention – when analyzing streaming texts. (Having said this, a lot of content that is available on streaming portals was actually produced for broadcast TV, or was produced with both "linear" and "nonlinear" audiences in mind, so it's not a clear-cut issue.) In any case, the practice of televisual textual analysis is changing with the times. When writing about television today it is therefore essential to think carefully about the intended *and* actual reception of the text you're studying, so that you're doing justice to the complexity of your object.

These suggestions are just a starting point, of course. And while I've used Netflix as my main example here, there are hundreds of other streaming services around the world that merit your attention as researchers – many of which pose their own unique methodological and analytical challenges (see, for example, Dovey; Vašíčková and Szczepanik). Whatever angle you take, and wherever your geographic focus lies, there are many fascinating stories to be told about how these portals variously inflect, construct and reconfigure our cinematic and televisual cultures.

## References

Dovey, Lindiwe. "Entertaining Africans: Creative Innovation in the (Internet) Television Space." *Media Industries Journal*, vol. 5, no. 2, pp. 93–110.
Lobato, Ramon. *Netflix Nations: The Geography of Digital Distribution*. New York University Press, 2019.
Lotz, Amanda. *Portals: A Treatise on Internet-Distributed Television*. Maize Books, 2017.
Madrigal, Alexis. "How Netflix Reverse Engineered Hollywood." *The Atlantic*, 2 January 2014, www.theatlantic.com/technology/archive/2014/01/how-netflix-reverse-engineered-hollywood/282679/
Thibault, Ghislain. "Streaming: A Media Hydrography of Televisual Flows." *View: Journal of European Television History and Culture*, vol. 4, no. 7, 2015, http://viewjournal.eu/archaeologies-of-tele-visions-and-realities/streaming/
Vašíčková, Dorota and Petr Szczepanik. "Web TV as a Public Service: The Case of Stream.cz, the East-Central European Answer to YouTube." *Media Industries Journal*, vol. 5, no. 2, pp. 69–91.
Wolff, Michael. *Television is the New Television*. Portfolio/Penguin, 2015.

# 25 Analyzing and writing about credit sequences

*Monika Mehta*

> Investigations of histories of cinema largely rely on archival documents and interviews. While these are important sites for documenting and analyzing cinema's histories, an examination of paratexts such as credit sequences shows that material histories are imprinted on the film. In this chapter, I show that analyses of credit sequences can provide generative insights into film production. Credit sequences are valuable for exploring: linguistic choices, formal elements (for example, visual design), production aesthetics, industrial practices and hierarchies, shooting locations, audience address, and state-regulations. Using examples culled from Bombay cinema, I demonstrate how credit sequences advance our understanding of authorship, production norms of different industries, and film's relationship to nation-building.

Scholarship on paratexts generally and credit sequences more specifically invites us to reflect upon our viewing practices: Where do we begin watching or paying attention to a film? Is it when the film's story begins? Do we fast forward a DVD or skip the introduction on a Netflix show so we can start the screening? Do we walk into a film late to avoid the opening credit sequence and leave as the end credits roll? These choices have implications for what we deem worth watching, and consequently, worth analyzing. In 2004 when I first viewed Benny Torati's film *Kikar Ha-Halomot/Desparado Square* (2001), and even later, in 2006, when I wrote about it, I was engrossed in how the film staged a Tel Aviv neighborhood's love for Hindi films, in particular Raj Kapoor's *Sangam/Confluence* (1964). In 2017, when I screened the film for my graduate course, I had been teaching and researching paratexts such as credit sequences for about five years. This time I paid attention to *Kikar Ha-Halomot/Desparado Square*'s credit sequence where *Sangam* appears not as a sign of love but as a copyright acknowledgment. This industrial pact is rendered in a global English in contrast to a local Hebrew chosen for other production credits. The two languages address differing and unequal linguistic constituencies; while English currently enjoys a global circulation and prominence, the same cannot be said for Hebrew. For me, credit sequences are valuable paratexts that help in examining linguistic choices, formal elements (for example, visual design), production aesthetics, industrial practices and hierarchies, shooting locations, engagement with audiences, and state-regulations. Below, I share what I have learned about Bombay cinema through the analysis of credit sequences and offer guidance about how and why to write about them.

Credit sequences can assist us in engaging with scholarly debates on language and nation-building. After India's Partition in 1947, many Muslim members of the Bombay film industry left for Pakistan, and Hindus who worked in the Lahore film industry arrived in Bombay. Even though in post-Partition India, "Urdu" written in the Nasta'liq script had become Pakistan's official language, and "Hindi" written in the Devanagari served as India's official language, a cursory glance at 1950s Bombay cinema suggests it was unwilling to part with Urdu. Credit sequences provide us an opportunity to compare and reflect on the Indian state and Bombay cinema's relationship to Urdu. For example, the opening credit sequences of 1950s Bombay films show a state issued censorship certificate that uses a Sanskritised Hindi in Devanagari script and administrative English in Roman script. In contrast, the film titles authored by production houses displayed three scripts – Devanagari, Roman, and Nasta'liq scripts (used for writing Urdu) – while the rest of the credits were generally in English in Roman script. A comparative analysis of credit sequences from 1950s and 1990s Bombay cinema reveals that post-economic liberalization and the rise of Hindu nationalism in India in the nineties, the practice of using three scripts had reduced substantially. We can also analyze the role of language in the filmic text in tandem with its use in the credit sequence. In the film *Kaagaz Ke Phool/ Paper Flowers* (Guru Dutt 1959) the protagonist's estranged wife and her parents are steeped in Anglo culture. The film mocks their pretentious ways and shows that they are selfish and uncaring. Interestingly while English and Anglo culture are derided in the text, English production credits written in Roman script sought to cultivate up-market audiences.

Scholarly discussions about production and authorship can be approached through an investigation of credit sequences. We can combine a paratextual analysis of industrial labor in a credit sequence with how such labor is represented in scholarly works and the filmic text. While auteur theory as it emerged in the 1950s enshrined the director as the sole author of the film, credit sequences show that filmmaking is a collaborative effort and not a product of a single person's vision. If films often conceal the labor involved in their production, the credit sequences reveal this labor. Industrial differences among cinemas can also be uncovered via the credit sequences. In the context of Bombay cinema, story, screenplay, and dialogues are often acknowledged separately and considered distinct forms of labor; they can involve two or more people, multiplying authorial imprints. Given that songs are central to Bombay films, the lyricist is an additional writer whose work contributes to the script. The playback singer who records the songs that the actor lip-syncs is also specific to commercial cinemas in India. Song sequences in films attach the playback singer's voice to the actor's body, thus providing us with an ideal body; and the credit sequence makes visible this division of labor. An analysis of how the credits are organized shows that

*Figures 25.1a–b* Images from the credit sequence for *Kaagaz Ke Phool/Paper Flowers* (Guru Dutt, 1959). In the first image, the film's title appears in Roman script. In the second image, the title appears in Devnagari and Nastli'q scripts grouped together. The sequence signals a hierarchy in which English is given priority.

this division generally favors the visual star rather than the aural one. Thus credit sequences alert us to cast and crew hierarchies.

We can also examine industrial, state, and technological shifts via analyses of credit sequences. Below, through an analysis of Zoya Akhtar's debut film, *Luck by Chance* (2009), I track how Bombay cinema transforms post-economic liberalization. Excel Entertainment, a company associated with upscale, urban narratives tailor-made for multiplexes and metro audiences, produced the film. The run-time of the opening and the closing credits in *Luck by Chance* is close to twelve minutes, a substantial amount of time for a feature film. The film opens with a censorship certificate. It shows a change in name from Central Board of Film Censors to Central Board of Film Certification in 1983, gesturing to regulatory as opposed to punitive practices. The certificate reflects a practice introduced in the mid-nineties of featuring names of the examining committee members in Hindi. It also states that the certificate is only for "theatrical films" alerting us to technological shifts – the rise of TV, video, DVD. Next, an image of a Hindu goddess appears. This is fairly standard practice where blessings are invoked for the film's success. Subsequently, a relatively new statement appears, one which emerges in the late 1990s as standard practice: "All characters in this film are imaginary and any resemblance to any person living or dead is purely coincidental." This disclaimer is part of corporate language, included in the credit sequence to avoid lawsuits. It also lends a professional and global sheen to the film as it mimics legal language introduced by Hollywood. Bolstering this, the closing credits duly note the roles of accounting and legal firms and issue copyright acknowledgements. In later credits, brand partners also signal the rise of corporatization. New job designations, including First Assistant Director, Second Assistant Director, Continuity and Wardrobe supervisors, just to name a few, both mimic Hollywood production practices and signal Bombay cinema's efforts to globalize via corporatization. Finally, the opening credits in *Luck by Chance* offer the most moving account of authorship. While the credits in English list the members of cast and crew who are given more importance, and earn both more fame and money, the visuals recognize below-the-line authors – who are generally unnamed and uncredited – for example, the people making the sets, unfurling the film banners, ironing costumes, and styling actors' hair.

The examples that I have given above show that analyses of credit sequences can provide insights into a film's production process. How does one begin such an analysis? For me, it begins with thinking about the kinds of questions that I can ask (see Box 25.1). As I watch a credit sequence, I take notes on the linguistic choices, visual design, the names and titles of the cast and crew involved in the film production, the organization of the credits, and brand and media partnerships. I then follow a comparative approach; for example, I think about linguistic choices in the credit sequence in relation to the film. Do they address different or similar audiences? Finally, I situate my analysis in relation to scholarly work in film and media studies such as authorship debates or theories of transnational cinema. Historically, studies of authorship have focused and venerated the role of the director. In contrast, the credit sequence reveals that many people and varied forms of labor are required to produce a film.

*Figure 25.2* This image from *Luck by Chance* (Zoya Akhtar, 2009) shows billboard painters whose labor is generally not acknowledged in credit sequences. Their image is paired with a well-known actress, Dimple Kapadia, who appears in the film.

*Analyzing and writing about credit sequences* 167

I close with a final methodological point: often materiality is viewed as external to films. Investigations of histories of cinema largely rely on archival documents and interviews. While these are important sites for documenting and analyzing cinema's histories, an examination of paratexts such as credit sequences shows that materiality is imprinted on the film. We just need to extend where we look.

> **Box 25.1**
>
> *Analyzing credit sequences*
>
> 1 Note the language(s) used in the opening and closing credit sequences. Are these sequences subtitled? If so, in what languages? What linguistic, ethnic, class, national or regional audiences are addressed via these languages?
> 2 Compare the languages (s) present in the credit sequences with the one (s) in the film. Are the languages the same or different? Do they address similar and/or different constituencies? How do language(s) function in the film vs. the credit sequences (for example, define characters vs. convey information or imagine audiences)?
> 3 Describe the visual design of the credit sequence (for example, color scheme, font). Does this design complement the film's aesthetic or genre? Does it signal commercial or art cinema sensibilities? What might the credit sequences tell us about the production values of a film?
> 4 How are the opening and closing credit sequences organized? What forms of labor and industrial alliances are listed in these sequences (for example, production alliances, brand partners, actors, editors)? In what order do they appear? Do the order, the visual design, and/or the placement of names in opening or closing credit sequences suggest an industry hierarchy?
> 5 Are the brand-partners mentioned in the credits highlighted or incorporated in the filmic narrative? If so, how? Do they help build the character(s), plot or action? Are these brands undermined in the narrative (for example, a diamond engagement ring being rejected instead of accepted)?
> 6 How do varied forms of labor presented in the credit sequences support, challenge or add to arguments about auteurship and authorship (below-the-line or above the line)?
> 7 Do the opening and closing credits appear against a black screen, stills from the films, or scenes from film? Do sound(s) or soundtracks accompany the closing and opening of the credit sequences? How do sounds and images interact with or impact the credit sequences? Do the visuals and sound interrupt the credit sequence, or, alternately, does the text obscure viewing?
> 8 How do the credit sequences position or imagine audiences – as reading publics, fans, distracted, arriving and/or departing viewers? Compare this with how the film positions and imagines its spectators.
> 9 Note the locations where the film was shot and the crew(s) employed at these different locations. Are these locations local (town, city), national, regional, or transnational? Does the film mention or signal the locations

noted in the credits, or does it present these locations in other ways (for example, a field in Switzerland is presented as a field in India)? Does this information about location support and/or challenge scholarly claims about national and transnational cinema?

10   Note if the credit sequences include acknowledgments, dedications, or copyright information. Do these signal formal or informal industrial alliances?

11   Is a censorship certificate or rating card included in the credit sequence? How does the certificate or rating frame our entry into the film?

12   Do the credits mention the use of special effects or sets? Does this sediment or complicate our understanding of the film's genre? (For example, the use of special effects might support a film's designation as a science fiction film, but complicate its status as a "realistic" drama.)

## References

Akhtar, Zoya. *Luck by Chance*. Big Home Video, 2009.
Dutt, Guru, et al. *Kaagaz Ke Phool*. Eros International, 2004.
Kapoor, Raj. *Sangam*. Shemaroo Video, 2001.
Torati, Benny. *Kikar Ha-Halomot*. Sisu Home Entertainment, 2003.

# 26 "We are not thinking frogs"
## The archive, the artifact, and the task of the film historian

*Katherine Groo*

---

This chapter argues that film archives are sites of mediation and interaction. It makes the case for understanding the practice of film history as one necessarily bound to the close analysis and writing of film archives.

---

The first film archive I ever visited was the American Museum of Natural History (AMNH) in New York City. When I arrived on the first day of my research in the early 2000s, I slipped past the life exhibits of North American mammals and found my way to the fourth floor. There, tucked behind an exhibit on evolution, I found the door to the research library and a different collection of fossils: Betamax tapes and a small viewing room with a dozen or so screening stations, each equipped with a television monitor, a headset, and a player for the tapes. Not all of the technology worked, but I was grateful for the space and the solitude. I was also overwhelmed by the experience. I spent a week studying at the museum during my first visit, huddled in front of a screen, taking notes and drawing images, trying to remember everything I could. During breaks, I would walk the corridors and consider the strangeness of the place, the way that geological time collided with modernity, the way that the institution's iconography of American power – the statue of Theodore Roosevelt that adorns its entrance, for example – intersected with its humble library of plastic tapes and broken screens, the way that the archive hid certain aspects of its colonial history while keeping others on display. I had come to the AMNH to see their ethnographic cinema, but the entire institution demanded to be read. In this chapter, I want to make the case for close reading film archives and including this analytical work in any writing we might do about film history.

The AMNH was the first of many archives I would eventually visit. (Others have included the Library of Congress, the Human Studies Film Archive, the EYE Filmmuseum, the *Centre national du cinéma et de l'image animée*, and the British Film Institute.) While no other was quite like the AMNH, I have never found a standard or "normal" archival institution. Each one has its own idiosyncrasies, from the way it stores and circulates its materials, to the system it uses to classify its collections, to the way it accommodates (or does not accommodate) researchers and their requests, to the technology it relies upon at each step along the way. I have screened prints on a Steenbeck table (a device for editing physical film stock) in a basement and watched digital files in the comfort of my own home; I have handled nitrate with gloves in a temperature-controlled facility and accessed an entire national archive's collection from a computer in a weird soundproof vault. I saw a collection of 35mm films that a wealthy businessman funded, transferred to VHS tapes, inside of the mansion he once called home. I have walked through a forest to get to a bunker of films in cold storage, traveled by ferry to see the most contemporary archival practices, and strolled on foot to screening booths in city libraries.

Each institution has its own history and contemporary culture. Some archives are designed for access. They welcome visitors, keep their catalogues up to date, and open up to scholarly interventions of all kinds. Others are designed with no particular concern for the needs of researchers; they might discourage these kinds of incursions in explicit or implicit ways. Some archives are well funded through private donors, local initiatives, or the national government; others struggle to take care of their collections and keep the doors open. And, of course, archives have directors, each of whom has varying amounts of power to determine what and how they collect, exhibit, and preserve their artifacts.

I encourage students to visit film archives, both online and, if possible, in physical brick-and-mortar spaces. If you are at a college or university, start with your institution's library or special collections. Many cities and towns have municipal archives or historical societies that preserve photographs and films of local interest. Consider also that the remnants of film history are scattered around the world, in unlikely places – not just in big cities. Seek out archives and talk to archivists.[1] Ask them about the history of their institution, their acquisition priorities, and their preservation program (if they have one). How does the archive understand itself and its collections? How does it organize its artifacts? But also ask yourself a few questions. What does the archive look, feel, smell, and sound like? How does the archive address you or frame your experience? Are you allowed to view original documents (an increasingly rare experience)? If not, what formats are available? As an exercise, try to screen the same item in as many different formats as you can. Take notes on these distinct experiences and consider: What is the difference between them? What technologies come between you and an original image or event?

What I began to grasp through my own encounters is that archives are not neutral, inert, or disinterested storage facilities where one goes to discover the material evidence of film history. Archives shape film artifacts *and* our experiences of those artifacts. Each archive makes choices and leaves impressions (through formatting, time stamps, proprietary watermarks, traces of both restoration and neglect). Archives structure our encounter with film history in fundamental ways. In his writing on the archive, philosopher and literary theorist Jacques Derrida argues that, "the archivization produces as much as it records the event," (17). What he means, quite radically, is that the archive is not a receptacle for history, but an active participant in its creation. It does not preserve historical events, but instead *determines* what we can ever know of history. In short, archives make Derrida anxious. They are sites of extraordinary power and they can be tools wielded to control what and how we remember (or fail to remember).

In my own view, the power of the archive is never as simple or monolithic as Derrida imagines. Film archives are complex sites of *mediation*. The archive plays a role in determining what we know about film history, but film artifacts can also *respond* to the archive, do things to it, work upon it. For example, in the Lumière archive – the Lumière brothers were among the very first filmmakers and are especially well known for a handful of early moving images, including a train arriving at the station and a baby being fed her first meal – I came across a set of films that had not circulated outside the institution. In many cases, they were frame-for-frame repetitions of other, more famous films that had been released on DVD or screened as part of a festival program. These films created a strange kind of mirror image. They contradicted the happy images of early twentieth-century family life and leisure that film historians had seen and studied and they pressed against the celebratory mythologies that had framed the Lumière archive for decades. They also made visible the entanglements between early film practice and colonial violence.

Crucially, film historians also interact with film archives. I am using the term "interact" here to signal far more than the mere fact that we visit archives and learn from archivists. Rather, I want to underscore the mutual, two-way encounter between archives and the historian. The task of the film historian is not transcription or reportage. That is, we are not responsible for describing what we find in the archive to those outside of it. We are not neutral observers of the archive, but close readers of it.

In the nineteenth century, historians strove for objectivity and adhered to what was known as a "correspondence theory" of historical practice. The historian was meant to erase themselves from the process of relaying facts about historical events and present those facts, as historian Leopold von Ranke described it, *as they really were*. What underpinned this approach was a belief that there was such a thing as a neutral historical perspective and that historians had a kind of privileged access to the events of the past. At the century's close, philosopher Friedrich Nietzsche rejected this philosophy of history. In an essay titled "On the Use and Disadvantages of History for Life," he argues that history is not discovered, but *made* in the present. Elsewhere, in *The Gay Science*, Nietzsche insists that it is impossible to separate ideas from the body that generates them. His body – including the many physical and mental illnesses it had endured – informs his understanding of the world. He writes, "We are not thinking frogs, nor objectifying and registering mechanisms with their innards removed [...]. Life – that means for us constantly transforming all that we are into light and flame – also everything that wounds us; we simply can do no other," (35–36). Waves of historical thought in the twentieth century demanded not only that we develop a better understanding of the historian as an active participant in the writing of history, but also that we open the field to *other* kinds of bodies and identities.

I understand my own historical practice as belonging to these contemporary critical frameworks. Film history is *always* mediated (by particular minds and bodies, by the archive, and by the artifacts themselves). The task of the film historian is not to conceal those sites of mediation or deny their existence, but understand and critique them, make them visible and available for further thought and reflection. Put another way, the writing of film history requires that we write deeply and carefully about film archives *and* our experiences of them. The practice of history is not only a process of retrieving something of the past, but also a generative, *creative* act of analysis that happens in contemporary institutions – and in the living present. We simply can do no other.

## Note

1 The Journal of Cinema and Media Studies publishes a quarterly roundup of "archival news" online and makes all of its past issues freely available. It is a terrific resource for learning more about contemporary archives. See Navitski, Rielle, editor. "Archival News." *Journal of Cinema and Media Studies*. University of Texas Press, www.cmstudies.org/page/CJ_Archival_past

## References

Derrida, Jacques. *Archive Fever: A Freudian Impression*, translated by Eric Prenowitz, U of Chicago Press, 1995.
Nietzsche, Friedrich. *The Gay Science*, translated by Walter Kaufmann, Vintage, 1974.
Nietzsche, Friedrich. "On the Uses and Disadvantages of History for Life." *Untimely Meditations*, edited by Daniel Breazeale, translated by R.J. Hollingdale, Cambridge UP, 1997, pp. 57–124.

# 27 Show me the data!
## Uncovering the evidence in screen media industry research

*Bronwyn Coate and Deb Verhoeven*

> Data can take many forms, can come from a variety of sources, and can vary in size. In this chapter, we focus on quantitative data and address how "big data" has created a range of new options for evaluating movie and broader industry performance. As a starting point, quantitative data provide the facts or evidence that at a summary level can be used as a reference to describe the state of the world as it stands. However, the use of data can enable further analysis using a range of techniques (such as data visualization) and quantitative methods (such as econometric modelling) to solve real world problems and address issues with policy relevance such as gender equality in the film industry.

Despite being famously characterised by writer William Goldman as an industry about which "nobody knows anything," the use of data has been a persistent feature of decision making in Hollywood. Data can take many forms, can come from a variety of sources, and can vary in size. The advent of "big data" for example, has created a range of new options for evaluating movie performance. Major studios rely on data analytics to assist on a range of decisions such as setting budgets based on the expected market reception, understanding the specific audiences for films in order to fine tune marketing campaigns, and determining the release pattern for films in cinemas. Furthermore, for an industry that has persisted with long-standing gatekeeping practices, data are core to revisionary movements such as #metoo, 5050 by 2020 and TimesUp which use data to produce evidence about the need for demographic and social change within the screen industry.

In this chapter, we focus on quantitative data which in the context of the screen industries can include information about phenomena relevant to the film industry such as films, cinemas, distribution, and attendance. For instance, in undertaking research about a film's theatrical performance, data related to a sample of films in time and space are required, including box office and film characteristics as a starting point. Extended data sources such as the demographic profile of audiences located in a cinema's catchment or public transport data or even climatic data could be relevant to understanding the performance of a particular title in specific times and places.

Data provide the facts or evidence that at a summary level can be used as a reference to describe the state of the world as it stands. At a basic level data are counted and measured to reveal evidence on what exists or that which is observed. Simple descriptive statistics can be used to present the results as percentages and averages which enable the interpretation of the significance of results. However, the use of data can enable a shift beyond simply describing the extent of a problem. Using data, we can, for instance, identify where policy should be focused and how best to intervene. Data can be analyzed using a range of techniques (such as data visualization) and quantitative methods (such as econometric modelling) to solve real world problems, like whether something is likely to happen or not for predictive purposes. Furthermore, innovative techniques combining methods and insights from a range of disciplines are an increasing feature of research exploring the screen industry. For instance, media scholar Jeffrey Klenotic uses geographic information systems and techniques of electronic data manipulation to explore the spatiality of cinema. As another example, in a project with Colin Arrowsmith and Stuart Palmer, we employed dyadic analysis to uncover evidence of reciprocity in film exchanges. The project uses network analysis to visualize a new approach to understanding the drivers of demand between different nations.

With new forms of evidence that are generated from the mathematical, the statistical, and the quantitative, our understanding of the screen industry is changing and also affecting change in the industry. By making transparent what has been previously invisible or obscured, policies designed to improve women's representation within the film industry (as one example) have become more prevalent. For instance, the Swedish film industry addressed gender imbalance by setting quotas for equal gender funding across all productions, with gender funding parity achieved within two and a half years of the policy being first announced. Data providing evidence, metrics, and benchmarks in relation to these types of issues can help make the film industry accountable for its actions and industrial practices.

The rise of big data has also facilitated the interoperability of different datasets. For instance, the Kinomatics Showtime Dataset (www.kinomatics.com) combines principle data regarding individual film screenings with information on film characteristics and specific geographic co-ordinates that capture where actual screenings take place across 44 countries. This enables analysis at different scales including the global, national, and granular levels, down to a specific city or region covered within the data. Through data exploration, it is possible to see where patterns emerge and how differences in scale change what is observed from the data. Insight from the exploration of big data can then inform more specific research questions to be addressed. In this process it may be apparent that further datasets may need to be added in order to sharpen or extend the analysis. For instance, research by Verhoeven, Coate, and Zemaityte (forthcoming) from the Kinomatics project combined data from the Kinomatics Showtime Dataset on screenings of films directed by women with open source data on various socio-economic indicators produced by the World Economic Forum to create cinema gender gap indices across different countries to enable comparability on an equivalized basis.

While evidence and quantifiable data are of high importance, depending upon the problem or issue posed, they won't tell us everything about all the reasons behind the underlying causes. For this, qualitative data may be required. As such the type of data needed depends upon the purpose for which it is to be used and most importantly what the question or problem is that is being addressed. While there has been push-back within parts of the social sciences (see, for example, the book by Meyrick, Phiddian, and Barnett, *What Matters? Talking Value in Australian Culture*) against the use of quantitative data concerning cultural goods such as film, it is not so much a problem with data *per se* but rather how data are used that is critical.

For issues that may be more subjective or involve human judgement such as the artistic quality of film, then rich qualitative data may be more useful than a five-star rating system. However, a broad spectrum of issues concerning the screen industry lend themselves to analysis using quantitative data. It is not the case that one type of data is better than another. In addressing complex real-world problems, such as the issue of piracy faced by the screen industry, both qualitative and quantitative approaches can be complementary to facilitate a deeper understanding. For instance, equipped with quantitative evidence on the extent of piracy, data can be modelled to understand how this impacts films' financial performance at the box office whilst qualitative data collected from individuals who engage in piracy can assist in understanding why piracy occurs in the first place.

A further consideration is that regardless of the type of data, the ability to do good research depends not only on how the methods, be they qualitative or quantitative or a combination of both, are applied but also on the credibility of the data used. With quantitative data, preparing the source data for analysis is a vital step, including cleaning which involves procedures to check data integrity (including its completeness and accuracy) ahead of its quantitative analysis and testing.

For researchers wishing to employ methods and approaches that can provide data-driven evidence, the first step is to identify the data source to be used. For some research this will involve planning in advance to collect the data while in other cases data will be present from open access secondary sources. Good empirical research depends heavily on data quality and integrity as well as the researcher's ability to ask the right questions to draw from the data what is interesting and revealing that may not have been obvious before.

# References

Coate, Bronwyn, Deb Verhoeven, Stuart Palmer and Colin Arroswmith. "Using big cultural data to understand diversity and reciprocity in the global flow of contemporary cinema." *Proceedings of the International Symposium on the Measurement of Digital Cultural Products*. UNESCO Institute for Statistics, 2016.

Goldman, William. *Adventures in the Screen Trade: A Personal View of Hollywood and Screenwriting*. Warner Books, 1983.

Klenotic, Jeffrey. "Using GIS to Explore the Spatiality of Cinema." *Explorations in New Cinema History: Approaches and Case Studies*, edited by Richard Maltby, Daniel Biltereyst, and Philippe Meers, Wiley-Blackwell, 2011, pp. 58–84.

Meyrick, Julian, Robert Phiddian, and Tully Barnett. *What Matters? Talking Value in Australian Culture*. Monash University Publishing, 2018.

Verhoeven, Deb, Bronwyn Coate, and Vejune Zemaityte. "From #metoo to #methree: Re-distributing gender in the global film industry." *Media Industries Journal*, forthcoming.

# 28 Researching and writing across media industries

*Derek Johnson*

> The challenges of writing and research across media industries can be overcome by looking not at the sum of these industry relationships, but instead the *intersections* from which they emerge. By adopting a set of interrelated research and writing strategies, media scholars can transform lists of media *franchises* into more critical assessments of the *franchising* processes through which agency and constraint unfold within and across entertainment industries.

Although it may seem the media industries have become more recently enamored with the idea of leveraging brands and franchises across different platforms, these strategies have proven central to long-term projects of conglomeration and cross-promotion stretching across popular entertainment history. As such, the ability to research and write about relationships among different media industries is a vital skill for both media historians investigating these longstanding institutional articulations and scholars concerned with more contemporary forms of "media convergence" (Jenkins).

Yet this skill proves hard won in existing research on media industries and the ubiquitous franchises that cross these boundaries. Too often, attempts to examine industrial partnerships and convergences operate through lists that catalogue major media conglomerate holdings and cross-reference against the footprints of particular franchise brands. Of course, there *is* great value in understanding, for example, that Disney leverages the *Star Wars* franchise to generate successive product for its film division while also supporting new television series carried on platforms like Disney XD and Disney+. As that web of content spins out even farther to support comic books for subsidiary Marvel Comics, as well as video games and other consumer products, we grasp the scope of Disney's corporate footprint and its reliance on familiar brands to manage the risk of that grandeur. Nevertheless, in equating product offerings with relationships between industries, such lists do not easily reveal the complex interactions and negotiations through which corporate media cultures actually produce these relationships. Rather than a "critical media industry studies" perspective that would be attuned to "particular organizations, agents, and practices within what have become vast media conglomerates operating at a global level" (Havens, Lotz, and Tinic 236), these lists substitute attention to finished product for critical analysis of negotiated industry process.

At the same time, attention to content finely differentiated across different media industry sectors presents additional challenges: to engage in textual or formal analysis of what seems to some like homogenized cultural product, I continue to struggle with a tendency to dive too often into a litany of details in which all but the devoted fan might become easily lost. Moreover, such analysis has required me and many others to think across media each understood through their own disciplines and theoretical underpinnings. In short, writing about media franchising and the relationships they support across industries has presented a significant challenge.

Self-reflexively, I have tried to overcome these challenges by looking not at the sum of these industry relationships, but instead the *intersections* from which they emerge. My first book, *Media Franchising*, explored how the licensing, spin-offs, and global formatting practices that unite television, film, comics, and games have created uneasy negotiations of unequal creativity and power among producers who share corporately-owned intellectual property resources from different industrial positions. Instead of seeing an expression of unified corporate authority, I revealed contestation over cultural reproduction among multiple stakeholders including licensed partners, creators positioning their interpretations against one another, and consumers collaborating in this proliferation of production. In doing so, I helped develop strategies that went beyond measuring single franchises to enable critical assessment of *franchising* processes through which agency and constraint unfold within and across entertainment industries.

First, I prefer to look to the moments of *industrial intertextuality* (Herbert; Hunting and Gray) in which relationships between media sectors are actually produced. Instead of fixed footprints, intertextuality enables a focus on dynamic articulations through which specific media industries become temporarily united in specific historical contexts. Concern for industrial intertextuality helps reveal which of the textual details within arcane franchise worlds actually matter as points of leverage and connection between different institutional forces. As media scholars Kyra Hunting and Jonathan Gray argue, the ad-break interstitials that reference Disney film characters on the Disney Junior cable channel are important not because they evidence Disney's homogenous offerings across media, but instead because they offer a point of connection, a gateway between the original programs and characters in the Disney Junior line-up and the distinct content and marketing appeals offered elsewhere. In my own book, I examine the storytelling practices of television series spun-off from franchises like *Battlestar Galactica* and *Star Trek* to consider how television writers reflect on their own use of a legacy brand and in doing so seek to distance themselves from it. Concern for content produced in these industrial contexts need not be exhaustive or attempt to sketch the full scope of ever-expanding brand mobilization, but can instead zero in on the specific moments in which value and meaning are generated across different media businesses and contexts of production.

Second, concern for ownership needs to be matched with concern for *partnerships* of the sort enabled by licensing agreements and other instruments of collaboration across industries. When I think about relationships across media industries in terms of partnership – even within conglomerate structures of ownership – I find more room to recognize negotiation, struggle, and competition between imperfectly aligned institutional stakeholders. Licensing agreements clearly lay out the uneven terms of industry relationships in the limited rights extended to licensees by licensors; but even different corporate divisions meant to work in "synergy" operate through distinct corporate cultures and unequal claims to status and authority underneath a shared conglomerate umbrella. Examining the structure of Time Warner following its awkward merger with AOL, or Disney's use of "country managers" as part of its global expansion, scholar Simone Murray reveals the emergence of a "silo mentality" in which conglomerate subsidiaries nevertheless stand apart (429). Inspired by this, Media Franchising considers how global media brands like Transformers supported parallel streams of distinct, localized management over decades across Japan, North America, and Europe. While franchise lists convey a unified conglomerate brand, attention to partnership enables perception of the alliances and fissures between these disparate industry forces. Even critics enamored with franchise footprints can recognize that efforts to examine partnership rather than strictly ownership would reveal even wider and more insidious forms of corporate oligopoly.

Attention to the intersections between industries can be achieved thirdly through research methods that consider not just intertextuality, but also the labor of *intermediaries* and *interfaces* that do the work of putting different industries into relation. Research focused on licensing, for example, can productively consider the professional practices, strategies, and identities of licensing agents – much as media scholar Avi Santo does in his investigation of the way intellectual properties like *The Lone Ranger* have been historically managed through licensing firms that wielded creative authority over the character. In *Media Franchising*, I similarly considered the productive power of licensing for companies like Marvel Comics as they sought to recover from bankruptcy at the turn of the century by extending to film studios, game developers, and other companies the right to use their superhero characters. Marvel's current power as a film studio itself thus owes in significant part to the work done in the interim by their licensing partners. As some media creators privileged within conglomerate relations frequently disavow or claim ignorance of coordinated relationships between media industries (preferring to cultivate understanding of their work as individually authored), it is often in the work of brand managers, marketers, and creators in the margins that relations between industries are forged. In an increasingly digital entertainment context, meanwhile, we might consider how new media platforms create productive linkages between different industries, consumers, and products. Filmmakers, for example, can share digital assets with licensed video game creators, and the players of those games can manipulate those same objects and use them to participate in the ongoing production of new media texts and experiences.

Fourth, in investigating the relationships between industries, I find it useful to balance *interdisciplinary curiosity* with attention to *media specificity*. To make sense of all these intersections, I prefer to look at culture industry not so much as a "totality," as Horkheimer and Adorno once described it, but instead as a shifting network of industries operating from distinct traditions, engaged in different practices, and following separate logics of production, distribution, and delivery (Miège). As such, I do not take my non-media-specific identification as a "critical media industry" scholar as license to sidestep specialized expertise in film studies, television studies, new media studies, comic studies, game studies, et cetera. I believe we can engage with each of these disciplines to explain how the relations between industries feed upon and extend the diverse media cultures examined in each. That engagement must simultaneously reach beyond the boundaries of any one media research tradition in order to identify the forces in operation across them all. At the same time, our research and writing can look productively beyond the boundaries of media studies strictly defined to consider the industrial relationships shared with consumer products companies, logistics, banking and finance, and other industries outside the scope of the media screen.

Finally, but perhaps most importantly, the researcher examining media culture across industries must foreground the stakes of that investigation. Our tendency toward list making and mapping runs the risk of becoming descriptive, where it is no longer clear why the footprint revealed ultimately matters. For a truly "critical media industry studies" to emerge, I believe we should attune ourselves, as media scholars Havens, Lotz, and Tinic suggest, to the potential contradictions at work in industry practice, and "more importantly, what implications these practices – and the texts they generate – hold in terms of larger social and cultural processes of representation and power" (249). The point of studying the relationships between media industries is not to catalogue the unfettered reach of media franchises and other ubiquitous brands, but instead to reveal at specific institutional intersections the dynamic struggle over meaning, identity, and the capacity to participate in the reproduction of culture. Scholars like Suzanne Scott thus provide useful models in their critical interrogation of the power dynamics whereby media industry convergences empower some producers and consumers while marginalizing others. Her investigation of the "fake geek girl" shows us how industries that imagine media franchising as a way to capture privileged male consumers participate in the boundary-policing that constructs female fandom as inauthentic, marginal, and unwelcome. In this way, the study of media franchising as a point of collision between industries can go beyond list-making to reveal the political struggles negotiated within and produced at these industrial intersections.

## References

Horkheimer, Max and Theodor Adorno. "The Culture Industry: Enlightenment as Mass Deception." *Media and Cultural Studies: Keyworks*, 2nd edn, edited by Meenakshi Gigi Durham and Douglas Kellner, Wiley, 1944/2012, pp. 53–75.

Havens, Tim, Amanda Lotz, and Serra Tinic. "Critical Media Industry Studies: A Research Approach." *Communication, Culture & Critique*, vol. 2, 2009, pp. 234–253.

Herbert, Daniel. *Film Remakes and Franchises*. Rutgers UP, 2018.

Hunting, Kyra and Jonathan Gray. "Disney Junior: Imagining Industrial Intertextuality." *From Networks to Netflix: A Guide to Changing Channels*, edited by Derek Johnson, Routledge, 2018, pp. 197–207.

Jenkins, Henry. *Convergence Culture: Where Old and New Media Collide*. New York University Press, 2006.

Johnson, Derek. *Media Franchising: Creative License and Collaboration in the Culture Industries*. New York University Press, 2013.

Miège, Bernard. "The Logics at Work in the New Cultural Industries." *Media, Culture & Society*, vol. 9, no. 3, 1987, pp. 273–289.

Murray, Simone. "Brand Loyalties: Rethinking Content within Global Corporate Media." *Media, Culture & Society*, vol. 27, no. 3, 2005, pp. 415–435.

Santo, Avi. *Selling the Silver Bullet: The Lone Ranger and Transmedia Brand Licensing*. University of Texas Press, 2015.

Scott, Suzanne. *Fake Geek Girls: Fandom, Gender, and the Convergence Culture Industry*. New York University Press, 2019.

# 29 The value of surprise
## Ethnography of media industries

*Tejaswini Ganti*

---

This chapter discusses ethnography both as a method of doing research about media industries, as well as a style of writing to present one's findings. It details how anthropologists use the term ethnography – both as a specific research practice and a representation of that research – and discusses the various insights offered by an ethnographic approach to the study of media industries. Ethnography grounds the study of media in a specific time and space and offers insights into the processes, possibilities, and constraints of media production that are not apparent from close readings of media texts or analysis of macro-level data about media institutions and commercial outcomes. It also describes the aims of ethnographic writing, which are to animate and make alive a particular sociocultural world for the reader.

---

In the summer of 2014, in the course of conducting research about the relationship between English and Hindi in the Bombay film world, I interviewed the head of a dubbing studio in India about the process of dubbing English-language content such as American television shows and Hollywood films into Hindi. After our interview, Meena (a pseudonym) gave me a tour of the studios and in passing mentioned that they not only dubbed American content into Hindi, but also periodically dubbed Chinese films into Hindi. Intrigued, I asked, "Wow, so you have some writers on staff who know Mandarin?" She replied, "No," so needless to say I was even more intrigued. "So, you find someone in the city who knows the language?" She said, "No, sometimes we get a synopsis of the film and then work from that, but if not, we just watch the film many times to figure out the story and then write the dialogues." She then proudly showed me a few minutes of a film in which they had done exactly that – the 1983 Hong Kong action, sports, comedy film – *The Champions* (Brandy Yuen). While I have no idea what the original dialogues must have said, the Hindi dialogues seemed pretty convincing in terms of matching the actions on screen.

Citing sociologist Paul Willis, cultural studies scholar Ien Ang states that the value of ethnography for researchers is, "a commitment to submit ourselves to the possibility of 'being surprised,' of reaching knowledge not prefigured in one's starting paradigm (1991: 50)." Over two decades of doing ethnographic fieldwork about the Hindi film industry, better known as "Bollywood," I have been surprised numerous times. Some of these surprises, like my opening example, have to do with production practices. Others have to do with social relations; for example, the density of kinship networks and endogamy within the industry made me resort to drawing kinship diagrams to keep track of how everyone was related. And others emerge from business practices, such as the fact that commercial outcomes are hard to track and verify.

In this chapter, I discuss ethnography both as a method of doing research about media industries and as a style of writing to present one's findings. For example, I have conducted ethnography within the Hindi film industry, which meant I spent long periods of time observing filmmaking, interviewing and interacting with members of the film industry, and even participating in some production activities. I have written an ethnography, *Producing Bollywood*, which examines the social world and production culture of the Hindi film industry and the changes wrought by processes of economic liberalization and new technologies of distribution and exhibition over the course of a decade (Ganti 2012b).

While I have interviewed hundreds of people over the course of my research about Hindi filmmaking, ethnography does not solely involve interviewing people. Instead, it is centrally about paying attention to what anthropologist Bronislaw Malinowski referred to as the "imponderabilia of everyday life," which is best achieved through long-term, sustained participant-observation (1984: 20). Spending time observing daily life at the sites of media production provides an important contextual frame for understanding media producers' self-representations and discourses about their practice. Paying attention to what people do, in addition to what they say, illuminates industry norms and expectations about appropriate or desirable practice. For example, early in my fieldwork I was quite surprised by the tremendous ambivalence with which many Hindi filmmakers viewed the song and dance sequences which are such a distinctive feature of popular Indian cinema. While filmmakers in their interviews consistently emphasized the absolute cultural and commercial indispensability of lip-synch song sequences for popular cinema, I noticed how they also frequently lamented and complained about their necessity during scripting sessions and informal conversations. I observed that rather than being an unquestioned feature of Hindi cinema, song sequences were often sites of tension, debate, and intense negotiation among members of the film industry (Ganti 2012a).

A short-term or "parachuting" approach to research can also make one miss or ignore important features of the production culture of a media industry because they may initially seem irrelevant to the "real work" of production. When I first started doing fieldwork in Mumbai, it took me some time to realize that the pre-production process mostly involved brainstorming or discussion sessions referred to as "sittings" between the director and key members of the production team when the script and music are finalized. Sometimes these sessions, especially those involving the film's narrative in the early stages, were so casual and meandering that I didn't realize that "work" was taking place. For example, one afternoon I was waiting in a producer's office while a screenwriter and director were talking about how to represent most accurately the behavior of college students in their screenplay. The conversation began with a discussion of some young film stars and their sartorial preoccupations, then detoured through the writer and director's own college years, continued with the conservatism of contemporary Indian teenagers, followed by the problem with Hindu priests, and ended with the British suffragette movement, before returning to the topic of characterization and setting for their screenplay!

Ethnography, furthermore, grounds the study of media in a specific time and space and offers insights into the processes, possibilities, and constraints of media production that are not apparent from close readings of media texts or analysis of macro-level data about media institutions and commercial outcomes. A focus on the processes and practices of production allows us to look beyond the instances of "success" – those films or shows that do get completed and distributed in some manner – since many films or television shows do not progress beyond a conceptualization or pilot stage, and some are abandoned halfway. Such "failures" also add to our knowledge about media production, offering productive insights and possibilities for theorizing about cinema and other media forms. I observed several instances where Hindi filmmakers attempted to adapt Hollywood films but decided not to follow through because they determined that Indian audiences would not be receptive to specific themes or plots (Ganti 2002).

As ethnographic analysis is inductive, generating assertions and conclusions based on the context being studied and the perspectives of the researcher's interlocutors, ethnographic writing aims to animate and make alive a particular sociocultural world for the reader. While I frequently use anecdotes as I did at the beginning of this chapter, in *Producing Bollywood*, I decided to experiment and wrote a chapter that aimed to provide a "thick description" (Geertz 1973) of an average day on a Hindi film set in order to impart the spirit and essence of the working style of Hindi filmmakers, as well as to bring to light prominent characteristics of the industry's structure and organization. I wrote this chapter in a narrative style, incorporating dialogue and conversations. I had three objectives with such a rendering: to make the quotidian life of film production palpable for readers; to provide the foundation for understanding prominent discourses of change and progress that were addressed in subsequent chapters; and to convey how one can discern valuable social and cultural insights through participant-observation on a film set.

Even though the chapter is written in a narrative style, it is no less analytical than the other chapters in the book, as ethnographic writing is also governed by very specific choices and inclusions and exclusions. I decided to create a composite portrait of a typical day on a film set drawing from my observations of a variety of film shoots rather than one particular instance. Creating a composite required me to make decisions; each character and conversation was created and chosen to convey specific points about the structure and working style of the Hindi film industry. The chapter illustrates some of the main features of the work culture of the Hindi film industry: the prevalence of face-to-face interactions; the significance of kinship as a source of talent; the set as a meeting space; the value of orality and reliance on memory rather than written records; and very visible manifestations of hierarchy. It also puts forth the flexibility – the ability to make impromptu decisions, the capacity to adapt to uncertainty, and a willingness to change the course of action – that is characteristic of Hindi filmmaking. Additionally, it portrays conversations about audiences, commercial outcomes, and Hollywood that are significant components of the industry's "production-talk," which provides insights into the prevailing ideologies of production and self-representations of the industry. Finally, it depicts the presence of Hindu rituals which have become incorporated into production routines, as well as the tremendous diversity – regional, linguistic, religious – of members of the film industry.

An ethnographic approach to studying and writing about mass media will focus on people, practices, and social relations rather than media texts or technologies (Ginsburg 1994). Viewing media makers or media audiences as complex beings who seek and make meaning through practices of production, distribution, or consumption involves paying attention to how they represent and characterize their practices, tastes, likes and dislikes. Such an attention to people and practice will always lead to the possibility of being surprised.

## References

Ang, Ien. *Living Room Wars: Rethinking Media Audiences for a Postmodern World.* Routledge, 1991.
Ganti, Tejaswini. "And Yet My Heart Is Still Indian: The Bombay Film Industry and the (H)Indianization of Hollywood." *Media Worlds: Anthropology on New Terrain*, edited by Faye D. Ginsburg, Lila Abu-Lughod, and Brian Larkin, U of California Press, 2002, pp. 281–300.
Ganti, Tejaswini. "No Longer a Frivolous Singing and Dancing Nation of Movie-Makers: The Hindi Film Industry and its Quest for Global Distinction." *Visual Anthropology*, vol. 25, no. 4, 2012a, pp. 340–365.
Ganti, Tejaswini. *Producing Bollywood: Inside the Contemporary Hindi Film Industry.* Duke UP, 2012b.
Geertz, Clifford. *The Interpretation of Cultures.* Basic Books, 1973.
Ginsburg, Faye. "Culture/Media: A (Mild) Polemic." *Anthropology Today*, vol. 10, no. 2, 1994, pp. 5–15.
Malinowski, Bronislaw. *Argonauts of the Western Pacific.* Waveland Press, 1984.

# 30 Listen up!
## Interviewing as method

*Alicia Kozma*

> This chapter examines ethnographic interviews as a critical method in production studies. Since writing and analysis from ethnographic interviews is heavily dependent on the research design of the study, the chapter reviews the process for constructing a project based on ethnographic interviews. Once this has been established, the chapter works through writing with other people's words and the place for the researcher within that process. To do so the chapter uses examples from an ethnographically-based project in production studies.

Movies are not magic, despite what film industries would lead you to believe (Sullivan 39). Movies – and their production, distribution, and exhibition – are the result of the collective efforts of a wide network of people. Uncovering those networks, their structures, and their implications, is the work of production studies. This type of cinematic research looks behind, rather than in front of, the screen to articulate the industrial system that produces cinematic texts. As such, production studies can necessitate alternative research and writing processes. One of the most valuable of these is the ethnographic interview. Ethnographic interviews give you the perspective of the living participants in and observers of your object of study, giving wholistic context and scope to changes within the production, distribution, and exhibition of filmic culture (Banks 547).

I use ethnographic interviews to uncover and map the changes in the neo-arthouse movie theater industry in the U.S., particularly how women's labor is constituted within it. Exhibition as a whole is understudied within cinema studies, and contemporary exhibition landscapes and practices doubly so. Theatrical exhibition has undergone major, rapid change since Hollywood fully embraced the digital turn. As a result, if I want to know how contemporary art house theaters are operating and what the work lives of their staff are like, I have to ask them. While it seems like a shockingly simple solution, it is a rare method in cinema studies; so careful research and writing procedures should be followed to make your work legible to the field.

When you write about screen media using ethnographic interviews, your research method is a critical component of your writing strategy; it drives all of your writing and the analyses contained therein. Careful planning and execution are paramount. There are three types of ethnographic interviews: oral history, personal narrative, and topic interview. Oral histories recount the way a sociohistorical moment is reflected in the life of a person who lived through it, personal narratives provide an individual's perspective of an event or experience, and topic interviews are someone's point of view on a particular subject (Madison 26). These three interview types naturally overlap. I use topic interviews (labor in neo-art house theaters) combined with personal narratives (specific women's experiences working in neo-art house theaters) on a microethnographic scale, which focuses on a shorter research period and a singular institution (the neo-art house industry itself). Your choice of interview type depends on the issue you are investigating.

The first step in this type of work is gaining approval for your study through your Institutional Review Board (IRB). The IRB is a group of people at your institution that ensures that research with human subjects is ethically composed and carried out. They protect the participants in your study from any harm that may come to them as a result of their participation. For ethnographic interviews, this means that your interview subjects have informed consent around their rights as study participants. This includes informing them of your rationale for the study, the types of information you want to collect from them, and what you plan on doing with that information (for example, writing conference presentations or journal articles), Most importantly, informed consent explains the process of anonymity to your subjects. Anonymity ensures that subjects won't face retaliation of any type as a result of speaking with you. For my study, which asked women about their work lives, this meant that anything negative they said about their theater, colleagues, or bosses couldn't be connected to them or threaten their employment in any way. I obscured their names using pseudonyms and their theater's geographic locations by dividing the county into broad segments (for example, a theater in the East or a theater in the Midwest). I also further anonymized their theater by giving them generic false names. This practice let my participants know that they could be as open and free in speaking to me as they liked. Anonymity is the key to truthful interviews. Your IRB application is also the place where you will fully define your interview questions. Interviews can be structured, semistructured, or unstructured. I use semistructured interviews because it allows me to ask questions I think are pertinent while also letting the interviewee share information I may not have thought to ask about. Your questions and interview structure should also serve to answer the question: "What type of data do I need?"

Once you have obtained IRB approval your next – and most important – step is recruiting your interview participants. I recruited my participants by cold emailing 50 women who worked at all organizational levels in neo-art houses. In my email, I outlined who I was, the project I was working on, the process for maintaining anonymity, and how I was proposing to interview them. Importantly, I included a link to my faculty profile on my institution's website, so they were able to see that I was a real person who really did work in cinema studies! Everyone is credentialed in different ways. Students can send information on faculty mentors; independent scholars, journalists, bloggers, etc. can send links to their established work; artists can send links to their portfolio. In determining what credentials to send ask yourself: "what will show this person my legitimate involvement in this project?" Your answer will be your credentials.

I also asked the participants I recruited to pass on information about me and my project to others they thought may be interested in participating. Being honest and open about what you are looking for and establishing your credibility as a researcher form the best approach to recruitment. Interviews can be conducted in person, over the phone, through email or chat application, or via video message service, but they should always be recorded in some format, either an audio/visual recording or handwritten notes. Your process for recording interviews and for allowing participants to exert their rights over the recording will be outlined in your IRB application.

Once you have conducted your interviews you need to transcribe and selectively code your data. Transcription ensures you have an accurate written record of the conversation to supplement your recording. Coding data allow you to categorize independent variables (for example, demographics and geographies). You can code the interview itself, although you don't have to do so. I chose to code the demographic and financial data I collected in my study and to use the interview text itself as a qualitative context for my quantitative coded data. Your final stage is answering your research question by *writing through your results*. This process relies on the idea of grounded theory – developing answers to your research questions through the data you have gathered. Your analysis and conclusions must come from the interview data you've collected; let the data guide your writing process. During transcription and coding, you will notice recurring themes, ideas, contexts, and questions. Use these trends to answer your research question.

This may be a new analytic process for you. Often when we write about screen media we take an object, form a hypothesis around that object, and use our writing and analysis to prove our stated thesis. Writing from ethnography demands that you let the data, as representative of your interview subjects, guide your writing. The writing process requires you to be open to the data, wherever it may take you. You may end up changing your hypothesis or your assumed conclusions, and that's ok! For example, when I was working on my project, I had assumed that the women I interviewed would be concerned about not getting credit for the work they did at their jobs and that their concern would cause tension with their employers. But as I transcribed and reviewed my data, I realized that my assumption was not a reality for my interview subjects, so I had to remove that assumption from my writing.

The point of conducting ethnographic interviews as a production studies method is to expose those corners of the film industry that remain hidden or clouded in secrecy by signal boosting the voices of the people who do the work day in and day out. To do so means their voices – not the voice of the researcher – must be amplified in the written text. Writing through ethnographic data means letting your scholarly ego and preconceived notions go and letting the data you have collected weave your research, analytic, and written path. By doing so you have the opportunity to shed light on unexplored areas of the film industry while giving voice to those people who help maintain it every day.

## References

Banks, Miranda. "Oral History and the Media Industries." *Cultural Studies*, vol. 28 no. 4, 2014, pp. 545–560.

Madison, D. Soyini. *Critical Ethnography: Method, Ethics, & Performance*. Sage, 2005.

Sullivan, John L. "Leo C. Rosten's Hollywood: Power, Status, and the Primacy of Economic and Social Networks in Cultural Production." *Production Studies: Cultural Studies of Media Industries*, edited by Vicki Mayer, Miranda J. Banks, and John Thornton Caldwell, Routledge, 2009, pp. 39–53.

## 31 The need for translation
Difference, footnotes, hyperlinks

*Tijana Mamula*

> This chapter is built around two closely related and only apparently contradictory observations: one, that translation matters; two, that it should not be trusted. Starting from that dual premise, it asks the question: How can screen media scholarship make more room for linguistic difference both through and within the practice of translation? A notion often voiced in the field of translation studies is that footnotes are the death of a translation. By adding a footnote, you distance the text from its original form, you contaminate it. But doesn't that contamination need to exist, and to be made explicit? The move to digital publishing is opening countless possibilities for the inclusion of notes, asides and links to all manner of written and audiovisual material, far exceeding the purview of the traditional footnote. Rather than denigrating the footnote as the death of translation, then, this chapter urges the young scholar to embrace the death of the footnote itself and its rebirth in the form of the hyperlink – where both of these are understood as metaphors for difference.

It has been a few years now since scholars began to notice the dearth of translation and the overwhelming reliance on critical writing of Anglophone origin in the field of screen and media studies. We have begun to reflect on this lack, calling for the production of more translation and for the acceptance of the practice of translation as a legitimate academic activity in its own right – in much the same way that literary translation is held in high regard in the field of language and literature studies. In many ways, this renewed interest in translation is linked to the field's growing concern with the ways that transnational and multilingual dynamics have shaped the history of screen media and continue to affect their development.[1] In addition to responding to the world's ever increasing globalization, these are all indicators of a desire to invite *linguistic difference* into screen media production and scholarship.

My reflections here align with that trend, and this chapter hinges on two closely related, and only apparently contradictory, observations: one, that translation matters; two, that it should not be trusted. Starting from these two ideas, and moving anecdotally, I consider how we can make more room for linguistic difference both through and within the practice of translation. I also ask how we can think the inherent value of translation as something that provides access to that difference rather than serving to eradicate it.

Several months ago, I attended a translation workshop where a long debate developed about how to translate into a foreign language a sample English text dealing with the traditional British "Sunday lunch." A substantial block of participants felt that in many cases it would be not only justified but necessary to translate the word "Sunday" itself into another day, such as "Friday," since for many cultures Sunday is not a day of rest. In order to make the text comprehensible to a foreign audience whose day of rest and familial congregation is another day, such as Friday – the thinking went – the text would have to be changed into one dealing with the British "Friday lunch." The facility with which this sample text was emptied of foreignness and difference, albeit hypothetically, troubled me deeply. Yet I also recognized that it is not uncommon practice. In Italy, for example, which has a long and robust tradition of dubbing all imported films and television shows into Italian, foreign cultural references are very often replaced with Italian ones. Thus, an American sitcom joke about, say, a Chevy might become one about a Fiat; Nina Simone might transfigure into Mina; "Silvio Berlusconi" might stand in for "Rupert Murdoch." Whether a specific reference is too obscure to be given to the audience *untranslated* is up to the individual translator to decide. But the general approach to translation is industry-wide, and – the difficulty of translating humor notwithstanding – the eradication of linguistic and cultural difference that it promotes is a systemic problem.

At the workshop, the debate on the British Pick-your-own-day lunch brought up translation theorist Lawrence Venuti's famous distinction between "domestication" and "foreignization," which might be best understood as less of a dichotomy than a *spectrum* along which translators position themselves. In Venuti's sense, turning a Škoda into a Ford would domesticate it; keeping it a Škoda would foreignize it; saying something like "a well-known Czech consumer car" – at the risk of sounding at once pedantic and unfaithful to the original – would sit somewhere along the spectrum, neither at one extreme nor the other. It is clear that, when viewed from the perspective of a systemic need to allow more foreignness into English-language screen media studies, foreignization denotes – as it already did for Venuti, who describes the choice as an *ethical* one – a position of greater openness that leaves far more room for change.

The difficulty that often arises in opting for either domestication or foreignization without commenting on the choice led us workshop participants to discuss another notion often voiced about translation: namely, and problematically, that footnotes are the death of it. In other words, to note how and why something is not *directly translatable* means to have failed in your task as translator. Why? Because by adding a footnote, or some other kind of translator's note, you distance the text from its original *form*, you contaminate it. But doesn't that contamination need to exist, and to be made explicit? We also say that things get "lost in translation." More often, though, what really happens is that they get *buried* by the demand that the two forms – of the original and the translation – coincide, and by the avoidance of the footnote to which this gives rise.

I am an avid reader of poetry. Like most readers of poetry, therefore, I have had plenty of occasions to notice and reflect on the fact that translated poetry is often published alongside the original text. In Italian, we call this *testo a fronte*: the two versions literally facing each other, page to page. The reasons for this are not difficult to grasp. It is widely accepted that the genre's formal constraints – issues of rhyme and meter and so on – make it particularly difficult to translate. Poetry translation often pits form against content in a way that comports the loss of either one or the other: you sacrifice a line's rhyme to retain its meaning, or keep its assonance at the cost of its sense. As a result, translated poetry allows at once for an absolute elimination of foreignness, where translations become adaptations or "versions," and for its irreducible presence, the *testo a fronte* like a giant footnote, declaring and explicating the original's otherness with respect to the translation. In other words, the imperative to con*form* in poetry translation is so binding, and so impossible, that it automatically leaves the door open to some necessary intrusion of foreignness and admission of untranslatability.

This is not so, alas, in most non-fiction writing, where content tends often (though by no means always) to take the lead. The assumption is that, with the binding *form* out of the picture, we can do away with the foreignness too: that we do not need the footnote. In the context of screen media, it is especially significant that traces of the translator's intervention have also, traditionally, been absent from moving image distribution. The nature of a theatrical film projection or a VHS subtitle track is such that it simply allows no space for anything resembling a "footnote."

Very recently, I happened to watch the movie *Annihilation* (Alex Garland, 2018) on Netflix with my mother. We had the audio set to Italian, so that my mother (a Serbian woman whose main second language is Italian, though she speaks another three besides) could follow it more easily, but we had also forgotten to disable the Italian subtitles. Both the dubbed dialogue and the subtitles were therefore in Italian. And yet they were completely different. While my mother conjectured as to why, I (a native Serbian who has spent half her life in Italy but speaks English best of all) kept on going back and forth between the translations, trying to gauge which one was closer to the original English, or indeed to reconstruct the English based on the discrepancies between the two. After a few minutes we both remembered that, of course, the dubbing would have been more radically transformed to synchronize with the actor's lip movements. But the process was instructive. Although the dubbing's imperative to synchronize took it further from the original, the subtitles too were skewed by length constraints: with the exception of very short sentences, subtitled dialogue is always compressed and synthesized with respect to the original (a general rule of thumb is that subtitled text should linger on the screen for the length of time it takes you to read it *twice*; which is longer than it takes an actor to say the same thing). Each veering from the original in different ways and for different reasons, the dubbing and the subtitles acted something like mutual footnotes. By confronting the two versions, I was able to access the original English in a way that the exclusive presence of only one version – no footnote to keep it in check or explicate its choices – would have foreclosed.

Which brings my argument to a head. The landscape of screen media production, consumption, and studies is in the process of being radically transformed. The move from print to digital publishing is opening countless possibilities for the inclusion of versions, notes, asides, links to other translations and other writings, to dictionary definitions, Wikipedia entries, Google searches, and all manner of audiovisual material, that far exceed the purview of the traditional footnote. At the same time, my Netflix experience is only the mildest example of the translational heterogeneity being written into online screen media distribution. From YouTube's automatically-generated closed captioning, to Viki's user-generated subtitles – a collectivity of translators for any one text, with all the inherent difference that comports – to the comments sections embedded in both the format and the culture of so many video and streaming platforms, contemporary screen media translation is radically diverging from the univocal, top-down, translator-to-audience systems of theatrical and home video distribution. Rather than talk about the footnote as the death of translation, then, we might consider the death of the

Figures 31.1a–b Images from *Annihilation* (Alex Garland, 2018) with Italian subtitles presented by Netflix

footnote itself and the birth, instead, of the hyperlink – where both of these, as should be clear by now, are understood as metaphors for *difference*.

In the broadest terms, therefore, my advice to the young scholar of screen media would be this: if, like me, you are multilingual, then use your knowledge of different languages to translate as much and as widely as possible, and, of course, to make a habit of consulting non-Anglophone sources. And if you do not speak more than one language, then open yourself to linguistic difference in other ways. This might mean learning another language *just* well enough to read or watch what you need to in it, but not necessarily. It could also mean consulting multiple translations of a single work when the original is inaccessible to you (I recently met a Hegel scholar who did not read German but had, to compensate, read and compared every English translation of Hegel ever published); or embracing subtitled, foreign-language films; or considering the ways that various screen media and critical writing produced *in* English by *non-native* English speakers is, in its increasing global presence and popularity, transforming the contemporary mediascape and indeed the English language itself. It can even just mean talking (or chatting) about the media that interests you with people who have different linguistic perspectives on it.

More specifically, though, what I want to say is: exhume the buried footnote; draw out the hidden hyperlink. Whatever your role in a given moment – whether you are acting as a reader, viewer, or writer – imagine always that at the end of every translated sentence there stands an invisible or potential *translator's note*; an unspoken trace of linguistic difference. So, use the technology that you have literally at your fingertips to cross-reference and *materialize* that trace. Today, the writer's tools are no longer just pen and paper, and a text's home is hardly ever only (and often not at all) a self-contained physical object of restrictive size and weight. The computers, tablets, smartphones and e-readers that we use to read, view, and write are part of an infinitely expansive network of people, objects, and events that cannot be disentangled from linguistic difference – from their existence within and in relation to a world in which multiple languages are constantly used. To mobilize that network in your experience or production of translation means to relate to the world *as multilingual*. It also means to assume not just an openness towards translation much needed in the field of screen media scholarship, but also an active role in the shift away from the monolingual paradigm.[2]

## Notes

1 Lisa Patti and I have both been engaged in this line of research for quite some time. See, for example, our co-edited collection, *The Multilingual Screen: New Reflections on Cinema and Linguistic Difference*, which offers a wide-ranging sample of writings on the subject.
2 On the subject of multilingualism's centuries-long conflict with the monolingual paradigm, see Yasemin Yildiz's influential book *Beyond the Mother Tongue: The Postmonolingual Condition*.

# References

Mamula, Tijana, and Lisa Patti, editors. *The Multilingual Screen: New Reflections on Cinema and Linguistic Difference*. Bloomsbury Academic, 2016.
Venuti, Lawrence. *The Translator's Invisibility: A History of Translation*. Routledge, 1995.
Yildiz, Yasemin. *Beyond the Mother Tongue: The Postmonolingual Condition*. Fordham UP, 2012.

*Forms and formats*

# 32 Words and more
## Strategies for writing about and with media

*Virginia Kuhn*

> In this chapter I call for explicit attention to the formal qualities of the critical essay itself, as well as to the form of the media being reviewed. Verbal language remains the main critical mode; as such, I focus on the rhetorical use of text on the page, on screen, and in video. Reviewing and revising our critical structures can push back against some of the logocentrism and linearity of current institutional modes, encouraging polyvocality and a respect for alternative ways of knowing. Screen literacy requires the ability to both consume and produce meaning; writing with media is key to writing about it.

Over the years my work has taken many forms and has engaged numerous subjects, but it is always premised on the notion that being fluent in a particular language – whether verbal, visual, or aural – requires not only the ability to consume meaning, but also to produce it. We might refer to this as *decoding* and *encoding*, or simply, *reading* and *writing*. The underlying contention is that in order to fully appreciate the rhetorical choices that went into a text's construction, you must be forced to confront those choices yourself. As such, I define contemporary literacy as competent control of the available semiotic resources. At a fundamental level, this means being aware of the possibilities and constraints of composing in a particular medium or authoring platform, since these affordances shape what can be expressed within its confines. Here, for instance, I have a set number of words and a finite number of images available since there is a hard copy component of the platform, a book. Images are still quite costly to print, so I must be judicious in their use.

Digital platforms offer different possibilities; they have expanded the palette of resources, allowing the integration of sound, image, and movement in addition to words. As such, screen-based media, whether time-based like video, or spatially-oriented such as a website, demand a different set of considerations. And even as most platforms are either word-friendly or media-friendly (but seldom both), and even as they are nearly always in flux, there are a few guiding principles for writing about and in these environments. In what follows then, I address some general strategies for writing *about* screen-based media as well as a few more specific approaches to writing *with* it. These latter considerations may not seem immediately useful in your own compositions, but they can help with assessing the rhetorical effectiveness of media on the screen. I confine these remarks to the use of verbal language in print and screen-based media. Sound and image are important registers to consider, especially given their impact on representation and identity formation – issues that are not well understood. That said, verbal language remains the dominant form of critical inquiry and its use is radically altered in screen media, so words are the main focus here.

## Words in analogue media

Writing in physical formats (on paper) is fairly reified structurally, and the standard critical essay tends to proceed linearly: introduction, thesis statement, evidence, conclusion. Of course, this structure is not intractable, but expository prose is seen as objective and critically distanced, so tends not to deviate in form. This is shifting gradually, and the last few years have seen wider acceptance of non-hierarchical formats in favor of those that are more associational or database driven, due largely to the advent of digital archives. Early projects such as Soft Cinema, Labyrinth, Hypermedia Berlin, and the Perseus project were outliers. The signal of the wider acceptance of the database format is indicated by the Modern Language Association's support for the "Digital Pedagogy in the Humanities" project – a database of curated curricular materials organized around more than 50 keywords. Further, there is an increasing appreciation of the fact that the standard print-based essay can prove limiting when trying to write about contemporary media which are ever more structurally complex.

Decisions about how to structure a critical essay should be intentional, defensible, and articulable, with the formal elements serving the conceptual goals. When adopting an unconventional structure that will be unfamiliar to readers, it is wise to be explicit about its purpose and shape. I used this approach in a chapter I authored for an anthology I also co-edited titled *Future Texts: Subversive Performance and Feminist Bodies*. The essay offers a critical reading of *Sucker Punch* (2011, Zach Snyder), a feature length film that consists of live action footage and copious visual effects, punctuated by game-like sequences. These game sequences intrude on the main narrative and offer another plane of diegetic reality until the viewer is uncertain which is which. Because the form is so crucial to the content of the film, I struggled before finding a format that would suit my reading of the film and explained the structure early on in the essay as follows:

> Given the multidimensionality of *Sucker Punch* – it is part action film, part video game, part anime, and part music video – it is difficult to do it service in a conventionally formatted linear essay. To mitigate this difficulty and enact its key ideas, this essay's structure invokes the concept of layering:

Using three levels that mirror the type of *leveling up* one does in video games, each layer attempts to add depth and nuance to the larger concepts.
(Kuhn 2016, 3)

By disclosing these formal decisions and the reasons behind them, I hope to communicate the key concepts of my analysis, regardless of the relative success of the structure.

## Words on screen: chunking text and leading the eye

Generally speaking, writing for the screen differs from the page because the screen's light and concomitant eyestrain are considerations. Sans serif fonts are best on screen. The serifs – those little barbs on letters – are useful for reading on a physical page since they slow the eye. The optimum layout of text on a web page or *lexia* (as I will refer to it hereafter to avoid analogue metaphors) consists of "chunking" sentences into shorter paragraphs with lots of white space in between. Beyond these more local concerns, the structure of the larger container also dictates some of the formal elements of each lexia. No matter how vast a website, it can only be consumed one screenful at a time, which makes attending to navigation crucial. And since often the path(s) through these hypertextual structures are numerous, each lexia should also include the sort of recursive statements required when the preceding and subsequent lexia are neither consistent nor predictable. While books can be accessed in any order – when holding the physical object, one gets a sense of the whole and how that page was ordered – screen media, even when a site map is offered, are less clearly sequenced, and so the structure of the argument should shift: each lexia should include a certain degree of recursivity since one cannot know which screen will precede it. One way to accomplish this without an inordinate amount of repetition is to use a pop-up widow that appears only when hovered over (see Figures 32.1a and 32.1b).

This adds foundational information that can be accessed without disrupting the flow of the argument by sending a reader off to an index. I found this method particularly useful for definitional purposes in the first article created in the multimedia authoring platform, Scalar[1], and published in the *International Journal of Learning and Media*. The function is native to Scalar and I used it to define two of the article's main terms, filmic text and digital argument; the pop-up window is accessed with a simple hover gesture and disappears as the reader resumes reading.

Time-based media like video require even smaller text blocks than lexia, since viewers must be able to read the words before the screen changes. But the timing can be tough to gauge: leaving words on screen too long risks losing viewers (in this attention economy), while leaving them too short a time risks frustrating them.[2] There are several ways to mitigate this and aid reading. Horizontally scrolling text can lead the eye through a few sentences without becoming too taxing. The eye can also be led through a screenful of text one

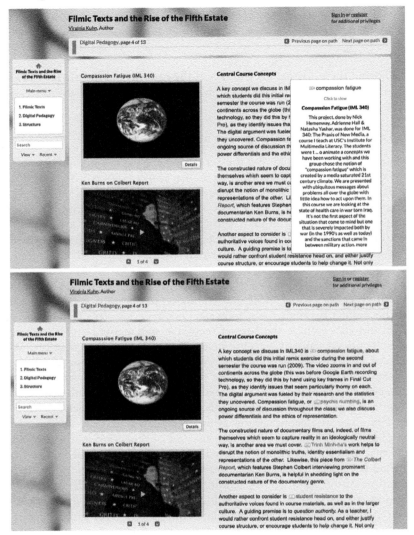

*Figures 32.1a–b* Screen shots from *Filmic Texts and the Rise of the Fifth Estate* showing Scalar's pop-up display. The first image shows the text box that is revealed by hovering; the second shows its disappearance as the reader continues reading the main page.

sentence at a time, by setting each line to appear for a few beats, before graying out as the next one emerges and lines up below it. Another option for shorter text is to have it appear on screen in full, but with key words bolded or highlighted for emphasis, which helps the eye to essentially read *over* common words, like articles and prepositions, that are less necessary to extract meaning.

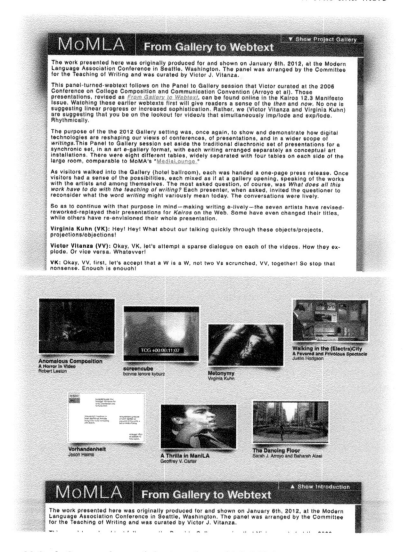

*Figures 32.2a–b* Screen shots of the interface of MoMLA

In contemporary screen media, words exceed their narrow usage in title sequences, credits, and those little yellow captions that are conventionally used in film and television. When the design freedom of digital fonts meets the movement of special effects in video, exciting new ways of meaning making arise. Kinetic typography animates on-screen text to form words in shapes that mirror its content: this is a good reminder that words have both graphical and ideational components and both impact meaning.

Screen media frequently combine spatially- and temporally-oriented elements in the same container, and their interplay can be tricky to negotiate. I have edited several collections of video essays over the last decade, three of which include a custom interface.[3] Although video essays are becoming more accepted as a critical pursuit, early on, it seemed important to foreground the textual components – the abstract or artist's statement and the citations. One way to emphasize the verbal components and signal that a move to digital scholarship is not a move *away* from words, but rather a way of extending and enhancing them, is to use a textual landing page as a gateway to the visual media. For example, in designing the interface of a 2013 collection of video essays, we placed screens with textual introductions at the opening of the collection as well as the opening of each project within it. Readers may read carefully, scan, or ignore the text, but they have to at least confront it and click to move on and open the project window (see Figures 32.2a and 32.2b).

Screens are ubiquitous in contemporary life. And if the events of the recent past have revealed anything, it is that the world's technologies for communication and expression have outpaced the media literacy necessary to decode their messages – from deliberate misinformation (fake news), election hacking, and data breaches, to identity theft, catfishing, and screen addiction. A more robust form of literacy on both a conceptual and practical level is required. As such, this is a propitious time for a reflection on how best to write with and about screen-based media. I have found that attending to the affordances of a platform and its available semiotic resources is the best way to ensure that the work created retains its structural and conceptual integrity.

## Notes

1 The Scalar platform arose from the team who created *Vectors: Journal of Culture and Technology in a Dynamic Vernacular* (launched in 2005) as a template that other publishers can adopt. Created specifically for born digital academic scholarship, Scalar includes rich annotation tools and the platform hooks into several media archives such as the Internet Archive; it is also free to use and open source. Since my publication, Scalar 2.0 has been launched and there are many models of its functionality on the site's featured projects area: https://scalar.me/anvc/scalar/.
2 It's useful to keep in mind that most video streams, which requires buffer time, making it easier to stop and back up than it is to move forward, so leaving text a beat shorter is often preferable to leaving it a beat too long.
3 These were published in *Kairos: Journal of Rhetoric, Technology, and Pedagogy*, a digital journal that has been publishing peer-reviewed natively digital scholarship for more than two decades. The expertise of the journal's publishers allowed for this customization. Journals such as this are still very few and far between.

# References

Gold, Matthew, Rebecca FrostDavis, KatherineHarris, and Jentery Sayers, editors. *Digital Pedagogy in the Humanities: Concepts, Models, and Experiments*. Modern Language Association, 2019.

Kuhn, Virginia "Filmic Texts and the Rise of the Fifth Estate." *International Journal of Learning and Media, Knowing and Doing*, vol. 2, no. 1, 2011.

Kuhn, Virginia. "Sucker Punch and the Aesthetics of Denial: Future Perfect Tense." *Future Texts: Subversive Performance and Feminist Bodies*, edited by Vicki Callahan and Virginia Kuhn, Parlor Press. 2016.

Vitanza, Victor, and Virginia Kuhn, editors. "MoMLA: From Gallery to Webtext." *Kairos: Journal of Rhetoric, Technology, and Pedagogy*, vol. 17, no. 2, 2013.

# 33 Best practices for screen media podcasting

*Christine Becker and Kyle Wrather*

> This chapter offers a collection of best practices for media scholars and educators who may be considering starting a podcast. Based on a survey of scholars and researchers currently recording and producing their own podcasts, this chapter synthesizes their responses into advice for those interested in participating in this growing medium. These recommendations are organized into six categories: planning ahead for a podcast, gathering the right tools, finding a clear concept, recording, editing, and understanding podcasting as a platform. Together, these best practices offer general guidelines for the kinds of considerations, challenges, and opportunities that may face individuals or organizations that are considering publishing their own podcast.

The phrase "I'm thinking about starting a podcast" is practically a cliché. The appeal of podcasting as a communication form is simple: entree to eager listening audiences, unrestricted runtimes, and low production barriers. However, while making your own podcast may sound simple, creating and maintaining the structure, content, and quality of a show or series comes with challenges. Nevertheless, podcasting offers media scholars and educators in particular new ways to share their work and insights. Using an online survey, we queried a number of media and screen studies scholars who have created or collaborated on podcasts to garner what they've learned from the experience (Becker and Wrather 2018). From their responses, we assembled a number of best practices for those considering starting a podcast, including advice on planning ahead, gathering the right tools, finding a clear concept, recording, editing, and understanding podcasting as a platform for reaching audiences.

## Preparation

First, launching a podcast involves a significant amount of planning. Jennifer Proctor, who has produced several audio projects, suggests that creators should consider, who is the target audience? How might that shape the approach to the podcast, including how much context to provide for obscure concepts or histories? And that includes practical questions. If this is a niche podcast with a small audience, how will you fund it?

The survey respondents particularly noted the importance of planning for the technical and marketing aspects of creating a new podcast, such as finding a host for the digital files, a feed to podcast syndicators, and promotional websites and online presences. *Porno Cultures Podcast* creator Brandon Arroyo also remarked that planning out a release schedule is important for retaining listeners:

> I think the most important things to remember are that aesthetics and constancy matter. Before I released my first episode I made sure that I had many other episodes recorded so that I would be able to keep up with the demand of a once-a-month schedule.

While many of these advanced planning aspects may not be visible to listeners, they pay dividends in creating more audience-friendly content while making the podcast more manageable for producers.

## Tools

Beyond planning, podcasting requires not only access to audio and editing equipment, but also a degree of technical skill. Respondents listed a wide range of valuable recording equipment, from specialized professional microphones and recording decks to cheaper USB microphones. Once you have the tools for recording, finding the right place to record may take some experimentation. Jacob Smith of *ESC* recommends: "Get a good quality mic and find a quiet place to record your voice – like a closet. It might take a few tries to get the right mic and right place." The raw audio is then processed and edited using audio recording software such as ProTools, Adobe Audition, the open-source Audacity, or Apple's Garageband. Jonathan Nichols-Pethick of <*modern_media*> emphasizes that audio quality is vital for a podcast's success: "Too many people make the mistake of thinking that sound quality doesn't really matter. It does. […] So, get a good audio recorder or studio setting for interviews with the best mics you can afford and that have some mobility." Like other creators, you must constantly balance the costs of equipment with your familiarity with audio production and editing equipment and techniques.

## Concept

Finding a clear concept and then establishing a consistent and comfortable voice is important for relating to audiences. For many of our respondents, at least part of the work of their podcasts is to translate media studies ideas and concepts to broader audiences. Jacob Smith explains that making these issues clear in podcast form is a matter of translation and explanation: "I didn't try to eliminate all the theoretical or academic content from my writing – the goal was to communicate those ideas in sound, but keep the ideas intact." *Phantom Power*'s Mack Hagood argues that podcasting offers opportunities to share media scholarship in new ways: "The mostly untapped potential of academic podcasts is that they allow for a different kind of academic discourse – using sound, silence, and music to change the temporal, affective, and cognitive modes of learning." To make this synthesis resonate, podcasters should focus on discovering their own style and approach to podcasting. Rather than following a specific model, *How Do You Like It So Far*'s Henry Jenkins suggests experimentation and self-reflection:

> Find your voice. Be yourself. Do not try to impress us with your scholarship. Think of this more as a teaching exercise or better yet, as a conversation with a group of smart friends, not all of whom are academics.

Above all, these podcasters suggest you think deeply about the ways your own work, knowledge, and interests might be used to enhance the depth and quality of your podcasts.

## Execution

You may have a killer concept, but only proper execution can fulfill it. Mack Hagood offers a striking characterization:

> For some reason, academics who wouldn't dream of publishing an article in crayon, with misspellings, meandering prose, and missing pages routinely publish podcasts with terrible sound quality, time-wasting, self-involved chit-chat, poor vocal delivery, and a complete lack of editing. Take the time to learn to create in audio. It's a sign of respect for your guests and audience.

In that same vein, respondents stressed the need to properly execute interviews. Henry Jenkins stresses, "The key thing is to ask questions that are particular enough to insure clear grounding for the listener and expansive enough to get your guest talking. Better to have too many questions on hand than too few." Similarly, Jennifer Proctor suggests,

> Look for the moment when your guest's voice heightens, and even if they seem to be going off-topic, follow them on their thread. When they're

most excited about what they're talking about, you'll often find your best gems and some good surprises that you couldn't have planned for.

Remember, you can always edit it down later.

## Editing

Don't think you're done once your interview or monologue is recorded; listen again and pare it down to its best parts. This will include minor tweaks, such as cutting out vocalized pauses (ums, ahs, stutters), but it might also include eliminating entire sections that are repetitious or tangential to the segment's central focus. Mack Hagood observes,

> I don't feel my job is to include everything they say. My job is to make an entertaining, thought-provoking podcast, which usually involves cutting out the majority of an hour-plus interview. Guests don't mind this. Cutting away the excess allows the audience to better focus on the important parts.

Brandon Arroyo agrees: "There is no way someone's going to enjoy listening to an unedited conversation. Most people don't have a great knack for talking smoothly; thankfully, the editing process makes everyone sound as good as possible." Above all, always keep the audience's attention in mind. Jennifer Proctor reminds us, "Don't assume an audience is going to hang on every word the way you might." Drill segments down to their essence.

## Platform

As you produce your podcast, take time to reflect back on what makes podcasting such a worthy undertaking. Our respondents repeatedly stressed that you must always think of your audience, which is likely seeking intimacy and immediacy combined with an in-depth discussion of big ideas. Also think beyond the audio, especially if your podcast covers visual media, and create a companion website to provide clips, images, and article links. Brandon Arroyo considers such extras as "a way for listeners to stay engaged with the conversation once they've finished listening to the show." Finally, make sure you utilize every social media platform you have access to in order to publicize your podcast episodes. Arroyo explains, "The single most significant factor in listenership is how much exposure the episode gets on social media. If I can post it to a Facebook group with a big following, more people listen."

## Conclusion

With so many suggestions to juggle, you might find it helpful to bring a co-producer on board to help you navigate this world. Amanda Lotz, who produces *Media Business Matters* along with Alex Intner, confesses, "I'm really glad that it isn't a solo effort. It would probably be dead by now if so." But you should also realize that the medium is still in its early creative stages and feel emboldened to forge your own path. Jacob Smith emphasizes, "There are (as yet) no rules or best practices, so be bold, do what feels right and comfortable, develop the material you think is important." Jennifer Proctor echoes this suggestion, "Podcasting is still something of a wild west, so it's a place to take risks and be creative in the way we share information and tell stories." Although it does seem like everyone wants to start a podcast these days, only your podcast will convey your voice.

## References

Becker, Christine, and Kyle Wrather. "Screen Media Podcasting Survey." Google Forms, 1 September 2018, http://goo.gl/oMi71i

# 34 Confessions of an academic blogger

*Henry Jenkins*

> My blog, *Confessions of an Aca-Fan*, launched in 2006 and has now hosted more than 2000 posts including interviews with more than 350 media scholars and producers. This chapter adopts a style appropriate for blogging – intimate, personal, concrete, practical – as it offers insights about the value of blogs as a form of public-facing academic writing and offers some thoughts on what might allow someone to succeed at this practice.

When I first launched my blog, *Confessions of an Aca-Fan* (henryjenkins.org), in June 2006, I had no idea that, a dozen years later, I would still be going strong. Some early readers saw the blog as a publicity stunt for the launch of my book, *Convergence Culture: Where Old and New Media Collide*. To some degree, they were correct, but it meant so much more than that to me, then and now.

I was frustrated by the enormous time lag in academic publishing: the months, years, between when a piece was written and when it appeared in print. This slow turnaround time felt fatal at a time when our culture was undergoing such dramatic and rapid shifts, making it hard for any of us to respond meaningfully to what people were calling "the digital revolution." I also felt strongly that scholars of media change needed to address a larger audience, that we needed to reach beyond the academic bookstore ghetto and speak to people who would never read what we comically call high impact journals. As a professor, I wanted to profess – to make knowledge known beyond our classrooms. Blogs offered that immediacy: write something, hit a button, and it is out in the world. Blogs offered that expanded reach: accessible to anyone who could Google. For these and many other reasons, blogging may persist among academics as others have shifted to other social media platforms: Twitter or Instagram does not allow the sustained analysis that a good blog post can offer. Other academic blogs may range from collaborations among a small number of authors (such as David Bordwell and Kristin Thompson's *Observations on Film Art*, davidbordwell.net) to larger scale institutional efforts (such as *In Media Res*, http://mediacommons.org/imr/).

Academic prose can often feel abstracted from the human realm: we are taught not to use "I" when writing for an academic audience. But, from the start, blogging was a highly personalized mode of writing. The earliest blogs were curated sets of links, which reflected the idiosyncratic interests and assessments of their hosts. Over time, bloggers added commentary and shared experiences. So, academic bloggers need to learn how to embody their ideas, to share their feelings and experiences, not in an exhibitionistic way, but as one of the resources from which they draw their insights. You want to make readers care about what you write, and that means, often, starting with why you care about a particular topic. To me, the problem is an epistemic one: I need to be transparent about how I know what I know. My blog was thus a "confession" from an "aca-fan," that is, someone who drew on what they knew as a fan as well as what they knew from academic research.

A blogger forms a relationship with a community of readers. In my case, I regularly hear from fans, gamers, journalists, creative industry people, brand executives, classroom teachers, activists, and parents who have found something meaningful on my blog. That readership is international – a quarter of my readers come from Brazil. Early on, I consciously built up this readership by exchanging guest posts with other blogs and by selecting topics that might engage specific networks of readers. What I write about shifts over time as my interests change, but I also maintain some awareness of what interests my readership. Introducing new topics may draw new readers into the fold and expand the perspective of my regular followers.

Accessibility does not mean dumbing down. Through the years, I've discovered that I can explore any topic through my blog. But I need to start where my readers are. I avoid using specialized terms or at least use them sparingly: combining *subjectivity*, *patriarchy*, and *hegemony* in the same sentence is rarely a good idea. Define terms, spell out their origins, and demonstrate their use value. If an everyday word will work as well, use it. I keep in mind that nobody reads everything I write – not even my family – so I need to introduce core concepts (in my case, *transmedia storytelling, participatory politics, the civic imagination*) afresh each time they are discussed.

My blog writing is much closer to the ways that I might address my undergraduates than the ways that I would speak at an academic conference. My students say that they hear my voice when they read my posts – an effect I consciously achieved, early on, by reading my early posts aloud to develop a syntax that felt good on the tongue. As with much lively prose, I try to avoid passive constructions, look for active verbs and concrete nouns, and am not afraid to use slang. My academic voice has also shifted through my blogging practice, resulting in more lively writing across the board. Scholars do not want to be bored any more than the lay public does. Academics are just often less attentive to issues of writing style than they should be.

Early on, I took a certain amount of flack from other bloggers about how long my posts were. I would cite the old Mark Twain line that I would have written less if I had more time. As a blogger working on a regular schedule, I can't afford to be too precious with my words. I learn to write quickly and trust my instincts. But as an academic blogger trying to expose people to new ideas, I often need to use more words than a writer who is simply reproducing the established wisdom. So, I don't feel guilty about the length of my posts. Being long-winded may turn some readers away but it also engages those who want something more substantive. That said, I generally break anything longer than 2000–3000 words into multiple posts, which keeps readers coming back for more. Reflecting the particulars of reading on a screen environment, I tend to break down paragraphs into smaller units than I would use in a journal article or book chapter.

Blog posts are a form of multimodal writing. Minimally, a good blog post includes links. Such connections may allow your reader to dig deeper into your topic, much as a bibliography provides resources for future scholars. Keep in mind that each link may draw someone away from your page, but a rich set of media resources may give people reason to return in the future. A blog post may also include images, sound files, and embedded videos. The exercise of looking for ways to illustrate your concepts may also make your writing more concrete, insuring that you anchor big ideas more often with specific examples. Including multiple or color illustrations may increase printing cost in traditional publishing so academics learn to do without, but you are free – in all senses of the word – to experiment in this alternative medium.

A blog is a place to reflect, to sketch out and test ideas with a larger public. I was shocked the first time I saw that people were using my blog posts in their curriculum. I am less surprised now and even write some posts specifically for instructional use. But I want instructors to signal to their students that blog posts are written quickly, that the thinking is not as carefully developed as more formal essays, that posts are always provisional. That said, remind students that any scholar is constantly testing and revising their earlier formulations as we respond to new information or encounter new circumstances.

Beyond this, blogs make visible the conversations and debates that inform knowledge production. I want my blog to be dialogic, and through the years I have developed multiple strategies for incorporating other scholars. As a teacher, I look for graduate student papers that might interest my readers. My mother used to hang my best artworks on the refrigerator door; my blog allows me to do the same thing for my students. And getting this work ready to post gives me an excuse to keep mentoring them beyond the limits of the semester.

I frequently interview other thinkers, mostly scholars but not always. I typically send my interview subjects roughly a dozen questions: some designed to solicit a straightforward exposition of key concepts that readers need to understand a topic, some designed to challenge or update their thinking, to link it to ongoing discussions on the blog. I always ask more questions than I expect to have answered, since doing so allows my subjects to pick and choose which ones interest them the most. I have found doing these exchanges in writing forces people to reflect more deeply on their responses. I don't have the time or money to transcribe interviews. People can respond to the questions and return the interview at their own pace; I keep enough interviews in play that I always have new material coming in. But this approach also means that there are many amazing people I meet through my work who do not have the time or professional inclination to do this kind of interview. This is one of many reasons I have launched a podcast, *How Do You Like It So Far?*, with my co-host Colin Maclay. Here, we can interview activists, media-makers, and others who are more likely to give me an hour to talk than take more time to write out their responses. My blog interviews are a big ask, and I find many list them on their CV as though they were publications.

Sometimes I engage in a more extended conversation, which involves the back and forth exchange of emails. I follow this format when I want to explore the relationship between my research and theirs, as opposed to simply creating a frame through which they can explore their ideas. And finally, I have organized a number of large-scale conversations that might bring several dozen scholars together, hoping to address an ongoing divide in my field – as we did with an early forum that mixed male and female researchers on fandom. Here, each person made an opening statement describing the trajectory of their work so far and then the two participants were encouraged to have some back-and-forth interactions as they discuss connections across their work.

Of course, my incorporation of these other voices is not altogether altruistic: the quickest way to burn yourself out is to try to produce this much content all on your own. I am often asked how I have been able to sustain the blog for so many years. One of the best pieces of advice I got when starting the blog came from *Boing Boing*'s Cory Doctorow. He said I should set a schedule for blog posts and stick with it. On any given day, there will be a dozen reasons not to blog, but you need to push past them. Otherwise, you miss a day, then two, then a week, and pretty soon, you are not blogging anymore. I had aspired to be a journalist in my youth so I joke about "putting out the morning edition." Over the past dozen years, I can still count on two hands the number of times I have missed a blog deadline. When I launched, I was on sabbatical and got in the habit of posting five days a week. I tried to keep it up once I returned to regular teaching but it was impossible. So, I am now down to two days a week – more if I have the content to justify it.

I keep a file where I list whatever ideas I have for future blog posts, and throughout the rest of my professional activities, I am always looking for potential content. If I review a book for a press, I jot down questions for a future interview. If I meet someone interesting at a conference, I collect their contact information with an eye towards incorporating them in some future exchange. I see the blog as a way of promoting emerging scholars and encouraging discussions around important topics. And I use the blog to illustrate long-standing concepts through contemporary examples or to update cases I have written about elsewhere. Having a blog has encouraged my tendencies as a networker and gives me a reason to be more attentive to emerging work in my field.

One thing that has discouraged other academics from blogging is the realization that the current tenure system often does not recognize and reward the tremendous amount of work which goes into their production. Blogging is not quite scholarship as it has been traditionally understood, though it does allow me to explore ideas with a larger public, to expand my networks, access new information, and get feedback on my work in progress. Blogging is not quite teaching as it has been traditionally understood, but it does allow me to work closely with my students to improve their writing and it does generate materials that are used in classrooms around the world. Blogging is not quite service as it has traditionally been understood, but blogging does allow me to engage with a wider public, to insure that academic insights have broader impact, and to help promote the work of emerging scholars whose voices need to be heard by others in the field.

Younger scholars may best enter this space via collaborations, since doing so lowers the time commitment and expands the reach of your promotional networks. Online projects such as In Media Res, FlowTV, and Antenna (now defunct) provided a starting point for many early career scholars to experiment with blogging and expand their followings before spinning off their own blogs. The word spreads quickly when you couple blogging with effective use of social media practices. I send notice of each of my posts via both Twitter and Facebook, and hashtags increase the likelihood that these notices will spread to unanticipated audiences.

I never would have imagined that *Confessions of an Aca-Fan* would still be going strong more than a dozen years later, but maintaining this blog has impacted every aspect of my academic career and though on a bad day I want to walk away from it all, it's hard to imagine ending this sucker.

# 35 The research and the remix
## Video essays as creative criticism

*Jeffrey Middents*

---

This chapter explores how crafting video essays can become a way to perform criticism using creative license that is backed up with critical knowledge. By re-examining the processes involved in developing three video projects that play up the interplay between audiovisual texts, the author explores the relationship between video essays and more traditional written projects. The chapter centers around a case study on auteurism and Alfonso Cuarón which combines images from the 2018 film *Roma* and sound from the 2001 film *Y tu mamá también*.

---

In mid-December 2018, I was asked to contribute short remarks for a timely dossier on director Alfonso Cuarón's latest film, *Roma*. Following a large middle-class family in Mexico City in the early 1960s, the film centers around a young domestic worker named Cleo (played by newcomer Yalitza Aparicio) as she weaves in and out of the family's daily life while managing her own. Epic and intimate all at once, *Roma* received accolades after its debut at the Venice and Telluride Film Festivals in early September. Moreover, the film had achieved notoriety earlier when it was *not* selected for the Cannes Film Festival because its distributor, Netflix, planned to release the film almost simultaneously through its worldwide streaming platform as well as in theaters. Its mid-December release therefore brought unprecedented international attention to a Mexican film, with assumptions that the film would be nominated for multiple awards.

As a scholar who has written about Alfonso Cuarón and taught his work in a number of classes, I wanted to visit the film through the familiar lens of auteurism. *Roma* explicitly invites comparison to his earlier films: in one scene, for example, the family goes to a 70s-era film where astronauts are shown floating in space suits outside their rocket – a clear reference to Cuarón's previous film, *Gravity* (2013). Amongst my own community of scholars and students, a fun game developed trying to connect *Roma* to all of his previous films, a practice encouraged by the numerous reviews that cited his earlier work. The clearest antecedent, however, was Cuarón's breakthrough hit, *Y tu mamá también* (2001). Set in Mexico in 1999, the film follows two horny teenagers on a road trip to a mythical remote beach with an older Spanish woman, narrated by a disembodied male voice (Daniel Giménez Cacho) that provides both cultural context and personal histories for all the characters, a device reminiscent of the late films of director Jean-Luc Godard. One of these voice-overs explicitly relates a memory for one of the boys triggered by a passing sign:

> Tenoch realized he'd never visited Tepelmeme, the birthplace of Leodegaria Victoria – Leo, his nanny – who migrated to Mexico City when she was 13. Leo found work with Tenoch's family and had cared for him since he was born. He called her "Mommy" until he was four. Tenoch didn't share this with the others.

In fact, by the time we hear this, we have already met Leo, if very briefly, in a scene where a woman (played by Liboria Rodríguez) walks slowly through a large house where many telephones ring from all corners of the house, carrying a sandwich to teenage Tenoch. When she arrives to the room he is in, she hands him the sandwich (with the line "it has your favorite cheese") and then answers the phone, ringing mere feet away from him, before wiping the mouthpiece, handing it to him ("*es para ti, cariño*/it's for you, darling") and then, coming into the sunlight as she does so, ruffling his hair with an affectionate smile.

I could – and have, and will – write about the ways these two movies interplay with each other. That is part of what I do and how I was trained: with a degree in Comparative Literature, I am much more comfortable with writing, where the analysis of audiovisual texts relies on description. Much can come out of how we perform such descriptions – note that in my description of the scene above, I have chosen to present *Leo's* actions and gestures, not those of Tenoch; such a decision de-emphasizes the main character, played by now movie star Diego Luna, in favor of non-actor Rodríguez, who happens to be Cuarón's actual former nanny and the person to whom *Roma* is dedicated. As editing software has become more accessible, however, the growing trend of scholarly video essays has allowed scholars and critics to perform critical work in the language of cinema itself. Providing commentary on clips is a much more organic activity, given how discussing movies and the connections among them is a common practice in classrooms, conferences, theatres, and casual conversations.

For me, at least, crafting video essays has become a way to perform criticism directly, using creative license that is backed up with critical knowledge. In his 2016 metatextual video essay "What Makes a Video Essay Great?" film critic and video essayist Kevin B. Lee shows a distinction between some more academic "essay videos" (a term used by practitioner Thomas van der Berg) and the more common fan-based supercuts; in the same year, however, media scholar Lori Morimoto argues in the video essay journal *[in]Transition* that even these seemingly less rigorous exercises are "an exercise in both theory and praxis that attempts to blur the divide separating Quality/melodrama, video essay/fanvid, fan/producer, and academic/fan." *Crafting* video essays – and I use that verb deliberately – means getting over some of our own veneration for the very texts that we are examining, because it means changing or modifying the very objects themselves, not unlike how a car enthusiast will take apart an engine to see how it works inside. I have heard other video essayists explain that after watching a film they will pop it into an editing program to break it into smaller pieces and rearrange the elements. Remixing, as a DJ might do with music, brings about a deeper resonance when we bring our own critical interests and questions to the editing board – and, likewise, that editing process can expose new directions we might not otherwise see.

I found it daunting to try altering cinematic content completely, to allow myself to remix something new, until I started to play with audio. In 2017, I crafted a video essay called "Mi sueño es representar la belleza de la mujer de mi estado/My Dream is to Represent the Beauty of Women from My State: Framing Beauty in Latin American Cinema." The title comes from an early scene in Gerardo Naranjo's 2011 film *Miss Bala*, a film where a young woman who wants to become a beauty contestant quickly (and unwillingly) becomes embroiled in the Mexican drug trade. In the scene in question, Laura (played by Stephanie Sigman) is asked by local pageant directors to walk in a straight line, introduce herself, and repeat the line expressed in the title. Naranjo chooses to frame her in the center as she does this and, indeed, holds her in the center through most of the rest of the film, even as her surroundings grow increasingly violent. At the time, I recognized that this trope of holding a beautiful female character in the frame's center was something consistent across many Latin American films (indeed, much of global cinema). My idea was to take this line of dialogue and stretch it beyond its original scene. After presenting the scene in its unedited, original form, I then took the audio from the clip and edited similar scenes from *Miss Bala* where the framing was similar; in the process, however, I manipulated the audio by doubling the sound of her shoes clacking on the hard floor. I then repeated this two more times, with the third iteration using images from other Mexican films and the fourth from other Latin American films – each version doubling the time of the sound of her walk. The original idea was to comment on framing, beauty, and women in Latin American film and to emphasize women walking, as if they were in a non-stop fashion show akin to *Miss Bala*. Once I had selected an assortment of clips, I realized that not only had I picked women walking down the center of the screen, but I found that a good portion of these scenes also featured these characters *looking back*. This unintentional consequence led to further questions about gender in Latin America: who are all these women looking back at? Why do they feel they need to look behind them? Are men shot similarly also looking behind them? (This last question was easily answered: they do not.) Editing the clips in order to develop my original argument unearthed new dimensions to explore.

Choosing to intercut narration from *Y tu mamá también* with a single, otherwise unedited scene from *Roma* turned out to be challenging. For one, I felt the slow-paced *Roma* needed the narration to be broken up a bit, to be allowed to breathe in ways that the newer movie was allowing. While the focus was on Cleo, I also realized that the scene I had selected happened to feature dialogue referencing a play on death – something also done in *Y tu mamá también* when Luisa, the older Spanish traveling companion (played by Maribel Verdú), meets a young girl at their final destination and she "plays dead" in the water. I decided to then add narration originally ascribed to Luisa to this scene with Cleo, in a way to elevate the scene and its focus on Cleo. What results is an interplay between the two films, allowing for a dialogue across time, image and sound, done in the cinematic language in which both were crafted.[1]

Not all video essays are – or should be – the same, and the arguments you want to make will dictate how the essay will be crafted. Most of my essays forego voice-over narration, but sometimes (as with Kevin Lee's work) that is the best method to get your point across. Before beginning, watch a wide variety of video essays, both scholarly and popular, to get a feel for what is possible. *[in]Transition* is a great place to start, in part because they feature an open reviewing system where you can read refereed responses to the work. Christian Keathley and Jason Mittell's book *The Videographic Essay: Criticism in Sound and Image* features some great exercises that can both hone your skills and start you thinking more creatively. Storyboarding your idea, either with sketches or screen-grabs, allows you to preview your idea visually before you start processing through the editing software. Rest assured that such software is forgiving, and playing with many aspects of your essay before settling on a final version is one of the best parts about it. Workshop your essay as you might with a written version by showing it to others for constructive criticism. Finally, remember to think like an editor as well as a scholar, and realize that visual construction demands a certain economy – which is another way of saying: don't make your essays too long, lest you lose your viewer in the process.

*Figure 35.1* Still from the author's video essay "Memories of C/Leo: On Auteurism and *Roma*," featuring an image of Cleo (played by Yalitza Aparicio) from the film *Roma* (Alfonso Cuarón, 2018) and voiceover narration from the film *Y tu mamá también* (Alfonso Cuarón, 2001)

## Note

1 The final version is called "Memories of C/Leo: On Auteurism and *Roma*" (http://reframe.sussex.ac.uk/mediatico/2018/12/24/special-dossier-on-roma-memories-of-c-leo-on-auteurism-and-roma/) and is part of a dossier of essays responding to Alfonso Cuarón's film at the Latin American media studies blog *Mediático*.

## References

Keathley, Christian and Jason Mittell. *The Videographic Essay: Criticism in Sound and Image*. Caboose Books, 2016.

Lee, Kevin B. "269. What Makes a Video Essay Great?" *Vimeo*, https://vimeo.com/199577445 Accessed 10 January 2019.

Middents, Jeffrey. "Memories of C/Leo: On Auteurism and Roma." *Mediático*. University of Sussex, 24 December2018, http://reframe.sussex.ac.uk/mediatico/2018/12/24/special-dossier-on-roma-memories-of-c-leo-on-auteurism-and-roma/ Accessed 10 January 2019.

Morimoto, Lori. "*Hannibal*: A Fanvid." *[in]Transition: Journal of Videographic Film and Moving Image Studies* vol. 3, no. 4 (2016), http://mediacommons.org/intransition/2016/10/06/hannibal-fanvid Accessed 10 January 2019.

# 36 Foregrounding the invisible
## Notes on the video essay review

*Chiara Grizzaffi*

> This chapter dwells on the very peculiar process of reviewing video essays. In the first part, it addresses the novelty of the video essay as well as of the process of open peer review. Second, the chapter describes the structure of the video essay review, detailing its different sections – the opening paragraph, the analysis of the argument and of the formal strategies adopted to convey it, the interpretation – and providing examples and advice on how to write them. Finally, it urges potential reviewers to engage with video essays by losing some critical distance.

I wish I could say I was a precocious cinephile, but in fact, my interest in cinema grew slowly – but steadily – during my university years. I still remember my first film studies classes: it was as if someone had suddenly turned the light on in a dark room. There was a depth I couldn't even imagine in films, and the more I patiently started to learn how to see in the dark by myself, the more I was also able to get a better understanding of who I was as a spectator and as a scholar.

I experienced again the thrill of that discovery, the exhilaration you feel once you can finally see something previously invisible, the first time I encountered video essays and videographic criticism on film scholar Catherine Grant's blog *Film Studies for Free*. The video essay – a work that reuses and remixes the images of the film(s) it is ruminating on – is a form of criticism and analysis that can show and even let the viewer "feel" all the qualities of the cinematic work (Grant, "Déjà Viewing?"): something that was absent (though very well evoked) in written publications. Furthermore, as a relatively new critical practice, the video essay still presents the features of an experiment, of a playful, even "amateurish" (see Pisters 146) attempt to find a new form of expression for thinking about cinema.

How can we, therefore, write a review about a hybrid, elusive object, one that nonetheless finds its richness in its variety? I had to confront this issue the first time I was asked to write a video essay review for *[in]Transition* – the first peer-reviewed journal devoted to videographic film and moving image studies. *[in]Transition* works according to an open peer review system; each video essay is published along with commentaries from the author and two reviewers. Usually academic journals do not publish the peer reviews of articles, but *[in]Transition*

> takes the formerly invisible labor of the peer reviewer and makes it eminently visible. The open review, and the experience of writing one, sits somewhere between the "private" existence of the traditional peer review and the public performance of a commissioned book review – or even original scholarship itself.
>
> (Denson 142)

How should we approach such original scholarship? Generally, when someone writes an anonymous review that is not meant for publication, she doesn't have to worry too much about its written form, knowing that the correspondence between her and the author will remain private. In the case of journals such as *[in]Transition*, the review is available online. Thus, these reviews should also analyze the video essay, present an original interpretation of the work, and encourage the reader to engage with the work. To write reviews, I activate my experience reviewing films, an activity primarily devoted to the feverish but satisfying search for new meanings and to sharing those meanings with the readers in a clear and engaging style. In structuring my reviews, I do not have fixed rules, but in general I prefer to contextualize the work before expressing my evaluation of it: is the video about a very well-known and debated topic, or is it exploring a new territory? And what are the main challenges set by the chosen issue?

For example, in reviewing *The Spielberg Touchscreen* (2016) by Ken Provencher, I began by pointing out that despite the numerous videographic works devoted to Spielberg's work, Provencher's video essay "stands out for the novelty of his argument and the compelling way in which he presents it through its audiovisual form." In other cases, a small detail, whose importance is merely subjective, is the spark for the opening paragraph. When I was asked to review *Tag* (2015) by Rob Stone, the title raised my curiosity:

> As a non-native English speaker, for me it was extremely fascinating to find out that the word "tag" is the name of a popular playground game (known as *acchiapparella* in Italian). The connection with the game reminds me of the playful, cinephilic side of intertextuality.

*Tag* was, indeed, an intertextual analysis of a particular recurring motif in European and American cinema.

Once the main question addressed in the video essay is individuated, the central part of the review focuses on establishing whether the author has provided a convincing argument through the audiovisual form, which means through montage, through the combination of images, sound, voice, written text and so on. This is the part of the review generally devoted to describing and commenting on the thesis developed in the video and on the formal strategies adopted. The appropriateness of the formal strategies employed in relation to the intuition, the critical and theoretical reasoning the video aims to demonstrate, is of pivotal importance. A far too obvious or an excessively loose connection between the images and the voice over; a poor handling of audio volume in a video essay about sound; the invasive presence of superimposed written text in a work that is all about the visual composition of a scene: these are all examples of an inadequate use of the audiovisual form.

Conversely, it is extremely important to stress when the formal solutions of a video essay are able to show (and to make someone hear) something surprising. For example, in my review of Jaap Kooijman's *Success* (2016), a video essay about Diana Ross and Beyoncé, I emphasized how its visual and aural elements manage to "convey the complex and layered relationship between the star personae of Ross and Beyoncé" through the repetition of similar

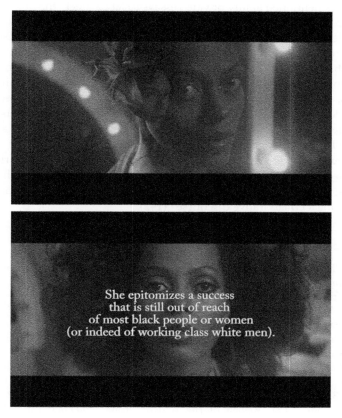

*Figures 36.1a–b* Images from *Success*, a video essay by Jaap Kooijman published on *[in]Transition - Journal of Videographic Film & Moving Image Studies*, 2.4, 2016

segments with the same written text superimposed, reverse motion, and a looped soundtrack – creating an "hypnotic experience." Through its audiovisual form, the video offers new perspectives not only about two well-known stars, but also about a 1982 article on Diana Ross by film scholar Richard Dyer.

Film scholar Christian Keathley argues that each video essay may be situated, in terms of aesthetic strategies, in a spectrum from an explanatory mode to a poetic mode. The explanatory mode generally entails an argument clearly developed using voiceover or written text; the poetic mode is characterized by a more experimental approach and semantic opacity (179–181). The works I review usually cover both sides of the spectrum, and I have realized that very often I find "the poetic in the explanatory", and "the explanatory in the poetic." In my view, an explanatory video essay should preserve, to a certain extent, the dialectic tension between words and images; conversely, a transformative, even apparently iconoclastic, video essay should offer glimpses of the underlying argumentation. The reviewer's aim should be to recognize these achievements.

The aforementioned ability of video essays to let us "feel" the qualities of the images, to engage us in a multisensory experience in which the object and the critical discourse around the object coexist, invites the viewer to enter this space of negotiation, thus renouncing her safe distance. Therefore, once the reviewer has assessed the originality of the video essay, its ability to engage with the existing bibliography (or videography), and the effectiveness of its formal strategies, it is essential to communicate to the reader the further observations that the video stimulates and how the video essay "feels" and make us feel: the enthrallment, the allure, the discomfort, the cringing, the poignancy – a range of emotions I have experienced in my years of research in videographic criticism. The review of a video essay cannot just be an instrument of scholarly validation: it becomes most effective when it expands and recirculates the work's meanings, creating a dialogue or, to use film scholar Shane Denson's words, "coauthoring a collaborative discourse" (142).

## References

Denson, Shane. "Open Peer-Review as Multimodal Scholarship." *Cinema Journal*, vol. 56, no. 4, 2017, pp. 141–143.

Grant, Catherine. "Déjà Viewing? Videographic Experiments in Intertextual Film Studies." *Mediascape*, Winter 2013, www.tft.ucla.edu/mediascape/Winter2013_DejaViewing.html Accessed 13 November 2018.

Grant, Catherine. *Film Studies For Free*. https://filmstudiesforfree.blogspot.com/ Accessed 18 December 2018.

Grizzaffi, Chiara. "'Success.' Review of *Success*, by Jaap Kooijman." *[in]Transition*, vol. 2, no. 4, 2016, http://mediacommons.org/intransition/success Accessed 13 November 2018.

Grizzaffi, Chiara. "'Tag.' Review of *Tag*, by Rob Stone." *[in]Transition*, vol. 2, no. 3, 2015, http://mediacommons.org/intransition/2015/07/29/tag Accessed 13 November 2018.

Grizzaffi, Chiara. "'The Spielberg Touchscreen.' Review of *The Spielberg Touchscreen*." *[in]Transition*, vol. 3, no. 1, 2016, http://mediacommons.org/intransition/2016/03/18/spielberg-touchscreen Accessed 13 November 2018.

Keathley, Christian. "La Caméra-Stylo: Notes on Video Criticism and Cinephilia." *The Language and Style of Film Criticism*, edited by Alex Clayton and Andrew Klevan, Routledge, 2011, pp. 176–191.

Pisters, Patricia. "Imperfect Creative Criticism." *Cinema Journal*, vol. 56, no. 4, 2017, pp. 145–146.

# 37 Review, edit, repeat
## Writing and editing book reviews

*Alice Leppert*

> Based on the author's experience as the book review editor for *Film Criticism*, this chapter provides an overview of how to write and publish an academic book review. It includes a discussion of what information and assessment a book review needs to include, tips for approaching and working with book review editors, and ideas for dealing with some of the unique challenges posed by the genre. It also gives a glimpse into the editing process and outlines the importance of book reviews in academia.

When I took over as the book review editor for the journal *Film Criticism* in 2015, the job was intimidating. I'd only written two book reviews in my life, both as assignments in graduate seminars almost ten years prior, and I never sought to publish them. At the same time, I was excited about the free books that quickly piled up on my desk and for the opportunity to stay up-to-date on the field and learn about all the new, exciting work coming out. Despite being a little rusty in the writing department, I remembered the basic formula for a book review, and I quickly learned that editing the reviews that I solicited was fairly simple. After all, the primary audience for a book review is someone who has *not* read the book, so if the review makes sense to me, it should make sense to the ideal reader. If it doesn't, it's pretty easy to pinpoint where the reviewer needs to clarify and what s/he needs to add for the review to be effective.

The first step to writing a book review is securing a publication venue (or designating a hypothetical publication venue if you are writing a review as an exercise), which requires a little bit of research on the appropriate journals. Journals take a variety of approaches to publishing reviews, so it's a good idea to contact the book review editor and ask how s/he handles reviews. *Film Criticism* generally publishes eight book reviews per year. Since this is a fairly small number, I select the books to be reviewed (with an eye toward including a variety of subfields and topics). Then I solicit reviewers, first from an internal list of reviewers who have contacted me in the past, and then if necessary, from a public call. Occasionally, I will accept unsolicited reviews if the book is recent and the subject matter doesn't overlap too significantly with recently published or solicited reviews. Potential reviewers should always accurately represent their research interests when contacting editors; include a CV or a brief description that explains their qualifications for reviewing the book in question. I am often puzzled by requests from potential reviewers whose research interests seem to have no bearing on the book they want to review, and thus I am very unlikely to assign them as reviewers. Once you are assigned a review, you should read recently published reviews in the journal to help supplement the basic formula for book reviews (especially to see if the journal's reviews deviate from the formula in any significant way) and, of course, follow the instructions provided by the editor. I regularly send back first drafts that have failed to follow the citation style and/or which exceed the maximum word limit, so getting this right the first time will ingratiate you with the editor and save you an extra revision.

A book review needs to fit a lot of information as well as critical assessment in a short space; *Film Criticism* asks for reviews of no more than 1000 words. The reviewer should provide a succinct explanation of the book's argument, ideally in her/his own words. For example, in his review of Dan Hassler-Forest's *Science Fiction, Fantasy, and Politics*, Matt Yockey writes, "Hassler-Forest convincingly argues that the immersive and always-transforming transmedia world-building practices of science fiction and fantasy are particularly useful for negotiating the contradictory logic of global capitalism." Though reviews should include direct quotes from the book, I usually encourage reviewers to state the argument without quoting it, as book authors are often *not* particularly concise when outlining their arguments. Reviewing Jon Kraszweski's *Reality TV*, Molly Schneider observes, "Kraszewski argues that scholarship on reality TV has not adequately addressed the role of the city in reality programs, despite the crucial ways geographical markers influence our understandings of these shows." The review should also give an overview of the methodology and/or organization of the book and a brief summary of each chapter. This is especially important, since many readers may be interested only in a chapter or two, rather than the entire book.

While the above guidelines generally apply to monographs, edited collections are especially challenging to tackle as a reviewer, given the constraints of space and the individual arguments of each chapter. The simplest way to approach an edited collection is to allow the editor(s) to be your guide. The book's introduction will lay out the overarching argument or intervention the collection seeks to make, so your review can assess the collection as a whole based on its editor(s)' stated aims. Usually the chapters will be arranged thematically or chronologically, with the editor(s) pointing to connections among them. Aim to mention briefly the topics individual chapters cover, and pull out a few for more in-depth discussion that seem particularly original, noteworthy, or that have the potential to make a significant impact on the field.

Throughout any review, the reviewer should be diligent about defining terms that may be unfamiliar. S/he can safely assume familiarity with jargon common to scholars in the field (for example, *diegesis*), but anything specific to a subfield (for example, national film movements or theoretical terms specific to a certain school of thought) should be briefly explicated. Finally, the review should offer an assessment of the strengths and weaknesses of the book, and put the book in broader context. What is its contribution to the field or its subfield? Does it advance a particular theory or methodology? What audiences might find the book useful? In her review of Elizabeth Ellcessor's *Restricted Access*, Ekin Pinar notes the book "would appeal to scholars in the fields of disability, new media, and cultural studies," concluding her review by assessing it "a great candidate for undergraduate syllabi focusing on disability and participatory cultures."

Despite having a pretty standard generic formula, there are still some significant challenges when it comes to writing book reviews. The most common revision I request is for authors to include a discussion of the weaknesses or limitations of the book. Many book review authors are graduate students and emerging scholars, and are thus understandably nervous about offending more established scholars with their critiques. On the opposite end of the spectrum, established scholars often review books by authors they know quite well and are thus reluctant to risk burning bridges, especially in small subfields. I try to reassure reviewers that no author expects to receive a wholly glowing review (that's just not how book reviews work), and that no book is perfect. In fact, many authors anticipate the sort of criticism they are likely to receive; it's very possible that they have heard similar lines of critique at conference presentations and from the anonymous reviewers of their manuscript. Occasionally, I'll receive a very critical review that launches into the shortcomings of a work before giving the reader any sense of what the book is actually about. In this case, I typically suggest that the reviewer first focus on nailing down the content and argument of the book before assessing its merits, as her/his critique will be meaningless at best and appear petty at worst if the review doesn't signal that the reviewer has read carefully and/or taken the book seriously enough. Essentially, a reviewer should approach a book review with neither an ax to grind nor uncritical praise to heap.

Book reviews are important to authors, reviewers, and readers. While book reviews may not seem to be the most exciting academic genre, that doesn't have to be the case. Despite their tight word limits, the best book reviews will still draw in the reader. Kristopher Purzycki opens his review with an evocative image:

> Spaces that once hosted an American cultural routine, vacant video stores have long been replaced by other enterprises. Across the dust-encrusted shelves of this once ubiquitous institution, Daniel Herbert's *Videoland: Movie Culture at the American Video Store* examines the

transformation of movie consumption and how various practices that nurtured the industry subsequently led to its demise.

Like any type of review, book reviews can help promote a product, potentially drawing in new audiences. Moreover, for scholars who spend years writing a book, its release can prove anti-climactic, as the stereotype of academic publishing tells us that no one will ever read what we have spent so much time and energy writing. Book reviews not only help a book gain a wider readership, but they also provide vital feedback to the book's author and an opportunity to reflect upon and assess new arguments and ideas for reviewers and editors.

## References

Pinar, Ekin. "Review of Restricted Access: Media, Disability, and the Politics of Participation, by Elizabeth Ellcessor." *Film Criticism*, vol. 41, no. 3, 2017, https://quod.lib.umich.edu/f/fc/13761232.0041.319/–elizabeth-ellcessor-restricted-access-media-disability?rgn=main;view=fulltext Accessed 14 December 2018.

Purzycki, Kristopher. "Review of Videoland: Movie Culture at the American Video Store, by Daniel Herbert." *Film Criticism*, vol. 41, no. 3, 2017, https://quod.lib.umich.edu/f/fc/13761232.0041.305/–daniel-herbert-videoland-movie-culture-at-the-american-video?rgn=main;view=fulltext Accessed 14 December 2018.

Schneider, Molly A. "Review of Reality TV, by Jon Kraszewski." *Film Criticism*, vol. 42, no. 3, 2018, https://quod.lib.umich.edu/f/fc/13761232.0042.319/–jon-kraszewski-reality-tv?rgn=main;view=fulltext Accessed 14 December 2018.

Yockey, Matt. "Review of Science Fiction, Fantasy, and Politics: Transmedia World-Building Beyond Capitalism, by Dan Hassler-Forest." *Film Criticism*, vol. 42, no. 3, 2018, https://quod.lib.umich.edu/f/fc/13761232.0042.304/–dan-hassler-forest-science-fiction-fantasy-and-politics?rgn=main;view=fulltext Accessed 14 December 2018.

# 38 Extracurricular scholarship
## "Writing" my audio commentary of *Losing Ground*

*Terri Francis*

---

This chapter discusses the audio commentary as a form of what the author calls "extracurricular scholarship" through the case of the collaborative commentary she recorded with film scholar LaMonda Horton-Stallings for the Milestone Films Release of *Losing Ground*.

---

The very first time that I remember seeing director Kathleen Collins's film *Losing Ground* (1982), I was a teaching assistant for a class called "(Re)Defining Black Film." I don't remember being thunderstruck by it. I took it as normal and fine that there was a film about a black woman professor. Almost everyone I know is a black woman professor! When I started teaching my own courses, I definitely included *Losing Ground* on my syllabus. For the first few years, I rented a 16mm print, but one year I was told it wasn't available and no further information was offered. As a solution, I began teaching the film's screenplay which was published in Black Film Center/Archive founder and film scholar Phyllis Klotman's book *Screenplays of the African American Experience*. In the years that I couldn't show the film print I would assign the screenplay, but of course we missed the atmosphere and the crucial voices and silences that make the film so impressionistic and revelatory.

Time passes and I have a surprise encounter that leads me back to the film images. At a New Year's Day brunch, one of the ladies in attendance sounded very familiar, but I couldn't place her until after I'd gone home and looked up her name: Seret Scott, the star of *Losing Ground*! Having missed her distinctive voice for so many semesters, I'd forgotten how I knew it.

Creating the audio commentary for Milestone Films's DVD release of the film allowed me to retrace how I (re)discovered the film for myself and how I'd encouraged Kathleen Collins's daughter Nina Lorez Collins to work on restoring and redistributing the film. I suggested the distribution company Milestone Films for the project and arranged for the film elements to be transferred to the Yale Film Study Center for safekeeping. (Nina) Collins visited me at my home in New Haven where I basically harangued her about the uniqueness of her mother's work and how much I missed having it in my classes, doubtless saying what she already knew: that her mother was a genius who created an incredible film that everyone needed to see. In the audio commentary as in my visit with Nina, I was able to express my real feelings about the film and what it means to me. Although my personal world is full of black women professors and authors, we represent a mere 3 percent of university faculty and how many of those, like the protagonist of *Losing Ground*, are in philosophy? How Collins brilliantly captures what it is like to watch students reacting to you and the range of the intense and intensely weird projections that they place on you. How stifling the classroom can be. How exhilarating it is to know you're right. And how much it's not enough. How precious the summer is for the freedom it affords us to focus on ourselves and our own ideas. How much we need to focus on ourselves. How much we long to infuse our work with creativity and a sense of liveness. How much we feel maybe a little inferior to or envious of or exasperated and abused by the artists in our circles. I understood Sara's search for aesthetic fulfillment, and I could easily imagine what it meant to have a student see in you the very qualities that you see in the works of art you've devoted your life to. I became deeply connected with this film over time, yet I never wrote about it. What I had to say about it felt to me almost too tender to express in academic prose.

Milestone proposed an audio commentary that diverged from the usual DVD extras yet returned to the genre's earlier form. As writer Andrew Eagan points out, audio commentary, largely absent from streaming services due partly to technology limits and licensing limits, remains an "extra" or "bonus" associated with physical media. Along with the main feature, these "deluxe" editions of a film include added material such as deleted scenes, interviews, trailers, production stills, and more due to the DVD's storage capacity. If such extras perhaps justify the cost of special edition DVDs, they also enhance the prestige of the film that receives such treatment, aimed as they are at film students and their teachers as well as fans and professionals in the film industry. BluRay and DVD commentaries are typically done by directors, actors, writers, or other key personnel in a film's production. However, the very first audio commentary ever recorded was done by the film historian and critic Ronald Haver for The Criterion Collection's 1984 Laserdisc Edition of *King Kong* (1933). Haver provided what he called "a lecture tour" that viewers could listen to while watching the film. Laserdisc technology, like DVD and BluRay technologies, allows sound to be recorded on separate tracks so that there can be a "lecture" or comment track as well as one for the regular film sound.

Our *Losing Ground* commentary would be a discussion between me and LaMonda Horton-Stalling, author of "Redemptive Softness," a crucial essay about *Losing Ground*. Though neither of us made *Losing Ground*, we both played important roles in ushering this nearly lost film into its new life with early twenty-first century audiences. Eschewing a script, we planned a conversation that would be mostly ad-lib on my part. I called it our black feminist viewing party.

One of the big moments for me in the Milestone commentary was when I realized how much I couldn't stand the Victor character and being able to be loose and frank about it. In earlier viewings, I was less critical of his arrogance and thoughtlessness. While I didn't feel the need to make a formal feminist critique in writing, the rhythm of our conversation in the studio as we watched the film allowed me to assert almost an alternative reading in which Sara and Victor are not equals and she is really the artist here while Victor is a hack. One of the principal ways that Victor saps her energy is his continuous talking and his constant need for her attention and company in order to validate and frame his own thinking. He's really another student who needs her authority, her ideas, her counterpointing but also resents it. In the audio commentary, I found what I now feel Sara lacks in the film, that is a colleague with whom to talk things over. Doing the collaborative commentary gave me an opportunity to tell my own story with *Losing Ground* and to explore my reactions to the film in a freeform, playful way.

I saw anew the thousands of acts of creativity that Professor Sara must perform in order to do her job and navigate her marriage. Her participation in the student film is analogous to my need for extracurricular scholarship through conversations and curating. By acting in the student film, Sara is able to access the truth of her feelings in all their rawness and she has to face the truths they reveal. By stepping into a fictional character she's freer to find a new, maybe more authentic, relationship to herself. The creative space is fraught with vulnerability because as a dancer and an actress, she doesn't have the masks of intellectuality and rightness to protect and reassure her. Sara is able to feel her own rage against her husband, and to see herself apart from her roles as daughter, wife, and teacher.

For me, watching movies is less escape and more arrival to myself. It's a private space of contemplation about how I view the world. The immediacy of public conversation mediates between the emotional contours of my engagement with a film and the accountability of published scholarly writing. Sometimes, at first, and maybe for a long time, you need to be all over the place. You don't always have all the evidence. And contradictions can unveil important paradoxes, whether in the particular movie I'm discussing or in the idea of and desires around black film, so why smooth them out?

Writing can't always be just writing. We do audio commentary all the time when we dissect a scene in class or gush over a beloved film star, detailing their attributes with friends. In recorded, spoken commentary we generate a reflexive art form where our dialogues with the screen and within ourselves meet. Talking is our path to the page.

## References

Eagan, Andrew. "No Comment: The audio commentary track, a staple of films on optical media, may not last into the age of streaming. Is it a victim of indifference by Netflix?" *Tedium* 21 February 2017, https://tedium.co/2017/02/21/dvd-audio-commentary-decline/

Klotman, Phyllis Rauch, editor. *Screenplays of the African American Experience*. Indiana UP, 1991.

*Losing Ground*. Directed by Kathleen Collins, performances by Seret Scott, Bill Gunn, and Duane Jones, 1982. Milestone Films Release, 2015.

Stallings, L. H. "'Redemptive Softness:' Interiority, Intellect, and Black Women's Ecstasy in Kathleen Collins's Losing Ground." *Black Camera*, vol. 2, no. 2, 2011, pp. 47–62.

# 39 The short, sweet art of blurb writing

*Leah Shafer*

> This chapter introduces writers to blurb writing. Blurbs are short, summative, persuasive texts that manufacture condensed copies of other texts. The chapter provides an introduction to the blurb as a purposive text that allows writers to curate, creatively cite, and appropriate the story and style of novels, films, video games, and other media for potential new consumers. Four guiding principles for the writing of blurbs are introduced: citation, context, character, and convention. Each principle is illustrated with a blurb. Overall, blurbs are described as tools for constructing an elaborate but economical cosmos that reflects and responds to their object of attention.

Blurbs are short, summative, persuasive texts that exist somewhere between advertising copy and annotated bibliographies. As texts about other texts, blurbs serve a critical function in a variety of situations. Blurbs can be used to: encourage audiences to screen a film; inform readers about a newly published book; serve as catalogue copy for a public archive; summarize complex research for a public poster session; summarize projects for a grant application; introduce a podcast segment; and so forth. Blurbs will likely serve an ever-greater role in media culture's attention economy as producers of all manner of texts compete for visibility and spread. As such, it is a writing form worth studying and practicing.

Blurbs are usually 50 to 150 words long, but they can refer to texts of any size, including ten-hour long documentaries and six volume novels. Part of the challenge and pleasure of writing a blurb is figuring out how to approach and exploit this radical disjuncture in scale. When you write a blurb you are curating and reassembling the most compelling bits of the text you're blurbing and using those bits to manufacture a condensed copy that you share in order to invite other people to consume that text. Blurbs harness the force of synecdoche when they create that condensed copy: they allow their writers to access and exploit the power of metaphor. With this power comes responsibility. The writer of a blurb is writing for an audience that will (presumably) encounter the text that is being blurbed, so the blurb creates expectations and sets a tone for that future encounter.

While blurbs are entirely referential, from the point of view of the writer they are standalone, purposive texts. Like thesis statements or advertising jingles, their form performs their function. The best blurb writers use the dynamic energy produced by the tension between form and function as an engine for sharp, evocative, persuasive prose that opens up a discussion with the text being blurbed. In mass media, blurbs are typically explicitly promotional and even the writers who write them have long considered them suspect: George Orwell called them "disgusting tripe" (Levinovitz). Gary Shteyngart wrote a satirical open letter renouncing the practice that described the chucking of his "blurbing pen" into a river. But, as the opening paragraph of this short essay suggests, there are many legitimate purposes for blurbs, and their promotional nature need not be regarded as a mark of debasement, especially when they allow the blurb writer to make discerning interventions for the benefit of the blurb reader. You can think about writing blurbs as an invigorating exercise in citation and appropriation, an opportunity to experiment with what Nicolas Bourriaud calls "relational aesthetics" (Boon 143).

When you write a blurb you are creating something that, as Maya Deren says, "itself constitutes an experience" (22). The size, function, and purpose of the blurb are productive obstructions that can yield considered creative work. The best blurbs construct an elaborate but economical cosmos that reflects and responds to the object of attention. Take, for example, this commendatory poem written by Ben Jonson for William Shakespeare's First Folio, an early example of a blurb. Jonson's blurb concludes:

> Shine forth, thou Star of Poets, and with rage
> Or influence, chide or cheer the drooping stage;
> Which, since thy flight from hence, hath mourn'd like night,
> And despairs day, but for thy volume's light.

Jonson's blurb is florid – it invokes, exalts, and rhymes – but it is also formally similar to blurbs we see today. It addresses the reader; it invokes the style of the text in question; it capitalizes on an interior, ontological tension in order to allegorize its content; it extols the writer; and, it persuades the consumer to consume by providing a representative taste of the text. So, just write like Ben Jonson.

I wrote film blurbs for the Cornell Cinema *Flicksheet*, a film calendar for Cornell University's film exhibition program, for fifteen years (cinema.cornell.edu). As a blurb writer, I learned to make choices about language and tone and to balance information with invocation. The choices I made as a writer of blurbs fall into four umbrella categories that I call the four Cs of blurb creation: *citation, context, character,* and *convention.* There is overlap between these categories, but using them to determine the approach most appropriate for each individual text being blurbed can help to clarify and organize the writing process. In order to unpack the four Cs, I offer an illustrative example for each. (All blurbs are by this blurber.)

Citation allows you to add authority to your claims. As you can see in this blurb for *Flat is Beautiful* (Sadie Benning, 1998), citing reviews can be a particularly useful tool when you want to give authority to an otherwise underrepresented artist or a text that utilizes unconventional tools and/or techniques.

> Pixelvision pioneer Sadie Benning's first feature length work is shot in Super-8 and Pixelvision with masked actors. This mesmerizing video about an androgynous 11-year-old girl's unhappy odyssey toward adolescence is weirdly moving and intuitive. "A major new work ... imbued with a unique ambience of fragile, lyrical entropy and charged, sleepy eroticism, Benning's tape has the quiet irresistible force of a masterpiece." (Film Society of Lincoln Center)

This blurb is about an experimental video by a queer 25-year-old woman that is critically acclaimed but not widely known. As such, citing this descriptive assessment signals critical approbation. The fact that the review was written by the Film Society of Lincoln Center also makes space in the blurb for the kind of critically sophisticated language that might otherwise read as too academic for a blurb with a wide public audience.

Context, whether embedded in a film's cultural critique, or coming out of the buzz surrounding a film's exhibition, can be a useful tool for the blurb writer. The indie film turned blockbuster hit, *Trainspotting* (Danny Boyle, 1996), was propelled to success in part by its dynamic soundtrack and music video style editing. The film's exhibition history and production style are invoked in this blurb, which employs intentionally fast-paced sentence-level construction to give the reader a sense of the film's frenetic energy.

> Telling the story of a handful of dazed, jobless heroin addicts stumbling through the underbelly of Edinburgh, this edgy, artful film became an international phenomenon this past summer as it tromped through an increasingly larger number of cinemas with the kind of wild, shrieking abandon practiced by its protagonists.

The memetic force of the condensed copy can be harnessed for the construction of a memorable blurb. Evoking the tone or character of a film through creative copying of the film's style can yield effective affective results. Perhaps the greatest appeal of the murder mystery *Fargo* (Joel and Ethan Coen, 1996), for example, lies in its outstanding performances, so this blurb draws that out.

> Whatcha got here is a good movie about some bad folks who did some not so nice things to some other folks up there in Northern Minnesota.

Jerry Lundegaard (William H. Macy), he hires these two thugs to kidnap his own wife, y'know, but things go wrong and in comes Marge Gunderson (Frances McDormand), a real nice lady and a police officer to boot. And that's the idea you got going here.

As you can see in this example, the Coen's quirky aesthetic and the film's memorable Minnesota accents opened a space for playful copying of the film's general character as well as its specific characters. Focusing on character(s) also creates room for including metadata about the cast, which (especially in the case of a film starring Frances McDormand) can be a compelling factor to readers otherwise uninterested in a film.

The more conventional the text you're blurbing, the more unconventional you can be with your blurb writing. *Fargo*, for example, is a conventional success: it premiered at Cannes and won several Academy Awards. The blurb does not need to legitimize or contextualize the film as much as it needs to copy and to celebrate it. In the case of *Titanic* (James Cameron, 1997), the film is such a profound commercial success, the audience for the screening is so guaranteed, and the story of the film itself needs so little introduction that the blurb can be extremely playful. The blurb is, in some ways, so unnecessary that it forms an opportunity for meta-commentary:

A really big boat sinks.

Writing blurbs allows you to exercise restraint and indulge poetic license in the same small space. Aspiring blurb writers can get practice by studying poetry that follows a form (like villanelles or haiku) and then using that form to describe a favorite text. Another generative exercise would be to take a long form movie, book, video game, or album review, and condense it into a 50- or 75-word blurb. Practicing this purposive, performative form draws you into generative conversations with other texts: these conversations are opportunities for experimenting with and honing diverse prose styles. If you hew to the four Cs and engage and exploit the memetic force of the copy, you can write sharp, sweet, short blurbs.

## References

Boon, Marcus. *In Praise of Copying*. Harvard, 2010.
Deren, Maya. *Essential Deren: Collected Writings on Film*. Documentex, 2005.
Levinovitz, Alan. "I Greet You in the Middle of a Great Career: A Brief History of Blurbs." *The Millions*, https://themillions.com/2012/02/i-greet-you-in-the-middle-of-a-great-career-a-brief-history-of-blurbs.html
Shakespeare, William. *First Folio*. Iaggard and Blount, 1623.
Shteyngart, Gary. "An Open Letter from Gary Shteyngart." *The New Yorker*, April 14, 2014.

# 40 Bridging the gaps between scholarly essays and mass-market film writing

*Nick Davis*

> This chapter draws on the author's years of experience as both a university-based professor of cinema studies and a film critic and journalist for popular publications. On these bases, the chapter argues that skills developed in each of these arenas – often presented as irreconcilable in goals, expression, and audience – can enrich one's work in the other and create professional opportunities in both. The author gives examples of how scholarly questions, frames of reference, and modes of analysis can elevate popular writing and distinguish a critic's voice. At the same time, the concision, clarity, and attention to craftsmanship that magazine editors and fan communities value can help to distill and anchor the arguments in academic writing. The chapter includes a handful of sample assignments that can cultivate these abilities in students and help them acquire useful professional skills.

For years, as an English major in college and a Ph.D. candidate in English and Film & Video, I remained unsure whether I wanted to be a professor of cinema or a movie critic for a mass-market publication. Today I work in both capacities, a fact entailing more lucky breaks than I can list, especially given how jobs keep evaporating in both fields. No reproducible script exists for securing a livelihood as a scholar or reviewer, much less in combination, despite a profusion of gifted, impassioned aspirants with sterling CVs, whose points of view would enrich both worlds. I can share, however, some approaches that worked for me, plus some assignments I devised to prepare undergraduate students with similar goals. The main advice I will stress is that – despite rumors you may hear about indecipherable academics or an anti-intellectual press – these two ways of thinking and writing about movies can serve each other beautifully, helping you to land opportunities in either area and to appreciate movies from even more vantages.

Here is a prompt I often circulate to students two-thirds of the way into a film analysis course, limiting their submissions to 500 words:

Your hometown paper seeks a young reviewer to write capsules about "modern classics" available on Netflix. As part of your application, they request a fresh, convincing take on a well-known film that convinces folks to take another look at it – one that, without employing much discipline-specific vocabulary, feels like a case you couldn't make without college-level training. Extra points if you can make this film relevant to your local community.

Some respondents use this invitation to comment more on aesthetic choices than a newspaper critic typically does. Others distill theoretical insights into colloquial but still-provocative terms that illuminate how a movie perpetuates or resists typical rules of the cinematic game. Joining the strongest elements of multiple submissions, we see how it's possible to accomplish both:

> In its most famous scholarly account, "the male gaze" encompassed not just macho characters or voyeuristic cameras leering at women but also Hollywood's insistence on realism as its preferred style – as if gender, like all of life, naturally *is* how studio movies depict it. *American Beauty* (Sam Mendes, 1999) is frustrating but interesting because it seems to applaud Lester's chauvinistic swagger in word and deed, yet the film's colors and sounds are so blatantly artificial that they suggest one peculiar man's outlook, not a series of universal laws.

Some instructors offer this kind of assignment as a warm-up to longer, thesis-driven papers. I reverse that sequence for a few reasons. First, I believe concise arguments are harder to deliver than expansive ones, especially when trying to signal layered insights in prose that any distracted commuter can grasp. Second, students, like everyone, often need to sit with complex ideas for a while before they can encapsulate or teach them to someone else; for many, the sheer notion that camera placements, color palettes, editing rhythms, and soundscapes are doing more than broadcasting "tone" or facilitating "flow" is itself a novel idea. Third, most full-time critics I know get progressively less space to critique an increasing number of movies, with anodyne blockbusters ceded half-page spreads and trickier, smaller movies afforded one or two paragraphs. I never presume that most or even many of my students intend a career in movies or as critics, but for those who do, learning to say something meaty (and proofread, and punctual!) in a short space offers an ideal pre-vocational workout.

At a time when undergraduates understandably expect classes to impart portable skills, these capacities for synthesizing and translating specialized concepts for non-specialist audiences strike me as eminently practical for any career path. What doctor, teacher, trader, lawyer, social worker, plumber, therapist, or consultant does not perform versions of this task every day? More specifically to film, the tally of aspiring critics who can express how a movie made them feel well exceeds the number who can persuasively trace those emotional responses to specific elements of a film's structure, perspective, and audiovisual engineering. Practicing deep formal analysis and learning to convey nuances without rarefied jargon can help in securing or retaining positions as a staff writer or freelancer. Editors usually reject what sounds "academic"; however, if rendered transparently, the stylistic accents, historical contexts, or sociopolitical ramifications that academics take seriously can register happily with others as uncommon expertise. By the same token, the more I applied journalistic mandates for clarity and concision in my scholarly writing, the more forceful my arguments became and the more widely they traveled.

I say none of this to imply that we should always judge scholarly writing on a standard of lexical transparency, or to suggest that jobs miraculously materialize for any researcher or reviewer who can couch dense concepts in crystalline prose. What I mean to emphasize is that pressures that seem to exist in academia against vivacious, digestible language, especially in early-career moments of establishing credentials and branded agendas, often emerge as specious or self-imposed. Thesis- or dissertation-writing, for example, often compels a performance of intensely specialized diction for fellow experts, but a hairpin turn soon follows whereby employers, colleagues, students, and presses beg for simpler articulation (very different from simplified ideas). Public writing and mass-market editors are great helps in instilling this knack.

I also found that my involvement in fan communities that scholars often denigrate substantially improved my scholarship. Rarely did any faculty mentor push me to note how minutiae of costume design or of musical instrumentation could enrich my formal or theoretical unpacking of a film. By contrast, online Oscar obsessives, religiously fixed on category distinctions (how are sound *edits* working with or against the sound *mix*?) and on discrete achievements in otherwise-mediocre films, gave me rich, focused feedback in these areas. Like every other academic, I know my work does not speak equally to every colleague in my field and that I am still an apprentice in many respects. I will say, though, that my eye and ear for granular details and my ability to write plainly, even on highly theoretical topics, have been singled out at moments when I needed to pass a high-stakes professional test – even as I credit these facets of my writing at least as much to input from non-academics as to formal schooling.

Popular publishers' demand for lively sentence-level writing – whether to lure clicks on Rotten Tomatoes or to furnish layout teams with eye-grabbing pull-quotes – also helped me to spruce up analytical prose and to enjoy drafting it. This is why I challenge (and alarm) my students by issuing single-sentence assignments that I grade on the usual A-to-F scale. I want to hear what insights they can unfurl over many pages, but they must also marshal syntax, sound patterns, and precise semantics to distill complex, intriguing ideas at the most condensed scales. I have orchestrated assignments where students post their favorite sentences from their own reviews on the internet, where constructive, moderated comments help them see the difference that careful grammar and verbal panache can make in hooking readers. Some writers and readers prefer a more aphoristic style: "*The Social Network* (David Fincher, 2010) is not a film for the generation brought up on Facebook. It is a film for the generation that does not understand Facebook." Other critics, writing on the same film, construct sentences more intricately, as some filmmakers do with their shots:

> However extraordinary Mark might be in terms of his programming and entrepreneurial abilities, his sexism is far from unusual in the world that he inhabits; misogynistic in its very structure, this film depicts men as chauvinistic and women, denied any complex characterization, as almost without exception belonging to three stereotypical categories.

Variety is the spice of life, and I like displacing myself as the sole arbiter of students' prose.

Conversely, exporting university-trained skills into my film reviews, festival journalism, or talent profiles has helped me place such pieces in auspicious venues. Like many peers, I started solo as the proprietor of my own film-criticism website. My reviews ran long, with phrasing, allusions, and argument structures that betrayed my background in scholarly essay-writing. I was never going to work at *People* Magazine – but cultivating a personal voice, even while trying to broaden its range, helped me find the readers I wanted to engage and impress, including from publications like *Film Comment*, which I had read avidly since college. Now, when writing about a film artist I admire, I often approach their work from angles informed (but not constrained) by my academic work, which usually differ from those that other journalists or interviewers adopt. In profiling Kristen Stewart, I cared less about her dating history or *Twilight*-fueled celebrity than her curious status as a Hollywood megastar who had honed a superficially "inexpressive" style of close-up acting more indigenous to Antonioni, Bresson, or Denis films, three directors I had studied in scholarly contexts. I withheld these names in print, but the ideas about Stewart I explored in a widely-read cover story that later attracted similar jobs were inspired by spectatorial habits I formed on campus.

Similarly, when I interviewed Todd Haynes or corresponded with Barry Jenkins, we could dig into more esoteric films or far-flung national traditions that respectively inspired *Carol* (2015) or *Moonlight* (2016) because professors and department colleagues had put those movies on my radar. Indeed, Haynes and Jenkins are two among innumerable directors who were themselves ardent film students and globally-oriented cinephiles, frames of reference that many magazine writers cannot summon in spontaneous conversation. Just as rare is deep liberal-arts exposure to topics a script might confront, or to patterns of bias or inclusion that a movie's aesthetics might sustain or contest. Being able to critically engage a film's subject or the politics of its camerawork, or to spot a salient influence in a movie you can only see once before reviewing it, or delineating what is unique and what is tacitly appropriated in Hollywood's most "original" features are all useful, marketable abilities for a critic or journalist. They also make every film-watching experience more rewarding and multi-layered – and isn't that what it's all about?

# 41 Writing across the page without a line

*Holly Willis*

> What does it mean to write across the page without a line? To write beyond the security of a well-honed critical practice? This chapter describes the evolution of my own writing practice and the subsequent creation of a craft-based writing workshop dedicated to the exploration of techniques for writing about – or alongside, next to, or near – film, video, still images, sound, and other media forms. Moving beyond the conventions of scholarly writing, the course explores forms that have been variously dubbed creative nonfiction, the hybrid essay, memoir, the fourth genre, the lyric essay, the video essay, and poetic or vernacular criticism; and it considers writers who have contributed often stunning examples to the form. While writing constitutes one of the main activities we engage in as scholars, we devote very little attention to it as a practice and craft within academia. This chapter describes attempts to redress this gap.

In the fall of 2014, after many years devoted to both academic writing and arts journalism, I decided I wanted to experiment with my writing practice. I applied to and was accepted into a writing workshop with novelist, filmmaker, and Zen priest Ruth Ozeki titled "The Art of Time in Story" at Hedgebrook, a writers' retreat for women, and found myself soon thereafter on Whidbey Island during a wet and foggy week in November. I brought with me the idea for a new book on women media artists and was interested in imagining how I could bring the quality of time into my writing about film and video. It was hardly a radical intervention, but it was what I could muster, and I was pleased to be accepted.

During the workshop, five other women and I meditated with Ozeki every morning, wrote for three or four hours alone, and then gathered for an afternoon workshop in which we explored sense memory and deep contemplation as it relates to writing. We also talked about our own writing practices. I remember one of my co-writers saying to me as we stood in the woods before returning to our cabins one morning, "Write from the heart." I nodded, but rolled my eyes as I turned away. "Write from the heart?" Hah!

I write from the brain! However, sitting in my cozy loft bed, with the little wood stove nicely stoked, I began a new story, nonfiction, about a spider, my mother, and an ill-fated pregnancy. At one point, I leaned my head back and imagined my heart opening, and within a few seconds I had written the most beautiful sentence I have ever written. Sure, the story itself was a messy muddle of air and spider webs, breathing and bleeding, but there it was, a glimmer of stunning revelation. To this day, whenever anyone reads the story, they point to that sentence.

I realized that week that I wanted more than anything to continue to write these kinds of sentences. I wanted to write my way across a blank page, to tell the stories of what has been lost, what is known and unknown, what is terrifying, ineffable, curious, necessary. Critical writing had given me the ability to question and critique, to interrogate the role of power and ideology, which I value enormously. But how might I integrate a kind of writing that is deeply personal along with the emancipatory impulse of critical thinking?

Later, thinking about my experience in Ozeki's workshop, I realized that while writing constitutes one of the main activities we engage in as scholars, we devote very little attention to it as a practice and craft within academia. We expect that our students know how to write, and lament when they do not write well. While we might query the structure of an argument and the marshaling of evidence, we rarely attend to emotion and feeling, nor to the poetic implications of words, sentences, punctuation, rhythm, lineation, even the design of the page.

Based on my own experience and the exciting proliferation of hybrid writing that has been happening over the last decade, I decided to redress the gap in critical writing with my own students in the Media Arts + Practice program in the USC School of Cinematic Arts with a course titled "Creative Critical Writing." I was particularly inspired by the work of Claudia Rankine, and her extraordinary 2014 book *Citizen: An American Lyric*, a genre-crossing, searing, and personal exploration of race in America. The book epitomizes a genre of critical writing that hovers between poetry and prose to create vital, often thrilling reading experiences deeply attentive to language, rhythm, and structure while questioning issues of identity, power, race, and class within our current, intensely neoliberal culture. Other inspirations include Bhanu Kapil (*Humanimal*), Tisa Bryant (*Unexplained Presence*), Maggie Nelson (*Bluets*), Wayne Koestenbaum (*My 1980s and Other Essays*), Lisa Robertson (*Cinema of the Present*), and Caroline Bergvall ("Fuses, After Carolee Schneemann"), all of whom have created poetic works that grapple with the world alongside other cultural artifacts.

Designed as a space for exploration and invention, as well as a political intervention that suggests that we ignore the form and voice of our work at our peril, the Creative Critical Writing Workshop is devoted to discovering and inventing techniques for writing about – or alongside, next to, or near – film, video, still images, sound, and other media forms in ways unfamiliar to most scholars.

The workshop evolves a bit each time I teach it. Overall, though, we think about text as texture; about writing that takes up space; the intersection of cinema and the word; a haptics of writing; the launch and the swerve; openings and endings. We watch typography in motion, listen to audio and voice experiments, meditate in gallery spaces, move our bodies like punctuation marks and generally try to disrupt the academic writing practices that demand logic, order, and coherence.

The writing prompts are very open and there is time devoted to writing in every class session, as well as to workshopping anything produced. None of the work is graded, and everyone in the class is expected to participate in the critique process. With the prompts, I try to provoke rather than direct, suggest rather than control. Here are a few examples:

## Voice

Near the start of the semester, we talk about voice, and the ways in which our academic voice is but one among many. I urge students to try out different kinds of voices:

Monday: describe something you did today, but instead of using "I," use the third person.
Tuesday: write as if you are whispering.
Wednesday: write in the voice you use when you speak to a lover.
Thursday: write in a voice that is convincing.
Friday: write in an anxious voice.
Saturday: write in a borrowed voice.

## Repetition

When T.J. Clark was a scholar-in-residence at the Getty Center, he came across two paintings by Poussin in the Getty Museum: "Landscape with a Man Killed by a Snake" and "Landscape with a Calm." He was so intrigued by the paintings and how they changed day by day with differing light and his own moods that he began a year-long process of recording his responses to the paintings each day. The result is *The Sight of Death: An Experiment in Art Writing*. Based on this idea, create an assignment for yourself that requires a similar kind of repetitive attention and writing, and see what it yields. Could you view the same frame of a movie, the same page of a book, or the same media installation for a period of time and reflect on it repeatedly?

## Lyric

Inspired by the lyric form and examples as varied as Lia Purpura's "The Autopsy Report," or Maggie Nelson's *Bluets*, take an existing piece (or two!) of your own writing that is perhaps more scholarly and reimagine it. Select individual sentences as excerpts and begin to play with them in a new document. Create a collage of sentences, and see if there is a new piece taking shape that you can explore with attention to the musicality of the language, unusual word order, and form.

## Fragments

Choose a subject – it can be as personal as things said to you that made you feel less human or as general as the color blue – and write a series of short fragments. Write two or three a day for a week or so, without any attempt to link them. Just let them be brief flares of truth or insight. After you have a collection, see how they might be assembled into an essay.

Student work in the class has been extremely varied. One student borrowed a technique used by Joe Brainard in his experimental memoir published in 1970 and titled *I Remember,* in which every paragraph begins with the phrase, "I remember." Her recollections listed a series of sexual assaults, building a powerful indictment not just of people she has encountered and their behavior, but of institutions, namely schools and universities, that sanction or ignore this violence. Another student wrote an essay about a body on a 12-foot piece of paper, with the words elongated length-wise; reading required bending over the very long table on which the page was displayed and moving slowly backwards, at once very aware of both your own body and the body being revealed along the length of the page. Another student "performed" her writing process, cutting and pasting phrases and fragments of writing while texting, checking Instagram, and sending emails. The performance also integrated video footage from the student's webcam of the student as she worked, nicely disrupting our experience of time and space. The performance reveled in the seemingly haphazard yet entirely quotidian assembly of a text through bouts of multitasking distraction. A fourth student responded to an inquiry from an academic journal after she submitted an essay; the editor requested that she "show her work." This phrase became the starting point for interrogating what it means to "show" one's "work" in a six-part essay series on *Medium* that integrates still images, gifs, and video. The expansive series beautifully demonstrates the iceberg structure of academic writing; what gets published is a tiny bit of a huge structure, much of which is forced into a kind of submissive silence.

Overall, the class has been by far the most exhilarating experience in my academic career. The students create stunning work, and the sense of release and creativity is extraordinary. Reflecting more calmly, I think that there are four things that seem necessary to me now when engaging in the practice of creative critical writing:

1   meditation, and the ability to quiet the mind, engage the body, and open to new ways of thinking and knowing;
2   an opening of the heart. I hesitate even to write this, but I still find that settling, softening and opening the heart allows for forms of expression unfamiliar to me in my analytical mode;

3 the creation of a circle of trust among participants in order to allow tender and delicate expression shared in a group; and
4 the movement between the meta and the immersive, by which I mean the ability to stand back and explore the radical potential of form and then to move in to feel the intimate and close-up.

We continue as a community exploring how to entangle and embody our felt experience in relation to the university, to academic writing, to authority, to power, and to this strange and beautiful act called writing. We continue to try to write across the page without a line.

## References

Bergvall, Caroline. "Fuses, After Carolee Schneemann." *The Brooklyn Rail*, 2005.
Brainard, Joe. *I Remember*. Granary Books, 2001.
Bryant, Tisa. *Unexplained Presence*. Leon Works, 2007.
Kapil, Bhanu. *Humanimal*. Kelsey Street Press, 2009.
Koestenbaum, Wayne. *My 1980s and Other Essays*. FSG Originals, 2013.
Nelson, Maggie. *Bluets*. Wave Books, 2009.
Rankine, Claudia. *Citizen: An American Lyric*. Graywolf Press, 2014.
Robertson, Lisa. *Cinema of the Present*. Coach House Books, 2014.

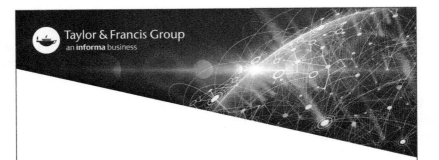

# Taylor & Francis eBooks

www.taylorfrancis.com

A single destination for eBooks from Taylor & Francis with increased functionality and an improved user experience to meet the needs of our customers.

90,000+ eBooks of award-winning academic content in Humanities, Social Science, Science, Technology, Engineering, and Medical written by a global network of editors and authors.

## TAYLOR & FRANCIS EBOOKS OFFERS:

- A streamlined experience for our library customers
- A single point of discovery for all of our eBook content
- Improved search and discovery of content at both book and chapter level

### REQUEST A FREE TRIAL
support@taylorfrancis.com